More Praise for *Drug Crazy*

"A rip-tearing, screen-worthy read full of narco raids and shootouts."   —*High Times*

"Never did I think one could learn so much about the drug crisis all in one place. Mike Gray has written a book of profound compassion that nevertheless deals intelligently with the facts. *Drug Crazy* is an antidote for passivity."
                    —Daniel Schorr

"What sets *Drug Crazy* apart is Grays ability to bring this sordid history to life. He combines a mastery of narrative with a chilling soberness of purpose."   —Paul Rosenberg,
                    Intellectualcapital.com

"Gray's analysis is, of course, controversial. It is, however, argued eloquently and persuasively, and deserves a hearing."
                    —*Kirkus Reviews*

Over the last fifteen years, American taxpayers have laid out over $300 billion to wage the war on drugs—three times what it cost to put a man on the moon. *Drug Crazy* offers a scathing indictment of our expensive and hypocritical follies, which have essentially benefited only two classes of people: professional anti-drug advocates and drug lords. Mike Gray has launched a frontal assault on Americas drug war orthodoxy, and his disturbing overview of the battlefield makes it clear this urgent debate must begin right now.

Mike Gray, author of the *China Syndrome*, has produced the award-winning documentaries *American Revolution* and *The Murder of Fred Hampton*. He has written for numerous publications, including *The Nation*, *The Los Angeles Times*, and *Rolling Stone*.

DRUG
CRAZY

DRUG

**HOW WE GOT INTO THIS MESS
AND HOW WE CAN GET OUT**

CRAZY

MIKE GRAY

Routledge
New York

Paperback edition published in 2000 by
Routledge
29 West 35th Street
New York, NY 10001

Originally published in hardcover by Random House, Inc.
Copyright © 1998 by Mike Gray
Printed in the United States of America on acid-free paper.

10 9 8 7 6 5 4 3 2 1

Cataloging-in-Publication Data available from the Library of Congress

ISBN 0-415-92647-5 (pbk.)

FOR P. N. HIRSCH,

a St. Louis merchant

who taught honesty by example

The night is far spent,

the day is at hand:

let us therefore cast off the works of darkness,

and let us put on the armour of light.

—ROMANS, 13:12

Acknowledgments

Thanks first of all to my wife, Carol, and son, Lucas, who stuck by through thick and thin with invaluable criticism and advice. And to longtime friends Jim Dennett and Andy Davis who helped keep the project afloat at critical moments. Thanks as well to Bob Lescher and Bob Loomis for their guidance over the last six years. And to Marcia Litman Greene, and the staff at the UCLA Research Libraries and the Chicago Historical Society, my deep appreciation for their assistance. Invaluable aid was rendered by the U.S. Border Patrol, U.S. Customs, the Drug Enforcement Administration, the RAND Corporation, the White House Office of National Drug Control Policy, the United Nations International Narcotics Control Board, and the Government of the Kingdom of the Netherlands. And finally, my thanks to Sergeant Joe Kosala and Detective Frank Goff of the Chicago Police Department, a couple of honest cops trying to keep the lid on against impossible odds.

Contents

DRUG
CRAZY

A Tale of Two Cities—
Chicago: 1995/1925

Goff is edgy about all the kids on the street. There are civilians all over the place and old folks on the porches even though it's been dark for hours. The temperature's barely into the fifties, but on the heels of a brutal winter in Chicago, any wind that's not from the north is an icebreaker.

Detective Frank Goff is in the backseat of a blue Chevy Suburban across from an aging brick six-flat on 113th Street. This is a lower-middle-class black neighborhood, mostly homeowners trying to keep their places up and not succeeding. The building Goff and his crew are watching is just a couple of blocks off State Street, "that Great Street," but when you get this far south—and this late in the twentieth century—it loses any resemblance to the boulevard of song and fable.

The van's windows are heavily tinted, but to be on the safe side Goff has added burlap curtains. He can still see through the mesh, but from the outside, the heavy cloth will shade any accidental kick of light from metallic objects. Scotty Freeman is at the wheel, and he's black, but Goff is staying out of sight. A white boy would look quite out of place around here. The two other guys on the crew, Fischer and Washington, are across the street in the vestibule of the six-flat. They're waiting for a coke dealer named Ramone.

It's been a long day. They started this morning cramped up in this same van, watching crack deals go down near a grammar school way out on the West Side. And that's what led them here. This elite team is with the school unit of the Chicago Police Department. It's Goff's job to make some kind of dent, however small, in the gang and narcotics activity that is devouring the city's school system. "To stop guns and narcotics around the school. That's our specific assignment. To get the drive-by shooters, to get the narcotics away from the schools."

Their target this morning was an enclave known as "K-Town" about fifteen miles northwest of here. Goff had been tipped that the area around the Marconi Grammar School was flooded with crack. He decided to drive a wedge in this operation. He got his team in position around 8:00 A.M., and what they saw over the next few hours would have left the average Chicagoan bug-eyed. But none of it was news to Goff. He sees this all the time. A car pulls up, a couple of guys get out, each one with a dozen "sixty-packs"—sixty little vials of crack, about a fifth of a gram in each. These guys are the wholesalers. They round up their street dealers and front each one a single sixty-pack. When the street dealer sells out his supply at ten bucks a pop, he keeps one hundred dollars, turns the other five hundred over to the wholesaler, and gets another sixty-pack. If you hustle at this game, you can be the richest kid on the block.

These street dealers, of course, are all quite young. They have to be. In Illinois it's a Class X felony to sell drugs within one thousand yards of a school, a park, or a church—which covers most of the city—and that carries a mandatory six- to sixty-year sentence. But the maximum you can give a juvenile is thirty days in the Audy Home. Common sense dictates that the dealers would use these youngsters on the street and keep the adults out of sight. The youngest kid Goff spotted this morning looked to be about eleven. He was not a full-fledged dealer; he would just take over when one of the older boys went to take a piss or something. His main job was lookout. They paid him to ride his bike up and down the street watching for the "Five-oh!" (as in *Hawaii Five-0*).

As for the buyers in this open-air drug market, some of them were quite young as well. The youngest was probably in the fifth grade, but they weren't all schoolchildren. The oldest was in his seventies. There was a mailman, a CTA bus driver—they were white, black, Spanish, you name it. At one point Goff spotted a pregnant white lady carrying a baby in a papoose sling with a gallon of milk in one hand walking down the street. Goff said, "What the hell is she doing here?" She bought a ten-dollar hit.

The impact of this kind of activity on an otherwise peaceful neighborhood is beyond belief. When the dealers move in, the most significant change, of course, is the guns. To protect their interests, the dealers bring with them a considerable amount of firepower, and they like to flash it so that everybody understands they're not kidding. Dealing in contraband is an inherently dangerous business. There are mountains of loose cash all over the place and if somebody sticks you up, you have to deal with it yourself because you sure as hell can't call the cops. Along with the constant threat of bandits, there is the constant battle over the marketing franchise. The only contract you have to do business on this street corner—a business that may be worth five thousand dollars a day—is the enforcer you've got stuck in your belt. And when the competition shows up, a century of civilization is stripped away and the neighborhood is transformed into Dodge City, circa 1850. The toughest sonofabitch on Main Street runs the show and the good citizens keep their mouths shut. Imagine half a dozen teenagers in Chicago Bulls Starter jackets with their caps on backward and automatics stuffed in their pants transacting business in your driveway. You don't see a thing. And that's what impressed Goff this morning as he watched from the van. Here were ordinary folks, working stiffs, trying to keep up the neighborhood, sweeping sidewalks, washing cars, never making eye contact with the dealers. The dealers might as well have been invisible.

A few hours after the top gun dropped off the first shipment, he came back to pick up the cash receipts and replenish inventory. From the backseat, two guys stepped out with guns at the ready just like Brinks guards, and scanned the street while the money was counted, bagged, and sealed. Apparently it tallied up. These guys split and a few minutes later another car dropped off the next round of sixty-packs. "They always keep it separate," says Goff. "The drugs and the money are never together."

Just like the Chrysler Corporation in a good year, this outfit was running three shifts a day, seven days a week. By noon, Goff and his team had seen enough to bust practically everybody in sight. He gave a shout over the radio and squad cars came screaming in from every angle, guys jumping out, guns all over the place, people running, handcuffs, faces on the pavement, everybody on both sides swearing motherfucker-this and motherfucker-that. They hauled ten kids off to the lockup, confiscated five automatics and a couple of Chinese AK-47s. And they shut down the operation, at least for the rest of the day. But Goff had no illusions that he'd made any permanent alteration here. "You know you ain't gonna stop it," he says. "It's a game."

It's a game, however, he can play with deadly skill. Unflappable, quick-witted, and creative, Goff has all the essential ingredients of an undercover cop. Now in his mid-forties with over twenty years on the force, his close-cropped graying hair and trim salt-and-pepper beard frame the kind of small-town good looks people trust at first glance. Cops and robbers alike say Frank Goff is a man of his word. He also reads the street better than most. "A lot of these guys that are users, they ain't bad guys. We see a lot of working guys, truck drivers and everything, people with jobs. They're not robbing people to buy this ten-dollar bag. Why arrest all these people? You know, they got a problem. So instead of just getting this kid selling a bag or two or this guy who buys a bag or two—we work our way up the chain." As soon as the dust settled, it took Goff about five minutes of threats and promises to find out where all this rock was coming from. The locals fingered "Ramone," a Gangster Disciple and known dealer whose address on 113th Street came up on the computer. Goff and his team headed for the South Side.

By sundown, Scotty Freeman and Darren Washington, the two African-American halfbacks on Goff's squad, are waiting in the darkened corridor of Ramone's apartment building as he comes in. When the hands reach out to grab him, he assumes he's a dead man. It seems that his little operation up in K-Town is a private sideline not sanctioned by the Gangster Disciples. Ramone thinks he's about to get whacked. He's so relieved when they say *"Police!"* he practically kisses them.

On the other hand, he has half a pound of rock cocaine in his pocket and a pair of Tech-9 assault weapons in his apartment. And since they've already checked his rap sheet, they know he has a major case pending. So in the time it takes to flip a coin, Ramone decides to become a C.I.—confidential informant—in return for a little slack. With Goff listening in, Ramone calls his supplier—"De-De"—and asks him to come by with another kilo. Then Goff and his men take up positions in the vestibule and in the van across the street. They're expecting De-De any minute now.

Over the past decade, Goff says, he's seen a sea change in the drug war in Chicago. "Ten years ago, if you stopped a dope dealer and he had a thousand bucks on him, that was a big deal. Today you can find that much in some kid's lunch bucket. And that's another thing that's changing. Before it was men. And they were mostly dealing reefer. Now, one of the hardest things to find is reefer. There's a big upsurge in heroin. Acid is back. Crack is all over the place. I absolutely guarantee that I could go any-where in the city and buy dope within three or four blocks. Very easily done. For instance, there's a place a block from the station house. This one operation maybe does fifteen or twenty thousand dollars a week."

Headlights sweep the street as a car turns onto 113th at the corner. Through the burlap, Goff watches as the guy parks in the spot they've saved for him in front of Ramone's six-flat. "That's the wrong car," says Freeman. De-De's supposed to be in a Dodge Shadow. This is a Ford. Freeman and Goff get out and approach the driver cautiously. They don't want to scare him to death. They flash their badges and politely ask him to move on. The startled citizen is gone in a flash. They get back in the van and wait.

A few minutes later, Bob Fischer comes out of the building. Goff cracks the window. Fischer says Ramone just got a call from De-De. "He wants Ramone to come down the stairs and pick the stuff up because he's having problems with his starter. He can't shut the car off." Just then another car turns onto the street. Fischer jumps in the back of the van with Goff to get out of sight. They watch the car roll up to them and pull into the open slot in front of Ramone's building.

"Blue Honda," says Freeman. Still the wrong car. They get out again. Goff crosses the street and moves up the sidewalk as Freeman and Fischer approach on the driver's side. No sudden moves. They don't want some poor taxpayer jumping out of his skin. The guy is half out the door when he spots them. He's got what looks like a pizza in a plastic bag in one hand and a sack of flour in the other. Goff says, "Sir, we're police officers, would you mind—"

BRRRRRRRUP! He's cut off by twenty-five rounds from the machine gun inside the plastic bag. Goff is hit in the neck. Scotty Freeman is down. Fischer, narrowly missed, blasts away with his weapon as De-De jumps back in and jams the Honda in gear. Goff, bleeding at the neck, empties his Beretta at the fleeing car.

Frank Goff has this recurring nightmare—he knows a lot of cops who have this dream—where he's firing and firing and nothing's happening. The bullets are just falling out of the gun barrel. Now he's living the nightmare. He can see the windows shattering, but these soft-point police bullets flatten on impact to prevent a ricochet. They're penetrating the glass but without enough force to do any damage to the driver. De-De, on the other hand, is using armor-piercing ammo. The round that grazed Goff's neck also went through both sides of a car half a block down the street. But while the police bullets aren't drawing blood, they still hit like a sledgehammer, and De-De is stunned. The windshield is so riddled he can't see out of it and he's bouncing off cars on both sides of the street. Goff jams in another clip and takes off after him on foot as the other guys look after Scotty Freeman.

Crashing his way down the street, De-De is not making very good time. Goff is gaining on him. De-De pitches a handgun out the window. Goff scoops it up on the run. It's a "throw gun"—an old pistol he tossed out so that Goff would think he's unarmed. But at the end of the block De-De's luck runs out. He hits a truck and careens across a front lawn and into a house. The startled folks on the front porch are apparently so used to neighborhood gunfire they don't connect it with this smoking wreck in their yard. They think it's a traffic accident. As Goff approaches at a dead run, his nightmare is suddenly compounded. Three little kids rush down from the porch to the driver's window, look in at De-De slumped over the wheel, and shout for Momma to call an ambulance. Goff is yelling, "Get away from the car!" but they're paralyzed. De-De lifts his head slightly, eases his hand down to the Ruger 9mm lying on the seat beside him, and without lifting the gun, fires ten rounds through the door.

The sound of the gunfire is contained inside the car, so Goff doesn't even realize he's being shot at until he's hit. One slug nicks his forearm, another his shoulder, but he can't fire back because of the kids. De-De meanwhile has recovered his senses. He jams the Honda in gear and roars off across the lawn. Goff blasts away at him as he careens around the corner, but De-De's taillights vanish in the distance.

At this point in an otherwise spectacular getaway, De-De makes his first mistake. He calls his girlfriend on the car phone and says he's been hit in a shoot-out. He tells her to open the front door. But he doesn't say anything about the cops, so she assumes it was rival gangbangers. She dials 911.

Meanwhile Goff and Freeman are getting their wounds tended by the paramedics. They were lucky. Aside from several 9mm holes in his jacket, Goff's three wounds are superficial. And Scotty Freeman was saved by his bulletproof vest. The shell just nicked the edge of it and deflected up under his collarbone. They're on their way downtown in the back of an ambulance when they happen to overhear a 911 call on the radio. A man with a gunshot wound needs an ambulance. Goff looks at Freeman. "That's gotta be the guy."

When the gang unit arrives at De-De's house to nab him, they find seven flattened bullets on the pavement beside his car. They apparently fell off his jacket when he got out. This time the slippery dealer offers no resistance.

As soon as Goff gets stitched up, he and Bob Fischer take a ride to the impound yard for a look at the unstoppable Honda. It's riddled with holes and all the glass is shattered, but the damn thing still runs. "Quite a testament to Honda," says Goff. But a look inside the trunk reveals one of the reasons—a sheet of boilerplate steel mounted at the forward wall. Goff recognizes this setup. It's what they call a "trap car." Behind that bulletproof wall there's usually a hidden compartment.

He checks the driver's side in front and spots a slight bulge under the carpet next to the rocker panel. It's a floor-mounted switch. Goff clicks it with his foot and the back of the rear seat falls forward. And there it is—bagged and ready for sale—seventeen pounds of powder cocaine. Along with bundles of cash. Tens and twenties mostly. It takes a quarter of an hour to count it. It totals $53,000.

Goff is impressed. "The day's receipts," he says. And a glance at De-De's ledger bears him out. The account book they found with the dope gives a glimpse of the incredible scale of the problem facing Frank Goff and his colleagues. In the first ten days of March, this mid-level delivery man for the Gangster Disciples took in $451,000.

If this story were fiction, we would now expect Frank Goff to get some kind of commendation. Maybe even a promotion. But three days later he got a blunt warning from his superiors: "Don't ever do that again." While it's true that Goff and his men recovered a dozen weapons, confiscated seven and a half kilos of coke and $53,000 in cash, and shut down a major crack operation, all in one eighteen-hour day, that wasn't their assignment. Their assignment was to keep crack away from the schools. And while Goff can argue that it makes a hell of a lot more sense to go for the roots of the vine rather than plucking the grapes one at a time, his superiors don't see it that way.

First of all, there was a total of seventy-two rounds blasted off in the middle of a residential neighborhood. It's a miracle there weren't six or eight bodies on the pavement, Frank Goff's among them. The brass isn't interested in this kind of Wild West gunplay, no matter what the results. To make sure Goff gets the message, they order him back into uniform. No more undercover work. From now on he and his men will ride in marked squad cars and stick to busting teenage dealers with dime bags.

Goff is disgusted, but not surprised. They have a saying downtown: "Big dope, big problems. Little dope, little problems. No dope, no problems." Downtown, they look on narcotics as a swamp, a sinkhole that can suck your career under in the blink of an eye. The river of money flowing through the streets, splashing over the curbs and into the pockets of everybody in sight, is unlike anything they've ever seen before. There are opportunities for disaster at every turn. Says Goff, "You walk in a room—you're making forty-five thousand a year—and there's a million dollars in cash, and the guy jumps out the window. Do you chase him? Or do you figure this is far enough?" But you don't have to be a police commissioner to see the possibilities. The headlines are full of it: TALES OF CORRUPTION AGAIN TAR N.Y. POLICE . . . 9 NEW ORLEANS OFFICERS INDICTED ON DRUG, GUN CHARGES . . . U.S. CHARGES 12 D.C. OFFICERS WITH A DRUG-PROTECTION RACKET . . . WIDESPREAD CORRUPTION IN L.A. NAR-COTICS SQUAD . . .[1] In one brief period, over twenty officers from Brooklyn's Seventy-fifth Precinct were implicated in drug dealing, gunrunning, and murder. In neighboring Brownsville, ten officers from the Seventy-third were tagged with running their own drug ring. In the Thirtieth up in Harlem—"Dirty Thirty"— two dozen officers were charged with shaking down dealers and selling the drugs themselves. Investigators said at least ten of the seventy-five New York precincts may be involved.[2] In Los Angeles, one of the sheriff's elite narcotics squads went down in flames when its members were videotaped stealing drug money from a motel room. No sooner was this team dispatched to jail than three deputies from another squad were busted with over a million dollars they shook out of dealers and money launderers.[3]

In Chicago, they seem to have figured out how to avoid all this untidiness. This is a city that understands corruption, and they have a biblical fix on it: "Lead us not into temptation." All ongoing narcotics investigations are handled by the narcotics squad, and the narcotics squad itself is focused entirely on small-time buy-bust arrests. There's almost zero chance of anybody in the lower ranks stumbling into a roomful of cash or a truckload of coke. And any serious attempt to follow the trail upward is discouraged. As they told Goff, "You're going after the right guys and somebody's gonna get hurt."[4]

Of course, there are a couple of ways to read that statement. It's clear the department has a legitimate concern about holding down the level of mayhem. But anytime the boss says, "Don't open that door," your average Chicago cop is going to suspect there's something behind the door. "I have a good idea," says Goff. "You can't really nail it down, but a lot of guys are thinking somebody's making bread somewhere."

Could it be that the "Chicago solution" is to intercept the corrupting cash at the highest level, and thus prevent it from trickling down and infecting the troops? Whether it's true or not, nobody argues that it's inconceivable. The Gangster Disciples—just one of half a dozen drug empires in Cook County—take in tens of millions a year, and their overhead is peanuts.[5] They pay no taxes, no benefits, no rent. They handle their own insurance, make their own collections, and the raw materials are so cheap they get a 300 percent return on the dollar. Which means the GDs could spend hundreds of thousands of dollars a year in bribes to Cook County public officials and it would be considered a modest cost of doing business.

But despite all the talk of high-level payoffs, Frank Goff has lately come to fear an even more ominous development in the ongoing battle. The Gangster Disciples have discovered politics. After a decade of learning how to manipulate the levers of power through surrogates, the GDs are beginning to look directly at the levers themselves. "It's just like the old mob days," says Goff. "We're talking about a street gang that can intimidate people, put up your fliers, tear down all the other people's fliers, get people to vote and register and come to the polls. This group can control a lot of votes. They finally realized that. They can elect whatever politician they want."

The political potential of the GDs spilled into the open one fall afternoon in 1993 at a downtown protest rally over school funding. Mayor Daley and his colleagues were watching from the fifth floor of city hall when Loop traffic suddenly ground to a halt as the march was joined by hundreds of orderly, disciplined young African-Americans. What impressed the seasoned city hall onlookers more than anything was the fact that the troops on the streets below had apparently been fielded at a moment's notice. They carried signs that said "21ST CENTURY V.O.T.E." According to the mayor's aides, that's the political arm of the Gangster Disciples.

"They've already elected certain people," says Goff. "Once you get that, once you can get the judges and the lawmakers elected, you can control everything."

. . .

In the courtrooms of Chicago, as in the creaking justice system throughout the country, the mills of the gods grind slowly. By the time the details have been worked out with De-De and his lawyers, twenty-one months have slipped past and it's winter again. The sentencing is finally set for December 8, 1994, and Frank Goff makes it a point to be there—but not with any sense of vengeance. Although De-De did his best to blast Goff full of holes, the even-tempered cop makes it a point not to take any of this personally. On the other hand, given all the backroom orchestration he's already witnessed on this case, Goff just wants to make sure the guy doesn't slip through the cracks.

The Cook County Criminal Courts Building at Twenty-sixth Street and California Avenue is five miles southwest of the Loop and light-years from the experience of the average citizen. The seven-story limestone facade with its chiseled motifs—*Veritas . . . Publicas . . . Justitia*—speaks of another era, and the broad steps rising to meet the fluted Doric columns no longer lead anywhere. The ornate bronze doors are permanently sealed. The entrance is now in the glass lobby to the south, which is able to accommodate something the original architects could never have foreseen—metal detectors.

The third-floor courtroom has also made a concession to the times: a wall of bulletproof windows now separates the officials from the onlookers. Inch-thick panels of Lexan angle upward from steel-framed partitions in front of the spectators, and the judge's words come to them through speakers in the ceiling. It would be hard to imagine a more telling symbol of the apprehension that permeates the criminal justice system.

Since this is a plea bargain, there's no jury, so Goff takes a seat in the box next to Scotty Freeman. When De-De is brought out from the holding cell, they're surprised to see that he's lost about twenty-five pounds. Goff leans to Freeman. "Doesn't look like jail set well with him." For his part, De-De fixes on the judge as the charges are read, never once glancing at his tormentors in the jury box. The judge asks him if he actually did all this. "Yes." Do you have anything to say? "Nope."

The sentence, of course, has already been hammered out among the lawyers. In Illinois, trying to kill a police officer will get you six to thirty years, so the state's attorney initially asked for twenty-five. But De-De is well-spoken, well mannered, and his family is well connected to the church. Over a hundred letters came from all over the community saying what a fine young man he is, that his parents are decent churchgoing people, that he got off on the wrong track and got crazy, that he should be released, that he was set up. And then the case was assigned to a liberal judge. The state's attorney said this particular judge could conceivably give De-De the minimum. Goff thought that was bizarre. "I just got some fifteen-year-old kid six years for selling twenty grams of coke." Now here they were talking about giving the same rap to a guy who had just tried to blow away three police officers. Goff said, "Okay, if the judge tries to give him six, I'll have his whole courtroom filled with Fraternal Order of Police members." Goff and the boys agreed to go down to twenty years. In the end everybody settled on fifteen.

Like a slave in the dock, De-De stands in prison garb, hands behind his back, head slightly bowed, as the judge hands him fifteen years for each attempt on three counts—Goff, Freeman, and Fischer—plus fifteen years for the dope and the pistol he pitched out the window—plus fifteen years for the dope and pistol in the car—a total of seventy-five years. But the sentences will run concurrently. Since he's already served twenty-one months—and since he's eligible for parole at the halfway mark—De-De will be back on the streets in five and a half years.

"It was good for De-De," says Goff. "In his gang he'll be elevated in rank. One: he kept his mouth shut—two: he did hard time in the joint—three: he tried to kill police. He'll be elevated substantially and he was pretty high to begin with. He'll be a regent. Or they may make him a governor." That would be good fortune indeed. A governor for the Gangster Disciples answers only to the top guy, Larry Hoover, the éminence grise who runs the show from a cell in Joliet.[6] If De-De becomes a governor he will control an entire section of the city, and through his hands will pass a torrent of cash.

Who gets what in the GDs is determined with absolute dictatorial authority by the lithe and enigmatic Hoover, the forty-five-year-old founder of the gang, now doing 150 years for murder. To some people, it may seem a little bewildering that a man behind bars can operate a major drug cartel as efficiently as if he were working out of a Michigan Avenue office suite. But if you're in the drug business it's self-explanatory. Sooner or later everyone in the trade, like De-De, will wind up doing a little time. If De-De has been straight with the organization and has not messed with the money, he'll be in good shape. When he arrives in Joliet, instead of getting his throat cut, he will find protection, camaraderie, and cash. And in prison as in the world at large, if you've got the cash you can have anything you want.

As Goff and Freeman are leaving the courtroom, it becomes clear why the Lexan panels were installed between the crowd and the court officials. The boy's mother is waiting for them and she's enraged. She berates Goff, but rather than waste her wrath on the white boy, she aims most of it at Scotty Freeman. "You should be ashamed to be in the same race as us!"

There was a final sinister sidebar to the events leading up to De-De's capture. "Everybody that was involved with that is now dead," says Goff. "All the players. The guy's house we went to— they killed, like, five or six people. They were trying to find the informant. They never did get him."

To an old Chicago hand like Studs Terkel, all this murder and mayhem has a slightly familiar ring to it. Studs has spent the last seven decades coursing the streets of the city recording the images that would emerge in best-sellers like *Working* and *Hard*

Times and *Division Street*. He says the last time the streets were this full of dead bodies, he was a teenager, and the man calling the shots was a punk from Brooklyn known affectionately as Big Al.

Alphonse Capone was born in the shadow of the Brooklyn Navy Yard in the last year of the nineteenth century. His parents, a young immigrant couple from a village on the Bay of Naples, were unable to divert him from the allure of street life, and by the time he was sixteen he was an enforcer for the Five-Points gang. In the summer of 1919, he suddenly needed to get out of town for health reasons, so he took a train to Chicago and got work as a bouncer at the Four Deuces, a famous saloon-whorehouse on South Wabash.

The Four Deuces was owned by Johnny Torrio, a dainty little immigrant from Naples with tiny hands and chipmunk jowls—hardly the image of a gangster. But his head, too large for his body, housed a first-rate criminal mind. Torrio may have been the first mobster of the modern era, the first real gangland businessman. He hated violence—"There's enough for everybody, boys." But if push came to shove, he always had a cageful of gorillas like Alphonse Capone to handle the pushing and shoving.

The event that would transform these two men from local pimps to international icons had taken place a few months earlier when Nebraska became the thirty-sixth state to ratify the Eighteenth Amendment to the Constitution: ". . . the manufacture, sale, or transportation of intoxicating liquors within, the importation thereof into, or the exportation thereof from the United States . . . is hereby prohibited." It would take effect just after the new year in 1920. "For John Torrio," writes biographer Robert Schoenberg, "Prohibition was an answered prayer. He always strove to turn crime into a regular business; now the fools had obliged him by making a regular business criminal."[7]

By erecting an artificial barrier between alcohol producers and consumers, the government had created a potential bonanza that can only be likened to the Gold Rush. No talent or capital was required, just guts and muscle. But the scale of the logistical problem was something the criminal element had never confronted before. While a speedboat full of Canadian whiskey might turn a tidy little profit, it made no dent in the thirst of fifty million drinkers. Supplying thousands of clandestine taverns on a daily basis called for organization, manpower, fleets of trucks, breweries, distilleries, warehouses—all the components of major corporations—and since they were dealing with contraband, they could hire only criminals. This simple dictate brought together thousands of muscle men, cutthroats, gamblers, and con artists who otherwise would never have spoken to one another, and welded them into a panoply of efficient law-breaking machines. It was this demand for integrated operations that would create the crime syndicate as we know it today.[8] As historian Andrew Sinclair put it, "National prohibition transferred $2 billion a year from the hands of brewers, distillers, and shareholders to the hands of murderers, crooks, and illiterates."[9]

The seeds of organized crime had been in place since the Civil War. In the 1870s, professional gamblers began banding together to defend themselves against civic-minded reformers and other do-gooders.[10] Men like John Torrio, who ran gambling and prostitution operations, had already planted seeds of corruption in city hall and the police department. Torrio was in a position to fertilize those seeds because he had what the others lacked: vision.

For nearly thirty years the Anti-Saloon League had lobbied for Prohibition, and on the eve of their triumph they issued a statement to the press: "At one minute past midnight tomorrow a new nation will be born . . . tonight John Barleycorn makes his last will and testament. Now for an era of clean thinking and clean living!"[11] For Bishop James Cannon, who had devoted his life to the temperance crusade, this was a moment of heady victory. For John Torrio and Al Capone, for the Purple Gang in Detroit, for Meyer Lansky and Frank Costello, for Charlie "King" Solomon in Boston and Max "Boo Boo" Hoff in Philly,[12] for

Samuel Bronfman and for Joe Kennedy and hundreds of other incipient millionaires across this great freedom-loving land, it was indeed the dawn of a new day. Unfortunately, it turned out to be the bootleggers instead of the bishop who had the most accurate fix on human nature.

Laying hands on the booze itself proved to be the least of their problems. A Niagara of whiskey began flowing over the Canadian border, which proved to be as porous then as now, and clandestine mother ships plied the seas off both coasts, off-loading European and Latin American produce onto high-powered motor launches for the midnight run to shore. And onshore, illegal distilleries and breweries of all sizes flourished everywhere. The "Terrible Gennas" who controlled Little Italy on Chicago's near West Side organized alcohol cooking as a cottage industry. They installed hundreds of stills in tenement flats and spare rooms, supplying the mash, yeast, and sugar, paying fifteen dollars a day to the man or woman or child who stoked the fire.[13] At the other end of the spectrum, there were huge distilleries operating openly wherever they could arrange political cover. Breweries were still allowed to make nonalcoholic beer, and a sizable draft of the product was either diverted before the alcohol was taken out or had the alcohol put back in later. But the most common ingredient in booze was industrial alcohol, which is used for manufacturing everything from paint and printing ink to plastics and cosmetics. To discourage people from drinking it, industrial alcohol was laced with poison, but this poison could be boiled off through redistilling. Industrial alcohol was siphoned into the illegal market at such a phenomenal rate that it ultimately accounted for half the booze drunk in the 1920s.[14] To give it the taste and color of scotch, you added caramel, prune juice, and creosote.

Torrio originally entered the market as a wholesaler, and with Capone as his right arm, they set up arrangements with importers in Detroit, New York, New Orleans, and Florida, with brewers from Joliet to Racine, and illegal distillers throughout the Midwest. They trucked the booze from all points to warehouses in Cook County and delivered it to hundreds, and then thousands, of retail outlets. While the prices were two to ten times what they had been—a keg of beer now went for fifty dollars—that figure included protection. To ensure peace in the marketplace, Torrio offered the perfect arrangement. The small-time operators were simply put on the payroll. The big-time operators were offered dependable supplies and protected territory. Everybody would respect everybody else's turf. No outsiders could move in. No speakeasy could buy from anybody but the designated chief of that territory.

Unfortunately, lucrative high-risk enterprises tend to attract the ruthless and greedy, which meant that Torrio's business partners included such volatile lunatics as the Terrible Gennas, Claude "Screwy" Maddox, and Dion O'Banion, a cherubic little Irishman who might either buy you a drink or shoot you in the back depending on his mood. O'Banion once set Torrio up by selling him the Siebens Brewery on the near North Side just a few hours before it was scheduled to be raided. Initially, Torrio refused to go after O'Banion, preferring diplomacy to slaughter in the interests of business. But the nature of the business demanded violence. There was no way to prevent it. All arguments, whether about territory, profits, or management philosophy, had to be settled by force. In short order, the streets of Chicago were red with blood, as were the streets of Kansas City and Detroit and almost every other major American city. The Cook County state's attorney, trying to stem the crimson tide, added a thousand men to the police force, got the county to triple the number of judges, and had absolutely no impact whatsoever. Over two hundred gangsters were gunned down, blown up, or knifed to death during the first two terms of his watch—on at least one occasion there was a machine-gun duel in broad daylight right in front of the Standard Oil Building on Michigan Avenue—but not a single gangster was sent up for murder.[15] In court, witnesses contracted a disease called "Chicago amnesia," and one prospective juror told the judge straight out he wouldn't vote guilty because he didn't want to get beaten to a pulp.

In January of 1925 a serious attempt was made on Torrio's life. Remnants of the O'Banion gang, rightly convinced that Torrio had signed off on the murder of their erratic leader, waited for Torrio outside his house with shotguns. They blew four holes in him as he was getting out of his car. Somehow he survived, but for a man who liked to hum opera to himself, this was no way to make a living. He turned the operation over to his less sensitive sidekick, Big Al.

At this point Capone took total command of an army of some five hundred men, and his ruthless approach to marketing soon eliminated or co-opted almost all of his competitors. He traveled through the city of Chicago in a seven-ton armored Cadillac with cars ahead and behind full of young men openly displaying submachine guns. Aldermen, senators, and judges took orders from Capone over the telephone, and his annual tax-free income was about to make him one of the richest men in America.

He was twenty-six years old.

And that is the striking thing about these Prohibition-era public enemies that jumps out at you from the old photographs. All the faces are so young. Street punks with machine guns.

But there's one other thing that resonates with our time. If you look at a gangland map of Chicago from the 1920s, you find a chilling similarity with the map of today. On the near North Side where the O'Banion gang once slugged it out with the Terrible Gennas, you now find the Vice Lords facing off with the Latin Kings. And where Terry Druggan and Frankie Lake once peddled synthetic scotch whiskey and needled beer, the Mexican Mafia now provides cocaine and heroin. And there can be no doubt who is the successor to Big Al. The vast territory that sweeps from the South Side and arcs around the Loop to the west is owned and operated by Larry Hoover and the Gangster Disciples.[16]

Chapter Two

May It Please the Court

It was late afternoon when Frank Goff and Scotty Freeman cleared the courtroom and descended to the marble lobby of the old Cook County Criminal Courts Building. As they passed through the line of guards and metal detectors and stepped out into the icy December blast, they witnessed yet another court phenomenon unique to our time: the arrival of the night shift.

Cook County runs the largest court system in the world,[1] and these days it's practically spilling into the streets. Over the past two decades the caseload has doubled, and then doubled again. But it would be political suicide to tap the voters for enough cash to quadruple the court system, so the County Board solved the problem by telling the judges, clerks, and lawyers to pitch in and work a little harder.

In a desperate effort to ease the docket, presiding judge Thomas Fitzgerald set up the first judicial night shift in the history of Cook County.[2] In October of 1989, five associate judges were yanked out of traffic court and sent to Twenty-sixth and

Cal, where they began hearing felony cases from four o'clock in the afternoon to midnight. Since the overload was driven mainly by the war on drugs—and since the regular roster of judges was fed up with drug cases—these courts would hear drug cases exclusively. Over the next eighteen months, the night shift ate through fourteen thousand cases and simply slipped further and further behind. In 1991 any pretense that this was a temporary solution was set aside when Fitzgerald added three more courtrooms.[3]

To a lot of people, the unsettling thing about the change of shift at 4:00 P.M. is the sudden change in racial composition. During the day, traffic in and out of the building more or less reflects the city's multiethnic nature. But when night falls the white faces seem to melt into the shadows and the corridors fill with blacks and Hispanics. There is an occasional white face among the accused, but it's always some luckless minor trader copping a plea. There will be no kingpins tried in night drug court. Black or white, if you can afford a La Salle Street lawyer, you will not be subjected to this cut-rate jurisprudence. This is strictly for those caught-in-the-act low-end traffickers who, by the sheer weight of their numbers, are threatening to grind the American criminal justice system to a halt.

The defense for these arrestees will be mounted by somebody like Tim Lohraff, a young idealist paid by the state to represent the indigent. Lohraff grew up on the far side of the lake in Buchanan, Michigan, and when he went off to college he had every intention of becoming a teacher. He was studying English literature at the University of Michigan when a summer job as a researcher exposed him to the romance of defending the defenseless. So he got a law degree from Illinois and he's been working for the Cook County public defender's office ever since.[4]

Lohraff, a white man of German and Irish extraction, is one of those people concerned about the perception of justice in night drug court. "I've been here a year," he says. "I've probably handled a thousand drug cases. I've had maybe fifteen or twenty white clients. I constantly ask the state's attorneys—'No white people sell or use drugs?' I mean, I'm not trying to go into statistics, but how does that play out night after night after night?"

At the cluttered defense table in room 302, Lohraff sifts through a mountain of folders and finds the next case. "This guy is kind of a quintessential example of what goes on in here every night," says Lohraff. "In this city most of the drugs are controlled through street gangs. They're organized in these military hierarchies, and the actual dudes who are on the corner hawking the stuff are the lowest of the low. They're the disposable, throwaway soldiers, the foot soldiers, and that's who this guy is."

Dwayne Thomas[5] is an eighteen-year-old black male who was already on probation for a drug offense when a couple of officers in a squad car saw him walking south on Ashland carrying a paper bag. When he spotted the cops he took off and ducked into an alley. They caught him, checked the alley, found the paper bag, and inside was a handgun. A felon with a gun is a violation of probation. "He wanted to go to trial," says Lohraff, "but you're really screwed when it comes to violations of probation. Winning one is next to impossible." So Lohraff quickly cut a deal. Tonight will simply be the final act in a script written last week by Lohraff and the state's attorney. If the judge agrees to the terms, the whole show will be wrapped up in about fifteen minutes.

Lohraff looks over the probation officer's presentencing report. It says when Dwayne Thomas was asked if he was a gang member, he answered, "I been in the GDs all my life."

"That's an interesting quote," says Lohraff. "It wasn't 'I been in the gang since I was eleven or twelve' but 'I been in the GDs all my life.' His mother was an alcoholic, his father had left. The GDs were—his *family*, you know? I mean the day he walks out of the joint, you know he's gonna be back on the same street doing the exact same thing he's doin' now."

Dwayne Thomas is led in from the holding cell, and in his sagging Cook County jumpsuit, it's hard to picture him as a member of the fearsome Gangster Disciples. Short, slightly built, downcast eyes, he looks far too young to be standing at the open maw of the state's awesome judicial engine. Tim Lohraff has done the best he could, but it wasn't much. Dwayne Thomas, after all, is only one of 120 clients Lohraff is currently representing. "What we do in night drug court is triage. Every file I get, I write on the outside of the file what the charge is—kind of like a doctor would, you know—cancer, heart attack, stubbed toe. If it's a Class X and the guy's never been arrested before and he's lookin' at six years, I'm gonna fight that one harder than the Class 4 where the guy can get probation. The people who are not looking at as much time basically get the shaft."

Dwayne Thomas glances up at Judge Dennis Porter. Black robed, sharp-eyed, efficient, Porter is leafing through the paperwork, trying to grasp the essence of the story as quickly as possible, because this is one of some 650 cases now pending on his call. But Porter has a reputation as one of the best judges in night court—the smartest, the most fair. "He knows the law cold," says Lohraff. "When Porter rules against us, we're pretty well screwed."

Judge Porter glances up from the paperwork to inspect the subject of all this legal effort. He nods to Lohraff.

"Judge, Mr. Thomas is standing before you. He is eighteen years old and comes from a home where his father left. His mother is an alcoholic who, according to Mr. Thomas, is the one that started him drinking. He stated that he has a problem with alcohol; he uses it almost every day. He's eighteen, Judge. We would ask the court to consider that he still has potential to reform his life. The state has agreed to three years in exchange for the defendant's plea of guilty, and in light of that recommendation the defendant would enter a plea of guilty."

The judge looks up. "All right, Mr. Thomas, by pleading guilty you are giving up certain rights, among them, you are giving up your right to a jury trial, a jury trial would be with twelve people who are registered voters, these twelve people come into the courtroom, listen to the trial, and they decide if the state has proven you guilty beyond a reasonable doubt. Any questions about what a jury trial is? All right, if you wish to plead guilty you will not have a jury trial. You can sign on that piece of paper your lawyer's giving you. . . ."

The words flow in a high-pressure torrent like the legal disclaimers at the end of a car commercial as Judge Porter races to fulfill the requirements of the Constitution. Each staccato burst of legalese is punctuated by "You understand?" Then finally, "Anything you want to tell me, Mr. Thomas, before I sentence you? All right, sentence of three years in the Illinois Department of Corrections. . . ." He checks the documents. "You've been locked up since April twenty-ninth? The defendant is credited with 197 days in custody. All right, good luck, Mr. Thomas."

Eleven minutes, thirty-nine seconds. Not a record by any means but right in there.

The success of Cook County's night drug court immediately attracted the attention of the federal government, and the Justice Department looked into it in 1994 and issued a highly favorable report. But buried in the accolades were some troubling footnotes. The researchers noticed that defendants often got probation but almost never got treatment: "This is a quick way to get rid of cases, but not necessarily in the best interest of defendants who have serious drug problems. . . ."[6] In other words, addicts who are given a pass on Monday will go back to the streets and get busted again on Tuesday, this time for violation of probation. Which, as Dwayne Thomas just discovered, is a cinch for three to five in Joliet. Thus probation, instead of being an act of compassion, becomes a trapdoor that guarantees a trip to the pen. "They give them just enough rope to hang themselves," says Lohraff.

The other unsettling note in the government report was the commentary from the people who work there, the lawyers, probation officers, and judges: "Night court is a production line . . ."; ". . . a cattle call . . ."; ". . . a mill, not a court of law."[7] But these reservations were far outweighed by the practical advantages of cranking out fourteen thousand verdicts a year without any new real estate. Several other cities are preparing to follow Cook County into the night.

The man who, more than anybody else, is responsible for the spectacular caseload at Twenty-sixth and Cal is a decorated Vietnam vet who did a tour with the first helicopter unit sent into that ill-starred war. Still lean and hungry, Commander Mike Hoke is now the top narc in the Chicago Police Department. His operation is based in an old gymnasium southwest of the Loop. The reason the narcotics squad is headquartered in the departmental gym is an interesting sidebar in itself. The building needed a new roof and the narcotics squad had a barrel of cash from confiscated drug assets. In the unerring logic of the City That Works, these two facts fit together hand in glove.

Set in the shadow of the Sox Park grandstands, the aging brick building offers no hint of its contents, and the three bearded guys in plaid shirts stashing their bowling satchels in the trunk of the blue Pontiac would not tip you off unless you were familiar with the habits of undercover cops. Up the narrow stairway, past the battery of secretaries at computer terminals, Mike Hoke issues orders from a paneled office lined with the wall plaques, photographs, and awards that speak of a career still on the move. At forty-five, he commands a company of 190 troops with a budget of $8 million, an operation that by itself is larger than most of the police departments in the country.

"I send out anywhere between two to ten teams a day," says Hoke, "and we ride up to a corner where we've got a complaint. And an undercover police officer gets out of the car, buys a small amount of narcotics, he gives a signal to an enforcement team, they ride up and take the person off to court. It's a felony to deliver narcotics. Our conviction rate's ninety-four percent."

But while this impressive level of success plays well downtown, Hoke himself is uneasy. He knows that practically everybody his guys will bring in tonight will be black or Hispanic. Like

Lohraff, he finds this disturbing but he says there's not a lot he can do about it. He is essentially running a fire department. "We respond to our clientele, which is the citizens of Chicago. Most of our complaints come from the black community—somebody who can't wash his car or let his kids go outside and play because of the gunfire. We have no open-air drug markets that are manned by white people and we have probably a hundred of them that are manned by blacks."

In other words, white crack dealers don't stand on street corners. They deal behind closed doors over the kitchen table, or the bar, or the office, or the conference table. As one young sorority girl–turned–dealer said, "You wouldn't believe the customers I had. Doctors, lawyers, business executives—all of them were white."[8] But since this kind of terrain is inaccessible to guys in squad cars, the practical effect is for white middle- and upper-class crack users to pursue their habit unmolested while the inner-city dealers are harvested like wheat through a combine.

It would be nice to think that this racial tilt in drug enforcement was unique to the Windy City, but a glance at the headlines anywhere reveals that the Chicago experience permeates the criminal justice system. The overall U.S. numbers are astounding. While the National Institute on Drug Abuse says that far and away the vast majority of people who have used crack are *white*, 96 percent of the crack defendants in federal court are black or Hispanic. The U.S. District Court for Southern California has not prosecuted a single white person for crack in over five years. In 1992 there were no federal prosecutions of whites for crack dealing in Chicago, or in Denver, Miami, Dallas, or Boston. The states prosecute an occasional white crack dealer, but the record there is better by only a point or two. California's numbers for this period were identical to the federal docket— only 4 percent of the defendants were white.[9]

Mike Hoke was born and raised down on Chicago's South Shore and he doesn't need a University of Chicago economist to tell him what's going on here. "When I grew up we had all these factories on the West Side that people, when you got out of school, could go work at, or the steel mills, or the army would take you. Now all these factories are closed. The army is gonna quit recruiting inside Chicago come this year. Dope dealing is probably the only growth industry inside Chicago."

There is another insidious fault line in the rules that works against African-Americans, and that is the legal distinction between crack and powdered cocaine. Chemically, the two compounds are identical except that crack has been mixed with sodium bicarbonate. The process is so simple that any fifth-grader with a little cocaine and a can of baking soda could cook up a supply on the kitchen stove. But when the sodium and carbon atoms bond with the cocaine hydrochloride, the substance becomes considerably more powerful, at least in the eyes of the law.

When the media discovered crack in 1985, it led to a feeding frenzy that whipped the country into a state of panic.[10] Congress, with a proud history of draconian drug laws, pushed through some of the most draconian yet. Today, when the kitchen chemist mixes sodium bicarbonate with cocaine, he is simultaneously increasing his potential prison exposure by several orders of magnitude. Say you start with a fifth of an ounce of coke—the weight of a couple of copper pennies. If you're caught with that amount of powder (or even ten times that amount of powder), you're probably risking a few weeks in jail. But the minute you combine that fifth of an ounce with two cents worth of baking soda, you're looking at a mandatory minimum five years without parole.

The cocaine itself is no more powerful than it was before, but combining it with baking soda causes the end product to vaporize at a lower temperature, and that means you can smoke it. Inhaling these cocaine fumes gets you considerably higher than snorting the equivalent amount of powder. The impact on the brain is instantaneous—an immediate, maximum upper. The exact same effect used to be achieved by rock stars in the 1970s and early 1980s with a technique known as freebasing. The powdered cocaine was treated with ammonia to remove the acid, then dissolved in ether to produce pure crystals that could be smoked. But when you light matches in the presence of ether, you run the risk of turning yourself into a human torch, as comedian Richard Pryor and countless others discovered. Crack, on the other hand, is nonexplosive, easy to make, and cheap. An individual rock the size of a match head can go for as little as five bucks (roughly three times the value of the coke it contains) and it's good for an instant trip to the cosmos. Unfortunately, easy come, easy go. The spectacular high is very, very brief. So if it happens to fill a void in your life, there is a tendency to spend every dime you can beg, borrow, or steal on the stuff. The emotionally disturbed daughter of a West Coast oil company executive tried a hit in her college dorm one night and proceeded to run through a $200,000 trust fund in six months.[11]

But crack is the fast-food item on the drug menu, and it naturally appeals to the low-end retail user who can't afford to buy powder cocaine in the sanctity of the locker room. And while we have to assume that these new laws were not intentionally racist, the practical effect has been to focus our wrath on the poor and leave the suburban cocaine users to their own devices. Today—although most drug users in all categories are white—blacks run a 500 percent greater risk of being arrested for a drug offense.[12]

Sitting behind his heavy oak desk on a fall day in 1993, Mike Hoke looks over the computer printout before sending it downtown. "For the first ten months of this year we've seized over six hundred pounds of cocaine, thirty-five pounds of heroin, and two tons of marijuana. We've locked up thirty-eight hundred people now this year, and seized three million dollars in cash. Ten months. And we have put some of these places completely out of business. But those are minor victories." He shrugs. "They're not major victories."

For an old combat hand like Hoke, this body-count approach to the war on drugs conjures up unpleasant memories. It's as if he senses a familiar aroma—the stench of the jungle. "This is a war that's not gonna be won on the streets of Chicago."

In its heyday, the Aragon Ballroom was surrounded by Chicago's upper-crust Jewish citizens—this is the North Shore, after all, only a couple of blocks in from the lake—but in the 1950s the Jewish community pulled up stakes and headed north to Skokie, leaving their magnificent old theaters and temples behind. Today, except for the wall of glittering high-rises along Lake Shore Drive, the area is solidly African-American and riddled with poverty. But the Aragon remains, and on a good weekend hundreds of white kids will stream in from the suburbs for bands like Smashing Pumpkins and Foo Fighters. On these occasions the neighborhood—though rife with crime and crawling with thieves and junkies—is totally safe for these young suburban innocents. They have no need to worry about the danger lurking in the shadows. Their security is assured because the local drug lord, "Mombassa," has declared it so: "You don't mess with the customers." Alphonse Capone couldn't have said it better.

The monumental Mombassa is a former basketball star who was on a fast track to the NBA when he banged up his knee and lost his scholarship. But he apparently did not leave South Bend empty-handed. He has such a sufficient grasp of business administration that he is now grossing around five thousand dollars a day, tax-free.

His nemesis, Sergeant Joe Kosala, runs the Twentieth District gang squad out of Damen Avenue. In the ongoing battle between these two primal forces, Kosala knows that nailing Mombassa himself is out of the question. He touches neither the drugs nor the money. So the most the cops can hope to do is shut the operation down for a few hours, but even that's not as easy as it looks. Though the alfresco drug bazaar in front of the housing project at 4846 North Winthrop is as wide open as a block party, it's proven nearly impossible to cuff the sales force. These youngsters are fleet of foot, and while most of the guys in the tac squad are young and lean, you can't outrun a desperate kid on his home turf. He knows where the pitfalls and loose boards are and you don't. But over time, Kosala has noticed that one of their favorite escape routes is through the abandoned town house across the street at 4847. Tonight he plans to cut them off at the pass.[13]

But just as the last of his guys are getting in position, one of the squads is spotted and they have to jump the gun. In the blackness, men leap from their cars and dash headlong into the unknown. This is the moment of maximum danger, with cops racing in from all sides, dim silhouettes stumbling through terra incognita, potential targets for a shotgun blast from any nook or cranny. Kosala, like Mike Hoke, is a Vietnam vet and he experienced his share of heart-pounding terror on a Mekong River gunboat. Fear is nothing new to him. But the rest of these guys are too young to have witnessed any of that carnage. They think they're immortal. One crew dashes into the shadowy gangway alongside the building and another goes for the basement as Kosala lunges through the back door and leads two men pounding up the stairs shouting *"Police!"*

If there can be anything more terrifying than a night landing on an aircraft carrier, this must be it. A scared kid will cut you down in a second because he doesn't know any better. Rushing into a black room with a gun in your hand, not knowing which door may suddenly kick open and spit fire or which floorboards are sawed through and ready to drop you into the basement—that requires more than just discipline. This is not TV.

The men fan out through the first floor, yanking doors open, poking around the sagging sofas and crates that serve as furniture in this clubhouse of the damned. The streetlight streaming in through the broken front windows casts an eerie camouflage of light and shadow over the cluttered rooms, but in seconds they've combed the first floor and they're moving to the stairway looking up. Kosala is a beefy Polish guy, over six feet and 220 pounds, but at moments like this he's positively light on his feet. Up he goes, ready to grab the rail if a step is booby-trapped, moving like lightning. He spins—there's a figure silhouetted against the window—

It's a dummy. Old clothes stuffed with pillows and propped up on a chair. It's a final little flip of the finger from Baby Doc's runners.

Down in the alley, the defeated team regroups, and Kosala drags out the dummy. He throws it on the ground and the squad proceeds to stomp it to death, pounding and kicking it until the stuffing is floating in the wind. For good measure, Kosala pulls out his .357 and puts a hole in the thing.

A few minutes later the squad is on the way back to the station, heading west on Foster Avenue, when the guys in the lead car spot something. They sweep across the left lane and screech to a halt. There, pinned in the headlights, half a dozen black teenagers are frozen in their tracks. The other cars slam on the brakes and suddenly the street is crawling with cops. In a flash the kids—four boys, two girls, the oldest maybe seventeen—are spread-eagled and braced against the wall. One of the cops recognizes the fifteen-year-old with the backward cap. He pulls him out of the lineup and tells him to empty his shoes. Sitting on the curb, the kid pulls off his sneakers, and the cop says, *"Dump 'em!"* Nothing there. *"Take off your socks!"*

These teenagers fit the profile so perfectly that it's impossible to believe they're not carrying anything. For ten minutes the cops pepper them with questions and pat them down, empty their pockets, and rain a constant stream of insults. "What's a girl like you doing with a piece of shit like this?" "Listen, stupid, I told you, dump your fucking socks." But the search turns up only an unused plastic baggie. Disgusted, they let everybody go but the barefoot fifteen-year-old sitting on the curb. They search him again.

It would be easy to chalk up this kind of abuse to racism, but the team happens to include an Oriental, a Mexican, and a

Puerto Rican. This is simply an explosion of frustration from otherwise professional cops who are fed up with the pursuit of Mission Impossible. As one team member put it, "We beat people without prejudice. We hate everybody equally."

The truth is, this time they didn't beat anybody. They just messed with a few heads for a little while. Finally, with a last needling insult and a couple of ominous threats about "next time," they tell the fifteen-year-old to take off. In an eyeblink the kid is into his shoes and on his feet. His friends are long gone now, out of sight. He heads west on Foster without glancing back and disappears into the night. With chilling insight, the cop at the wheel of one of the squad cars leans to the reporter in the backseat. "So what do you think the long-term sociological implications of this shit will be?"

The last time this country got a vivid reminder of why we have the Fourth Amendment was twenty years ago when Richard Nixon and his associates decided to use the awesome power of the White House to get even with a handful of people they didn't like. They rifled confidential medical files, digging up dirt for a smear campaign. They bugged phones and offices, invaded private lives, and launched campaigns of fear and intimidation under color of authority. It was, in fact, a textbook example of the very thing Thomas Jefferson and his colleagues were thinking about when they wrote these unequivocal words two hundred years earlier: "The right of the people to be secure in their persons, houses, papers, and effects, against unreasonable searches and seizures, shall not be violated, and no warrants shall issue but upon probable cause. . . ."[14]

President Nixon learned, to his utter astonishment, that on those rare occasions when the American people are willing to invoke the absolute terms of their amazing charter, the results are swift and terrible indeed. One television image summarized the collision in the late summer of 1973 as the wave of evidence began to crest against the president. Sam Ervin, the jowly, cracker-barrel senator from North Carolina who was running the Watergate hearings, paused in his questioning to give us a history lesson. He quoted William Pitt, the British parliamentarian, speaking on behalf of the American colonials at a time when their doors were being broken down by the king's soldiers. The king felt he could set aside English law in the colonies because so many Americans were engaged in smuggling, and the best way to catch a smuggler is to take him by surprise. Senator Sam, his rolling cornpone accent barely concealing his rage, reminded us of our heritage.

"The poorest man may, in his cottage, bid defiance to all the forces of the crown. It may be frail—its roof may shake—the wind may blow through it—the storms may enter—the rain may enter—but the King of England cannot enter. All his force dares not cross the threshold of the ruined tenement!"[15]

It may be hard for the current generation to imagine, but in the fall of 1973 kids went back to college wearing T-shirts that displayed the picture of a U.S. senator, and the Constitution, with inexorable certainty, functioned exactly as its authors said it would.

Unfortunately, a price has to be paid to support these principles, and it's a price we're not always willing to pay. In the drug war in particular, we have discovered what King George understood so clearly in the 1770s: it's practically impossible to catch buyers and sellers of contraband if you stick to the rules. The illegal transfer of goods between two people who are in agreement is a tough act to interrupt. With a murder, the victim's family demands justice; with a robbery, the victims themselves demand justice. The rapist, the embezzler, the con artist, all have people chasing them. But when somebody buys contraband from a willing seller, there's nobody to call the cops.

Likewise with six black teenagers walking west on Foster in the middle of the night. The only way you can really find out if they're dealing drugs is to throw them up against the wall and go through their pockets. This happens to be a blatant violation of their constitutional rights (try to imagine this happening to a white businessman on Michigan Avenue), but it's absolutely essential to the work of catching drug dealers. Consider the problem from Sergeant Kosala's viewpoint. Even if his men had found a bag of crack on one of the teenagers, they can't go into court and say, "Judge, the kid looked suspicious so we braced him and found this in his pocket." The judge would bounce the case in a second. So the facts are going to have to be altered to fit the Constitution. As Kosala says, "They lie, so we lie."

The night shift is in session again at Twenty-sixth and Cal, and once more lawyer Tim Lohraff is at the defense table trying to salvage what he can from a hopeless situation. Tonight two of his clients have already gone down in separate trials, both convicted on evidence that was almost certainly seized illegally. "A cop watching your average drug deal is hard put to make a righteous bust," says Lohraff. "All he can see is some guy giving another guy money, and a minute later a third person comes over giving the first guy something you can't see. Well, that isn't gonna work in court. So the script is: 'The suspect dropped a glassine bag to the pavement. The arresting officer recovered glassine bag and saw it contained a controlled substance.' And of course we all know what happened. Everybody in the building knows that the cop threw the guy up against the wall and found the shit in his pocket or his shoe."

But for Lohraff, there is something even more ominous here than the routine violation of his clients' constitutional rights. "There's a curious thing about these drop cases. They're usually the lowest level felony—straight possession. Yet the cop will testify in court and lie—which is perjury. So you have a cop committing a greater felony to convict a lesser felony. It's gotta have an impact on a cop to stand up and lie on a regular basis and think nothing of it."

Lohraff's adversary tonight is an able and aggressive young prosecutor from downstate named Ed Ronkowski and he's about as happy to be here as the rest of these people. Ronkowski, a square-jawed hard charger with his eye on a political career, literally wrote the book on drug prosecution for Cook County. His manual is used to train new state's attorneys in narcotics law. But like everybody here, he had to be dragooned into night court. In fact, this is his second tour of duty.

The defendant, not surprisingly, is a male black eighteen-year-old, and if the court is willing to believe the arresting officer, State's Attorney Ronkowski will have the kid's head on a pike. But there's no sense of triumph. Like Commander Hoke, Ronkowski thinks he may have seen all this somewhere before. "If you want to use Vietnam as a metaphor," he says, "we're at the point where the helicopters are leaving the embassy roof."

But it is on the other side of the bulletproof Lexan where the friends and family watch and wait that one gets the real sense of what this process is inflicting on us. Here are the brothers, fathers, mothers, cousins, mates, and children of the accused. They watch silently, expressionless, as the prosecutor's words fall from the loudspeakers in the ceiling.

"As you approached, what did you observe?"

"I saw the defendant drop from his right hand a packet of white powder."

"What was the lighting conditions at that time?"

"It was brightly lit from streetlights, the nearest one being twenty feet from the defendant."

"What did you do?"

"I walked over and picked up the packet."

And as the gavel falls, there is a murmur through the crowd. And throughout the evening, each verdict is followed by a ripple of sound. In this courtroom tonight you can close your eyes and imagine what it must have been like a couple of thousand years ago standing on the afterdeck of a Roman galley, listening to the crack of the whip and the murmur of the men at the oars.

"We're not producing justice here," says Tim Lohraff. "We're manufacturing revolutionaries."

Chapter Three

Long Day's Journey into Night

The wave of reform that carried Teddy Roosevelt to the door of the White House in 1900 had its origin in the steam engine, the evolutionary device that took us from the ox to the locomotive in a single leap. It wreaked havoc with the social order just as the microchip does today. When the North embraced the steam engine and the South chose to stick with the eighteenth century, the rift between the two cultures widened into the bloodiest conflict in history. The industrialization that followed the Civil War brought rising power to the cities, along with slums, saloons, political corruption, and a spectacular concentration of wealth in the pockets of a handful of men.

Ranged against these evils was a broad coalition that stretched from Kansas to Brooklyn—ordinary Americans fed up with machine politics and robber barons who trampled the little people underfoot. The progressive wing of the Republican party had undeniable claim to the leadership of this movement, for this was the party of Lincoln. These people had freed the slaves. And though it took a war to prove the point, the progressives had shown that the federal government could play a decisive role in the improvement of the human race. By the end of the century, these highly motivated reformers thought they could see the millennium—a chance to do away with not just corruption but evil itself. All they had to do was pass the right laws and humanity would purify itself.

When McKinley was assassinated in 1901, Vice President Teddy Roosevelt unexpectedly mounted to the throttle of this powerful social dynamo. One of his first moves was to dust off the all-but-forgotten Sherman Anti-Trust Act and go after major-league Monopoly players J. P. Morgan and John D. Rockefeller. The roar of public approval enabled him to make an end run around a surprised Congress, and over the next seven years he would change the country so profoundly that his face would wind up on the side of Mt. Rushmore.[1]

For the average upstanding American, the most visible evil of the day was the saloon, filled with brawling immigrants whose votes could be bought for a pint of beer. Here was the social sinkhole where the workingman spent his paycheck, then went home in a stupor to beat the wife and kids. Eliminate the saloon—no, eliminate *alcohol*—and you would dry up the taproot of crime and human weakness.[2] By the end of Roosevelt's second term, seven states already had prohibition laws on the books and the groundswell was clearly building to outlaw alcohol nationwide.

It was in this collision of social reform and religious fundamentalism that the narcotics issue first came to focus in the United States. Another time, another place, and the results might have been far different, but at this moment it would only take a handful of chance meetings to profoundly alter world history.

May 1, 1908, was a blustery Friday in Washington with broken clouds scudding in from the northwest. An intense cold front had moved up the Ohio Valley the night before and there were storm warnings along the Atlantic Coast from Maine to Florida. A few blocks north of the White House, a forty-one-year-old research physician named Hamilton Wright was crossing Massachusetts Avenue at Scott Circle when he heard somebody shout his name. He turned and there was Cal O'Laughlin, the Washington correspondent for the *Chicago Tribune.*

Wright was known to the press. After graduating near the top of his class at McGill University, he had gone to the Far East and established a laboratory in the Strait of Malacca to study tropical diseases. While still in his thirties, he became famous for discovering that beriberi was a bacterial infection. He was wrong, unfortunately—it's a vitamin deficiency—but that turned out to be irrelevant, since he had already married the daughter of industrialist W. D. Washburn, the powerful Republican senator from Minnesota. When Dr. Wright and his bride arrived in Washington just after the turn of the century, he discovered he liked politics better than medical research, and he let it be known through his father-in-law that he was available for some kind of suitable governmental employment.

Cal O'Laughlin was eager to help the son-in-law of one of the country's major power brokers. "In his usual direct way," Wright later noted, "he asked me if I would like to be a member of an opium commission about to be appointed by President Roosevelt." The commission was news to Wright. He didn't know much about opium but he had no trouble recognizing the possibilities. "I saw at a glance that it was bound to be a large and extensive bit of work."[3]

The opium commission that the *Tribune* had just got wind of was a creation of the U.S. State Department, and it had less to do with drug control than selling shoes. The object of this mission was to ingratiate ourselves to the Chinese in hopes of opening up their markets. By helping them with their notorious opium problem, we might be able to impress them with our moral concern, and simultaneously pull the rug out from under the British, who had created the problem in the first place. For most of the last century the British East India Company had been forcing China to accept Indian opium in payment for Chinese tea and silk. The Chinese fought a couple of wars over this issue, lost both times, and wound up giving the British the port of Hong Kong along with a burgeoning opium trade that began to disgust even the English. Though the Americans arrived late in the Far East, the opportunity to help carve up China's commercial markets—"one of the greatest commercial prizes in the world," according to future president William Howard Taft— had U.S. businessmen of every stripe lusting after a slice of the pie.[4]

Using the opium issue as a wedge, Teddy Roosevelt saw a chance to soften up the Chinese with diplomacy instead of gunboats, and it would be virtually cost-free since the United States was not a player in the opium trade. The State Department began agitating for an international conference, and the other great powers were soon shanghaied into signing on. The meeting was set for January of 1909, fittingly, in Shanghai. The Americans would send three delegates. The Episcopal bishop of the Philippines would head the mission, the number two man would be from the American legation at Peking, and the third slot was up for grabs. And on that windy morning in Washington, Cal O'Laughlin advised Hamilton Wright to talk to the White House right away. Wright got there "shortly thereafter," and eight weeks later he was named as the third U.S. delegate to the International Opium Commission at Shanghai. And though his career at the State Department would end in disgrace, he would leave a profound imprint on the twentieth century, for Dr. Hamilton Wright is personally responsible for shaping the international narcotics laws as we know them today.[5]

When Wright first began wading through the State Department files on the opium problem, he assumed he was dealing with some distant plague like yellow fever or leprosy. He had no idea there was widespread opium addiction in the United States itself. But he was trained as a researcher, so he set out to see for himself. He toured the major cities and sent out hundreds of questionnaires to prison wardens, police chiefs, doctors, and drug companies. The survey was not scientific, and the spotty responses left a huge margin for error, but Wright was now a man with a cause and he began to put the worst-case spin on everything he saw. In short order he managed to convince himself that the United States not only had an opium problem, but that it was *worse* than China's.[6]

In truth, there was an opium problem in the United States, but hardly the "numberless dope fiends" Wright began to see. At the turn of the century the typical American addict was a middle-aged southern white woman strung out on laudanum (an opium-alcohol mix),[7] and the highest credible estimates put the number of U.S. addicts at about three people in a thousand.[8] Others thought it was half that. Most of these people had become unwittingly dependent on the vast array of over-the-counter patent medicines that were laced with everything from morphine to cocaine. A popular cough syrup spiked with heroin was available by mail order: "It will suit the palate of the most exacting adult or the most capricious child."[9]

At a time when medical science was still bleeding people with leeches, bottled painkillers with this kind of power were a godsend. Doctors everywhere prescribed them freely for every conceivable ailment because the patients always said they felt better. It was not until the late 1800s that the public began to realize that some of their favorite medicines could be highly addictive. Ironically, just as Hamilton Wright was discovering that narcotics addiction in the United States was soaring out of control, it was actually on the decline.[10] All the leading authorities now agree that addiction peaked around 1900, followed by a steady drop. The reason was simple common sense coupled with growing awareness. The Pure Food and Drug Act of 1906 finally forced manufacturers to list product ingredients on the label, and when people began to realize their favorite nostrums were laced with addictive drugs, they stopped using them.

But for Hamilton Wright it was no longer possible to be objective about the facts. Having persuaded himself that opium addiction was a global scourge, he set out to eradicate it personally. Handsome and imposing, tall, square-jawed, with his hair parted in the middle and a trim little handlebar mustache, he looked like a well-preserved Yale quarterback and he had the ego to match. His tendency to go for the jugular, to overstate the case and stretch the numbers, proved to be a powerful weapon in the opening volley in the war on drugs. But his bulldozer style infuriated a lot of people. Chastened by the secretary of state's warning to watch his step, Wright sailed for the Orient in October of 1908 aboard the steamship *Siberia*.[11]

The Shanghai Opium Commission was a smashing success for U.S. diplomacy. The Chinese were deeply impressed with the American effort. This was the first time they had been treated as an equal partner in an international conference, and it was the first time in memory that the folks who called the meeting did not walk off with a piece of Chinese real estate. But the impact on the drug trade was negligible. The delegates at Shanghai were allowed to exchange information and make recommendations, but that was all. Nobody was obligated to follow through. And some of the key players—England, France, the Netherlands— did not share the American delegation's horror of opium. A British study had recently concluded that opium addiction was no worse than alcoholism, and maybe not as bad. As one public health official put it, "There is more violence in a gallon of alcohol than a ton of opium."[12] Most of the countries involved thought this conference had gone far enough, and when the Americans proposed a second meeting, the British torpedoed the idea. But Hamilton Wright and his colleagues had managed to get agreement on a few resolutions, and that would make all the difference.

The sleeper was Resolution 5, which called on all the signatory governments to clamp down on opium and its derivatives within their own borders. It was easy for the British to go along with this idea—in fact they proposed it—because it had no effect on the international drug trade. It was simply a way of saving face while the Americans held their feet to the fire. But in the hands of Hamilton Wright, Resolution 5 would become a sledgehammer to fashion his dream of worldwide narcotics prohibition.

In the spring of 1909, Wright returned to Washington triumphant, energetic, and fired with a sense of mission. His first job was to convince his bosses at the State Department to demand a follow-on conference in spite of British and Dutch opposition. And to embarrass the rest of the world into going along with his idea, Wright planned to transform the United States into a shining beacon of drug morality. For the next two years he was a one-man Washington pressure group, pitching to Congress, threatening and cajoling foreign ambassadors, twisting arms, and drafting model narcotics laws for the people of the United States.

Despite his relentless enthusiasm, Wright faced a couple of daunting problems. For one thing, there was the U.S. Constitution. A national drug law would call for a national police force—an idea discouraged by the Tenth Amendment. After a year of trying to work his way around this obstructionist document, he complained to his boss that "it has been a difficult business. . . . The Constitution is constantly getting in the way."[13] But the Supreme Court had recently opened the door to a possible way around the Founding Fathers when they ruled that the government had the right to regulate anything it was taxing.[14] Perhaps, thought Wright, the narcotics law could be disguised as a tax act. By the winter of 1909, he had drafted a model bill that would require anyone who dealt with drugs—doctors, druggists, manufacturers—to register, pay a license fee, and keep scrupulous records. And since the revenue men could refuse to license anyone they didn't approve of—addicts, for example—the government would have absolute control over the distribution of narcotics. But despite his certainty about everything else,

Wright was still grappling with the question of who would enforce the law once it was enacted.

The main resistance to federal police authority came from south of the Mason-Dixon line. The senators from Dixie did not want the federal government tramping through their carefully crafted segregation laws. A national drug law, enforced by a national police force, would breach the moat of states' rights, and God knows what would follow that. But Wright now saw a chance to remold southern prejudice into an asset, and it was at this point that his genius took an evil turn. Motivated no doubt by patriotism and a deep concern for the future of humankind, he decided to play the race card.

The "drug-crazed Nigger" was already a popular bogeyman among racists.[15] All Wright had to do was fan the flames. He began feeding the Congress lines like "Cocaine is often the direct incentive to the crime of rape by the Negroes. . . ." While it was true that blacks in the South used cocaine—it was sometimes supplied by white employers trying to get more work out of them—there is no evidence that African-Americans abused the drug any more than anyone else.[16] But to the southern senators, cocaine was particularly ominous because they heard that it transformed the black man into a powerful zombie who not only forgot his place but was impervious to bullets. Some say the reason the .38 caliber revolver was adopted as the police standard in the United States is because of the belief that the lighter .32 caliber slug could not stop a black man high on cocaine.[17]

In using racism in his quest for narcotics legislation, Hamilton Wright was following a hallowed tradition. Almost every drug prohibition ever enacted has had some racial or political component. When Muslims tried to stamp out coffee drinkers in the seventeenth century, it wasn't the caffeine they were after, it was the coffeehouses, which were filled with plotting malcontents.[18] In the United States, the first anti-narcotics law ever passed—the San Francisco opium ordinance of 1875—was aimed squarely at the Chinese. They had been imported by the tens of thousands to build the western railways, but when these monumental projects were finished, the Chinamen were a glut on the labor market. Their principal sin—working too hard for too little money—could hardly be outlawed, so the authorities had to find something else. One thing that set these people apart was their taste for opium. "Many arrests were made, and the punishment was prompt and thorough."[19]

Wright was happy to play the Chinese race card as well, warning that "one of the most unfortunate phases of the habit of smoking opium in this country is the large number of women who have become involved and are living as common-law wives or cohabiting with Chinese. . . ." The specter of unbridled Negroes and coolies waiting at the foot of the bed to carry off wives and daughters proved to be more than the Dixie Democrats could countenance, and they began to knuckle under to the doctor's relentless fear-mongering.

Looking back on Wright's dogged and uncompromising efforts with nearly a century of hindsight, one must marvel at his innocence. Today, we know that a narcotics habit can be a lifetime ordeal, and even addicts who successfully kick may go through rehab a dozen times before they make it. Yet Wright gave no consideration whatsoever to the problems of people who were already addicted. He seems to have imagined that he could cure them by simply passing the law. But it turns out his naïveté can be easily explained: Wright and his colleagues were the victims of a spectacular medical hoax.

In 1909, the medical profession was informed that a miracle remedy for drug addiction had been discovered. It was almost infallible and it took about five days, tops. This amazing revelation meant that opium addiction was no more difficult to overcome than nail-biting. All you needed to kick the habit was a little discipline and a long weekend. Not surprisingly, the man who planted this silly idea in the minds of the American medical establishment wasn't a doctor himself, although he was often referred to as "Dr. Towns" in the press. He was in fact an insurance salesman from Georgia—a self-taught farm boy who went on to become the Colonel Harlan Sanders of the drug-treatment industry. And like the silver-haired Colonel Sanders, his success was based on a secret formula.

Charles B. Towns arrived in New York in 1901 with a plump nest egg from his foray into the life insurance business, and enough guts to take on Wall Street. But as many another farm boy has learned, the Street devours amateurs and he was quickly picked clean. Defeated for the first time in his life, Towns was still in shock when an acquaintance came up to him one day and whispered, "I have got a cure for the drug habit—morphine, opium, heroin, codeine—any of 'em. We can make a lot of money out of it."

"That's a job for a doctor."

"It's a job for a man with an almighty nerve. You've got that. I've got the formula."[20] The formula turned out to be a powerful laxative mixed with a couple of deadly poisons. Needless to say, it had a profound impact on the patient. The first volunteer Towns and his partner experimented on tried to escape from the hotel room after the initial dose, and he had to be held down for two days to keep him from committing suicide. Then, "At the end of forty-eight hours, the divide was crossed. . . . He was offered a hypodermic of the drug . . . and he declined it."

"This is a cure!" cried Wright. Unfortunately, word of this vitriolic cure spread quickly on the streets, and after that it was impossible for Towns to get any more volunteers. So he finally kidnapped a junkie no one would miss—a racetrack tout—and locked him up like the first victim. Though the formula had been modified, this patient didn't like it either—"When I get out of here and tell the boys what you've been doin' to me, your life won't be worth twenty cents!" But after five days they sent him home "a well man."

Convinced he was onto something monumental, Towns began pushing for recognition in the medical establishment. In his high white collar and pince-nez glasses, he certainly looked like a doctor, but with no diploma he was easily dismissed as a snake-oil salesman. So he decided to leap over all these small-minded practitioners and present his case directly to one of the country's leading authorities on addiction and alcoholism. Dr. Alexander Lambert of Cornell University was, above all else, an open-minded scientist, and he agreed to let Towns demonstrate his cure on a few addicts at Bellevue. The results were impressive, or so they seemed, and the fact that Dr. Lambert had personally witnessed it was another star-crossed collision, for Lambert happened to be Teddy Roosevelt's personal physician. Word of Towns's magical mystery cure quickly made it to Washington, and everybody was so relieved that any questions were swept aside.[21]

The reason for the apparent success of this poisonous remedy was that nobody ever bothered to do a follow-up study. Since it was the rare individual indeed who showed up for a second treatment, Towns claimed his method was 90 percent successful. A full decade later, it finally occurred to Dr. Lambert that there was a gaping hole in the evidence, and he set out to track down a number of ex-patients to see how they were doing. He was stunned. Of some two hundred people he had treated at Bellevue, "I found that about four or five percent really stayed off."[22] So the 90 percent cure rate was in fact a 95 percent failure rate, but by then the damage had been done. The mistaken idea that there was a cheap, easy cure for addiction had become one of the founding myths underlying our narcotics laws. It explains to some degree why the several hundred thousand citizens who were already addicted—many of whom had acquired the habit innocently—would soon be simply cast adrift to fend for themselves. By 1920 Towns and his cure had been discredited, but our unforgiving approach to dealing with addicts was already institutionalized.[23]

The Second International Conference on Opium was finally set for December of 1911 at The Hague. By badgering his superiors at State, and threatening and tormenting foreign ambassadors and congressmen, Hamilton Wright had managed to pull this meeting out of the hat in spite of resistance from almost everybody else involved. His style—overstatement, bluster, and manipulation—infuriated the British. They accused him of misrepresenting the Shanghai agreement and exaggerating the dangers of opium in his report to the U.S. Congress. The State Department was alarmed. Afraid that Wright's heavy-handed approach could blow the whole deal, they asked him to find some other line of work. But he was now armed with the terrible swift sword of moral truth and he wasn't about to be deflected by a mere bureaucracy.[24]

Once again Wright confounded his critics. The British eventually calmed down and the Americans managed to get an agreement at The Hague that more or less formalized the document signed in Shanghai three years earlier. The Hague Opium Convention called for each country to exercise absolute control of the cultivation, manufacture, and distribution of cocaine, opium, and its derivatives. In his zeal to set an example for the less enthusiastic representatives, Wright made a sweeping promise. Without bothering to run it past the folks back home, he single-handedly obligated the United States to pass a federal anti-narcotics law. And when he got back to Washington, of course, he used this promise as a double-edged sword, telling Congress that this new treaty gave them no choice but to enact such a law.

Eighteen months later there was a follow-up meeting at The Hague to iron out the kinks, and this time Wright took the reins as head of the U.S. delegation. But this was to be the apex of the doctor's amazing arc. Though his relentless arm-twisting had created enemies around the world, it was not his enemies who would undo him. It was Demon Rum. Dr. Wright may have been a dauntless foe of the opium poppy, but it seems he couldn't keep his hands off the bottle. Alcohol at that moment in U.S. history was an evil equal to opium, and people were starting to talk about Wright's drinking habits. When Secretary of State

William Jennings Bryan smelled liquor on Wright's breath once too often, the two men got into an argument, Bryan threatened to fire him, and Wright left in a huff. Wright assumed that he was indispensable, and he wrote the president asking him to intervene. The reply never came. And thus, the man who had guided the nations of the world toward international narcotics prohibition was suddenly yanked off the stage. After an embarrassing round of begging for another assignment, he left for France to join the war effort as an ambulance driver, and he died three years later as the result of injuries from an auto accident. He was not quite fifty. His legacy, however, is with us still.

The anti-narcotics legislation that Wright fashioned finally made its way through Congress in the winter of 1914. The Harrison Narcotics Act, named for the Tammany Hall Democrat who ushered it through the House, appeared on the surface to be nothing more than a means of gathering information. It called on everybody in the drug trade to purchase a license and keep precise records. The debate had little to do with the evils of addiction, focusing instead on the nation's international obligation under The Hague Convention. At the final reading, the bill passed in a few minutes. *The New York Times* didn't even mention it.[25]

Although the medical profession had largely been brought around in support of the act, they were in for a rude awakening. Hamilton Wright had installed a couple of land mines in the bill, and the trip wire was hidden in a clause the doctors thought was supposed to protect them. There was one extra word in the sentence. A physician could prescribe narcotics "in the course of his professional practice *only*." The interpretation of this phrase was left to the Treasury Department, and to the revenue agents, giving dope to an addict was not "professional practice." It was simply feeding a bad habit—not only immoral, but now illegal.

The medical profession was completely unaware of this development. When one middle-aged morphine addict expressed her fear that the Harrison Act would cut her off, the surgeon general of the United States personally reassured her.[26] He said the act was intended simply to gather information. Meanwhile, down at Treasury, they were sharpening their lances.

It should be remembered that the men who were about to enforce the Harrison Narcotics Act were under the impression that a foolproof cure existed for addiction. If the Towns formula could cure an addict in five days, obviously withdrawal was no big deal. Any weak-willed pervert unwilling to take a simple treatment and get straight would have to be dealt with forcefully. Armed with righteous indignation, they set out to rid the nation of drug addiction. And thus Congress, without any clear sense of the enormity of what they had done, set the stage for the criminalization of a quarter of a million drug-addicted citizens.

Six weeks after the Harrison Act went into effect, the *New York Medical Journal* carried an ominous observation: ". . . the immediate effects of the Harrison antinarcotic law were seen in the flocking of drug habitués to hospitals and sanitoriums. Sporadic crimes of violence were reported too, due usually to desperate efforts by addicts to obtain drugs. . . . The really serious results of this legislation, however, will only appear gradually and will not always be recognized as such. These will be the failure of promising careers, the disrupting of happy families, the commission of crimes which will never be traced to their real cause, and the influx into hospitals for the mentally disordered of many who would otherwise live socially competent lives."[27]

The easiest way to understand the mind of a drug addict is to use food as a metaphor. Imagine you've just been told by the government that food is so bad for you it's been taken off the market. You might be able to handle it for a couple of days, and after that you wouldn't be able to think about anything else—*food*—how to get it, where to get it, and where to steal the money now that a hot dog with mustard is suddenly fifty dollars. But even this metaphor is an inadequate measure of the addict's urgency because a junkie, though starving, will trade food for dope. This consuming desperation, never clearly grasped by either the lawman or the average physician, would prove to be the fatal flaw in the plan to free humanity from the scourge of addiction. What Hamilton Wright and his colleagues had expected to be a brief skirmish would turn instead into the longest-running war in U.S. history. As one contemporary put it: "We had counted without the peddler. We had not realized that the moment restrictive legislation made these drugs difficult to secure legitimately, the drugs would also be made profitable to illicit traffickers."[28]

The man who wrote those words was in a position to know. In 1914 Dr. Charles E. Terry was the city health officer for Jacksonville, Florida. He's considered one of the leading authorities on this period, and his book—*The Opium Problem*—is quoted in every history of the era. Terry's study flew in the face of conventional wisdom when he found that most addicts were women, and that whites outnumbered blacks two to one. And the cure rate—even with the famous Towns formula—was never more than 5 percent. But his report contains one fact that is as stunning today as it must have been to Dr. Terry: "One of the most important discoveries we made at that time was that a very large proportion of the users of opiate drugs were respectable hardworking individuals in all walks of life, and that only about 18 percent could in any way be considered as belonging to the underworld."[29] In other words, 80 percent of his patients had jobs, homes, families, and reputations. And while it may seem bizarre to read that narcotics addicts can hold down jobs and be useful, productive citizens, it turns out there is no scientific evidence to the contrary. In fact, the medical literature is filled with thoroughly documented records of addicts who functioned normally throughout their lives. Among the mountain of case histories, one of the most remarkable is the story of Dr. William Stewart Halsted, "the father of modern surgery."

Halsted, the dashing young son of a distinguished New York family and former captain of the Yale football team, was already a prominent surgeon in Manhattan while still in his twenties. In the decade after the Civil War, Halsted was experimenting with the recently invented hypodermic syringe and the new drug, cocaine, and he made a significant discovery. When he injected cocaine into the skin, the nerves were deadened. It was the first effective local anesthetic and it was a major leap for modern surgery. Unfortunately, Halsted was also experimenting on himself, and he found that when he injected the drug directly into his veins, he got a rush that was better than sex. "Cocaine hunger fastened its dreadful hold on him," a colleague wrote. "He tried to carry on, but a confused and unworthy period of medical practice ensued. Finally he vanished from the world he had known."[30]

Halsted didn't vanish. He was shanghaied. His friends chartered a schooner with a trusted crew and sailed him to the Virgin Islands and back in a desperate attempt to wean him from his habit. They managed to keep him clean for a couple of months, but as soon as he hit the beach he started shooting up again. In a last-ditch effort he checked himself into a hospital in Providence, and after one relapse—through sheer willpower and inner strength—he emerged triumphant, completely cured. Or so the story went.

Shortly after that, in 1886, Halsted joined with Osler, Welch, and Billings—the "Big Four"—to found the prestigious Johns Hopkins Hospital. Halsted's skill and ingenuity as a surgeon made him world famous. His private life was exemplary. He married a thoroughbred southern belle and they lived together in "complete mutual devotion" until Halsted's death thirty-six years later. The fairy tale would have ended there except for a small black book with a silver lock and key.

In 1969, on the eightieth anniversary of the Johns Hopkins Hospital, the book was formally opened according to the instructions of its author, Sir William Osler, one of the four founders. In it was the "secret history" of the Hopkins, and here Sir William revealed that Halsted had cured his cocaine habit by switching to morphine. In other words, one of the four founders of Johns Hopkins was a morphine addict for over forty years, and while one of his colleagues knew all about it, the others apparently never suspected. According to all reports, it had no observable effect on Halsted's performance at home or at the office. Listen to British surgeon Lord Moynihan on Halsted's technique: "frequently light, swift, sparing movements with the sharpest of knives, instead of free, heavy-handed deep cutting . . . the minimum of hemorrhage instead of the severance of many vessels. . . ." Throughout his career Halsted tried to kick the habit and couldn't. He was never able to get by with less than 180 milligrams of morphine a day. "On this," said Osler, "he could do his work comfortably and maintain his excellent physical vigor."[31]

Halsted's story is revealing not only because it shows that a morphine addict on the proper maintenance dose can be productive. It also illustrates the incredible power of the drug in question. Here was a man with almost unlimited resources— moral, physical, financial, medical—who tried everything he could think of to quit, and he was hooked until the day he died. It brings into focus the plight of those addicts all over the country who were about to be cut off with nothing.

But the problem that seemed so daunting to medical men like Terry and Halsted looked like a piece of cake to the lawmen. Addicts—and the doctors and pharmacists who enabled them— were to be hunted down and forced to change their ways or else. Another hint of their naïveté about the scale of the problem is contained in the Harrison Act itself. It calls for an appropriation of $150,000 for enforcement. Eighty years later we are spending that much every three minutes.[32]

The Justice Department strategists understood quite clearly that the Harrison Act was on shaky ground constitutionally. Hamilton Wright and his colleagues had been so skillful in disguising it as a tax law that judges all over the country were interpreting it as a tax law. And when the first case reached the

Supreme Court in 1916, Justice Oliver Wendell Holmes, Jr., blew the government's brief out of the water. In a seven-to-two decision the court tossed out the indictment against a Pittsburgh doctor who had sold a narcotics prescription to an addict, and a host of other doctors, druggists, and addicts who had already been convicted had to be turned loose. The Treasury Department enforcers scrambled to deal with this unexpected damage and immediately began agitating in Congress for additional legislation. In the short run, they managed to keep the medical profession in line through intimidation. According to the Narcotics Division's own numbers, they indicted some thirty-five thousand people over the next couple of years without ever bringing the cases to court—thus terrorizing the medical profession into compliance without risking defeat at the hands of the judiciary.[33] Meanwhile, they went looking for a better case—something vividly outrageous that might change the minds of at least three judges on the high court.

At a different moment in our history, this kind of rough-and-tumble federal intimidation might have been met with public outrage. But in the second decade of the twentieth century, the American people were going through a sea change in attitudes. Among the major losers in this transformation would be the victims of drug addiction. Back in 1900, the country had looked upon addicts as unfortunate citizens with a medical problem. By 1920, they had become "drug fiends," twisted, immoral, untrustworthy. Like vampires, they infected everything they touched. There was no room for compassion here. The only way to get rid of a vampire is to drive a stake through his heart.

This image—the Drug User as Vampire—was to become a driving force in the public mind. And the origin of this powerful symbolism can be traced to a single individual: Spanish-American War hero Richmond Pearson Hobson. At one time, Captain Hobson, "the Hero of Santiago," was the highest-paid lecturer in America, and after each of his public appearances the women in the audience would line up to kiss the dashing young naval officer. He was known as "the most kissed man in America," and they even named a caramel candy after him—"Hobson's Kisses." President McKinley personally decorated him for valor in the Cuban engagement, where he was said to have single-handedly stopped the Spanish Fleet. In fact his mission had been a total failure. His assignment was to sail the aging U.S.S. *Merrimac* into the channel entrance at Santiago harbor and scuttle her there to trap the Spanish Fleet—as Hobson himself put it: "Homeric manhood, erect and masterful on the perilous bridge of the *Merrimac* . . ." Unfortunately the rudder jammed, the ship never made the channel, and Hobson had to be rescued by the Spaniards. But it was a short war and there were hardly enough heroes to go around, so the navy promoted him to captain and by 1906 the Hero of Santiago was a congressman.

Now accustomed to the limelight, Hobson became uneasy when he felt it edging away. So he reincarnated himself as a champion of the temperance cause and once again found himself at center stage. He had a way with words. He called liquor "the Great Destroyer," and when he coined that term in a House debate, his admirers demanded that a copy of the speech be sent to every household in America. But his most remarkable contribution was his quasi-medical analysis of the human brain. Hobson had no more medical training than the eminent Charles Towns, and he was equally undaunted. The brain, he explained, is divided into various vertical layers like a building, with the baser instincts in the basement. Alcohol attacks the penthouse—"the top of the brain . . . organ of the will, of the consciousness of God, of the sense of right and wrong, of ideas of justice, duty, love, mercy, self-sacrifice and all that makes character." Unfortunately, he said, Negroes and Indians were particularly susceptible to alcohol because their mental buildings were not as tall as the white man's. According to Hobson, when alcohol reached the top of the brain of Negroes, "they degenerate . . . to the level of the cannibal."[34]

When his campaign was crowned with success in the enactment of Prohibition, Hobson needed a new focus for his unlimited moral indignation, and he retired from the scene for a few months in search of a worthy demon. It's hard to imagine what took him so long. The evil drug heroin was practically tailor-made for a moral crusade. Not only could it be held accountable for all crime and vice, it had the added advantage of being a foreign import. In a frenzy of public appearances, lectures, and writings, Hobson introduced a chilling new concept. Heroin, he said, transforms the addict into a monster who has no control over himself and is compelled to spread his disease like Count Dracula. It was a masterstroke in the art of propaganda. "The addict has an insane desire to make addicts of others," said Hobson, and he horrified audiences with stories of wretched young zombies infecting their pals with heroin-laced ice-cream cones. "One addict will recruit seven others in his lifetime," he said, and he claimed there were over four million addicts in the United States—a figure sixteen times higher than the Public Health Service estimates.[35]

Hobson's impact would have been powerful under any circumstances, but the early 1920s saw the dawn of commercial radio and almost overnight the great crusader found himself addressing the whole country at once. NBC, one of the new national networks, gave him uninterrupted free time on four hundred stations—an unprecedented audience—and he warned America that there was evil afoot: "Suppose it were announced that there were more than a million lepers among our people. Think what a shock the announcement would produce! Yet drug addiction is far more incurable than leprosy . . . more communicable . . . and is spreading like a moral and physical scourge. The whole human race, though largely ignorant on this subject, is now in the midst of a life-and-death struggle with the deadliest foe that has ever menaced its future."[36]

In fact there was never a shred of evidence to back Hobson's pseudoscientific speculations, but his crusade quickly united all the old prohibition allies—the Kiwanis, the Masons, the Elks, the WCTU—and they simply overwhelmed the handful of scientists who tried to put the brakes on this juggernaut. And despite the fact that fifty years of medical research has consistently debased each of Hobson's assumptions in detail, his terrifying stereotype of the addict as infected bloodsucker lives on in the headlines—and in the American psyche—to this day.

But a phenomenon like Hobson is only possible when there is a receptive audience. His amazing success was the product of two powerful social currents that collided just before World War I. First, the moral surge that crested with national alcohol prohibition had been building for fifty years. And second, rural America's growing fear of the immigrant tide—specifically the flood of European Catholics pouring into the cities—had been hammered into a powerful sword by the Anti-Saloon League. "Besodden Europe," wrote one prohibitionist editor, "sends here her drink-makers, her drunkard-makers, and her drunkards . . . with all their un-American and anti-American ideas of morality and government. . . ."[37] The First World War would further inflame this xenophobic hotbed. When wartime propaganda painted the Germans as thick-necked beasts, the venom inevitably spilled onto Germans in America, and again the Anti-Saloon League wasted no time in lighting the torches: Pabst and Busch and most of the major brewers were Germans, so beer was obviously subversive. Drunken soldiers couldn't shoot straight. Worse, brewing used up eleven million loaves of barley bread a day that could have been used to feed our starving Allies. Clearly, brewers and distillers were guilty of treason. "In this orgy of simplicity," writes historian Andrew Sinclair, "the arguments of the drys seemed irrefutable. They were for God and for America, against the saloon and against Germany. The wets therefore must be for Satan and for Germany. . . ."[38]

The narcotics reformers naturally climbed on board this flag-decked bandwagon. To these people it was becoming clear what the evil Hun had in mind. An editorial in *The New York Times* passed on this rumor of German fiendishness: "Into well-known German brands of toothpaste . . . habit-forming drugs were to be introduced; at first a little, then more, and as the habit grew on the non-German victim, and his system craved ever greater quantities . . ." then the Huns would cut off the supply and the Yanks would be on their knees.[39]

By 1919 public attitudes about narcotics had shifted so radically that even government documents were referring to addicts as "dope fiends," and the Treasury Department decided the time was ripe to make another run at the Supreme Court. After three years of patient sifting, they found a case involving an outrageous hack named Webb who sold prescriptions for fifty cents apiece to any and all comers. His patients numbered in the thousands and he never bothered to examine anybody. He wasn't practicing medicine, he was dealing drugs. But the genius of the prosecutors was to proceed as if Webb were just an ordinary physician whose method of treatment happened to include giving his patients unlimited quantities of dope. The question they posed to the court was: is this legitimate medical practice? This time Justice Holmes came down on the side of the lawmen. "To call such an order . . . a prescription . . . would be a perversion of meaning. . . ."[40] It was a major win for Treasury, and because of the skillful way they had framed the case, they were now able to state that any doctor who prescribed narcotics to an addict was looking at a possible jail term. This decision was soon reinforced by a couple of others, and in no time at all the medical profession more or less washed its hands of the narcotics problem.[41]

It may seem strange that a guild as powerful as the American Medical Association would allow a bunch of Treasury men to wade into their profession and start telling them how to write prescriptions, but the fact is most doctors found the narcotics issue disgusting. Addiction wasn't studied in medical school, nobody seemed to know much about it, and the only experience for most physicians these days was the occasional junkie who showed up wild-eyed, unwashed, and desperate, terrorizing everybody in the waiting room. Every word from his mouth was likely to be a lie and if you turned your back he'd clean the place out. (The average physician would probably have been astounded to know that only a decade before, many of these wretched desperadoes had held down jobs, owned homes, and raised families.) The medical profession was more than happy to turn this ugly problem over to the Treasury Department.

But there's always somebody who won't go along with the program. In this case it was a doctor in Shreveport by the name of Willis P. Butler. Like his contemporary Charles Terry in Jacksonville, Dr. Butler was a local health official who happened to be in the forward trenches at the start of the drug war. In 1919, as the federal enforcement efforts began to cut into the availability of drugs throughout the country, Shreveport city officials became alarmed at the sudden increase in crime among addicts who were trying to finance their habit. "Thievery was bad," said Butler. "They were stealing stuff off front porches." State officials suggested that Butler set up a treatment program for addicts like the one they were running in New Orleans. He went down to take a look. "I saw right away that the clinic was trying to fool their patients off of drugs. They were mixing morphine in solution and reducing their dosage drastically." But the state medics were only fooling themselves. "The addicts knew what they were doing because some of them were doubled up in pain."[42] Butler had enough experience as a jailhouse physician to know this approach wouldn't work. So when he got back to Shreveport he came up with a triage system that some authorities still consider the best single model of community opiate control and treatment in American history.[43] In the four years the clinic was in business, Butler and his staff admitted some twelve hundred patients, and they were sorted into three groups: (1) addicts who needed some kind of immediate medical care; (2) those that were physically healthy; and (3) the incurable. Members of the first group had their habit maintained until they were cured of their other ailments, then they were put into a detox program that included up to a month of intensive hospital care. The second group got drugs until a bed was available, then they too were pressured into gradual reduction. And the patients that Butler and his staff determined to be incurable—often people with untreatable cancer or advanced venereal disease—simply got whatever drugs they needed. Once their dose was stabilized, everybody who could work was expected to, and if they didn't have a job, Butler would get them one. The same with a decent place to live.

It was this last group, the "incurable," that got Butler in trouble with Washington. Although the Treasury Department had originally encouraged the idea of public treatment facilities, federal policy had recently undergone a change in thinking. By 1920, Charles Towns and his magic formula had been completely discredited, along with every other form of treatment then available. The U.S. Public Health Service had reviewed them all and concluded that under the best of circumstances "only about 10 percent of cures have been reported. . . . Our present methods of treating drug addiction must be considered failures."[44] Rather than interpret this warning as a caution signal, Treasury took it as a green light. Since treatment didn't work—if in fact these people were going back on drugs the minute you turned them loose—gradual reduction was a waste of time. Cold turkey was the answer. And to make sure they stayed drug-free, the government would simply have to dry up all sources of supply—including well-meaning but deluded physicians like Willis Butler.[45]

But the success of Dr. Butler's operation was apparent even to the narcotics investigators who came to Shreveport to shut him down. First they checked the local drugstores, looking for evidence of criminal activity, and found nothing. Then they talked to the city's leading physicians and got a chorus of praise for Butler and his clinic. Then they met with the local federal district judge, and he warned them flat out not to make any move to close the place. He said he could personally testify that the clinic had reduced crime in the city. They got the same story from the chief of police, the sheriff, and the U.S. marshal's office. At this point, the agents recommended to headquarters that they just leave Dr. Butler alone.

In Washington, this finding was unacceptable. The federal government didn't have the authority to restrict maintenance to some physicians and not to others. Addict maintenance would have to be allowed nationally or not allowed at all. Discrimination on the basis of "responsible" prescribing would put the government in even more trouble with the Constitution, since this would clearly be the licensing of doctors.

In January of 1923 Butler was invited to a closed meeting in the office of the U.S. attorney and there he found three Treasury Department officials waiting for him. They were polite but firm. He was told that he was not in any way accused of wrongdoing, but his operation was going to have to close down. Other cities were asking questions. If Shreveport could have a clinic, why couldn't they? "No records were gone over," said Butler, "no patients, officials, or doctors were called, and nothing was gone into except the closing of the dispensary."[46] But he could see the handwriting on the wall. One way or another they were going to pull the plug. Defeated but unbowed, Butler agreed to shut the clinic down. But he kept on writing prescriptions for a handful of addicts on his own authority. Given his political clout, the T-men apparently decided they'd better not push him any further.

Six months after the clinic closed, the Shreveport *Journal* checked out the local scene to see what had happened since the federal intervention. It found that while street traffic in heroin and morphine had been practically unknown before the clinic was shuttered, both drugs were now being sold freely everywhere.[47]

In the Old Testament ritual of Yom Kippur, a goat was chosen by lot as a sacrifice to the wilderness demon Azazel. The priests would symbolically burden the scapegoat, or "goat of removal," with the sins of the people, then they would toss it off a cliff out-side Jerusalem, and the nation would be cleansed of its iniqui-ties. The ancient Greeks used human scapegoats—*pharmakos*—and it is from the healing process associated with throwing rocks at these people that we get the word "pharmacy."[48]

In the Roaring Twenties, the United States needed plenty of scapegoats, and the narcotics addicts were almost designed for the job. They were a tiny, powerless minority, and though their numbers might include plenty of powerful individuals like William Stewart Halsted of Johns Hopkins, they didn't dare open their mouths. Defenseless and indefensible, this pathetic aggregation turned out to be a godsend for the politicians. From this point on, whenever senators or congressmen found them-selves outflanked on the right, they could come down on addicts like avenging angels to prove how tough they were on crime.

And now there was plenty of crime to be tough on. Back in 1905 only two citizens out of a hundred thousand had died at the hands of another. Thanks largely to Prohibition, the murder rate in 1923 was four times that high and climbing.[49]

Chapter Four

The Devil and Harry Anslinger

In the beginning, Henry Joy thought alcohol prohibition was a good idea. One of the founders of the Packard Motor Car Company and something of a Renaissance man, Joy thought that eliminating booze from the American scene would cure a whole range of national ills. For one thing, he felt the increasing complexity of the factory demanded a sober workforce. The newly conceived assembly line was no place for drunks. What's more, the money that working men would save by not buying booze could be used to buy other things—toasters, washing machines, homes, cars—and once free of the sodden drag of alcohol, the economy could surge forward. But more important than the economic benefits would be the social rewards for the poor and downtrodden. Decades of fire and brimstone from the temperance crusaders had convinced most of America that the focal point of evil was the saloon. Shortly after the Anti-Saloon League was formed in 1893, Henry Joy and his wife, Helen, came on board with time and money.

When the Eighteenth Amendment—and the Volstead Act that spelled out the details—went into effect in January of 1920, the Reverend Billy Sunday said, "The reign of tears is over. The slums will soon be a memory. We will turn our prisons into factories and our jails into storehouses and corncribs. Men will walk upright now, women will smile and children will laugh. Hell will be forever for rent."[1] Unfortunately it didn't work out that way. By the end of the decade, the great evangelist would have to eat every syllable.

Alcohol consumption did drop dramatically, at least in the beginning. And the economy was booming—the prohibitionists took credit for that. On the other hand, crime was skyrocketing and becoming organized. The country was swimming in bootleg liquor and hardly a day went by without a headline about police corruption. Henry Joy, like most temperance activists, had assumed that when the Eighteenth Amendment passed, Americans would just stop drinking. It never even occurred to him that people would ignore the law. Then one day he found out his servants were making top-quality wine and beer for everybody in the house except himself and his wife.

Henry Joy inadvertently wound up with a front-row seat for the war on booze. His vast estate fronted on Lake St. Clair, north of Detroit. On the opposite shore was Canada, only minutes away by high-speed motor launch, and this waterway was destined to become a major midnight conduit for Canadian whiskey. Joy found it hard to get used to the sight of federal agents blasting away at smugglers trying to land on his beach, but he put up with it. Then one day in December of 1926 a carload of agents showed up at his estate and without bothering to identify themselves ransacked the boathouse and seized eleven bottles of beer from the old watchman. When they came back later, the old man didn't answer fast enough, so they broke down the door and roughed him up. Joy was outraged, but there was more to come. The next time the lawmen were in the neighborhood, they spotted an armed man in a boat just offshore and shouted for him to stop. The man—a duck hunter—couldn't hear anything over the sound of his outboard, so he cruised on, oblivious, and the agents blew him away.[2]

"I made a mistake. I was stupidly wrong," wrote Joy. "America must open its eyes and recognize that human nature cannot be changed by legal enactment." In a complete about-face he canceled his membership in the Anti-Saloon League and became a major supporter of the Association Against the Prohibition Amendment. This newly minted organization was headed by a blue-chip roster that included the three du Pont brothers, the head of General Motors, and the president of Morgan Guaranty Trust. Like Joy, most of these tycoons had been supporters of Prohibition until they were confronted with the reality. Now they were concerned about the future of the republic and there was plenty to be concerned about.

In the first year of Prohibition, crime leaped 24 percent in the nation's major cities, and before the decade was over the criminal justice system would be overwhelmed.[3] The federal caseload tripled and civil cases were brushed aside to make room for the flood of alcohol offenders. Drowning in the flow, judges began offering "bargain days" where a whole courtroom full of suspects would be allowed to plead guilty in return for a small fine. The federal prison system was operating at 170 percent capacity and the cost to the taxpayers was about to increase by an order of magnitude.[4]

Even more alarming to old-money aristocrats like the du Ponts was the dangerous erosion of respect for the criminal justice system. Prohibition enforcement tarred every institution it touched—Coast Guard, Customs, Treasury, Justice—and local cops and sheriffs in cities and counties all over the country. An officer could triple his annual income in a single day just by looking the other way. By 1929, one out of four federal agents had been dismissed for charges ranging from bribery, extortion, conspiracy, and embezzlement to drinking the evidence and submission of false reports.[5] In Detroit, where the liquor trade was said to be second only to the automobile industry, the graft paid to public officials topped $2 million a week, and this was at a time when you could get a hamburger for a nickel.[6] In New York the typical speakeasy had to shell out four hundred dollars a month between the Prohibition Bureau, the police department, and the D.A.'s office, and the lowly cop on the beat picked up an extra forty dollars every time there was a delivery.[7] A reporter for the *New York Evening Sun* summed up American history in 1930 as ". . . Columbus . . . Washington . . . Lincoln . . . Volstead . . . two flights up and ask for Gus. . . ."[8]

The havoc was not limited to institutional damage. The Volstead Act also produced alarming changes in drinking patterns. Beer consumption dropped dramatically, but the sale of hard liquor doubled.[9] Here was another law of the smuggling trade at work: you have to put the maximum bang in the smallest possible package. Beer is bulky. Whiskey is compact and easier to conceal. If you've ever been to a college football game, you've witnessed this phenomenon. Students are normally beer drinkers, but since alcohol is prohibited at the stadium, they sneak in a flask and become whiskey drinkers. This distortion of behavior was visited on the Jazz Age with a vengeance. Instead of buying a drink, they bought a bottle and they didn't get up until there was nothing left but the glass. In the decade before Prohibition Americans had been gradually turning away from alcohol—a tribute to the temperance advocates—and now the trend was dramatically reversed. Drinking became fashionable. If you didn't have a hip flask, you were out of it. And since the speakeasy had no liquor license to lose, there was no need to check ID. If you could reach the bar, the question was "What'll it be?" This laissez-faire attitude collided with another astounding evolution. Before 1918 the only females hanging out in saloons were hookers and dancers. If the ladies drank at all, they drank at home. Now women were flocking to the speakeasies in such numbers, they would give the era one of its enduring images—the flapper. As Heywood Broun complained, the old saloons may have been sinkholes but at least you didn't have to fight your way through crowds of schoolgirls to reach the bar.[10]

Confronted with the ongoing failure of law enforcement, the prohibitionists demanded more of it—tougher judges, harsher sentences, more draconian punishment. By 1929 the penalties had been ratcheted up by a factor of ten. You could now get five years and a $10,000 fine for selling one drink.[11] The enforcement budget was tripled, more agents were hired, the Fourth Amendment was practically set aside—and still it came, an unstoppable wellspring of booze flowing from breweries in basements, and from breweries that covered acres operating at full tilt with the complete cooperation of local officials, and from three hundred thousand private stills spread all over the country. A man who paddled his canoe the length of the Mississippi in the late 1920s said the scent of fermenting mash was in the wind from the headwaters of Lake Itasca to the dock at New Orleans.[12] An updated verse of the old railroad gandy dancer's tune said it all:

> *My sister sells snow to the snowbirds,*
> *My father makes bootlegger gin,*
> *My mother sells wine from the grapes on our vine*
> *My God! How the money rolls in.*[13]

In the end, the rapierlike coup de grâce to Prohibition would be administered by a woman. Tall, statuesque, strikingly beautiful, Pauline Morton Sabin came from the same rarefied atmosphere as Henry Joy. Her uncle was the Morton of "When It Rains, It Pours" and her father was secretary of the navy under Teddy Roosevelt. Like Henry Joy, Pauline Sabin had been an early supporter of Prohibition. "I felt I should approve it because it would help my two sons. . . . I thought a world without liquor would be a beautiful world." Now she would undo it with a fatal thrust.

A lifelong Republican and a skilled organizer, Mrs. Sabin watched with growing agony as the violence and corruption spread, but she was most frightened by the impact it was having on young people. The lesson kids were supposed to learn—"crime does not pay"—was an obvious lie. Crime paid very well and everybody knew it. And killers like Capone were becoming romantic heroes. In May of 1929 she assembled a couple of dozen like-minded social divas at the Drake Hotel in Chicago and they announced the formation of the WONPR—Women's Organization for National Prohibition Reform. "Many of our members are young mothers—too young to remember the old saloon," said Sabin. "But they are working for repeal because they don't want their babies to grow up in the hip-flask, speakeasy atmosphere that has polluted their own youth." Over the next two years three hundred thousand women joined the WONPR, and before it was over there would be 1.5 million.[14]

This defection was a disaster for the prohibitionists. They had always claimed that women backed the Eighteenth Amendment without reservation. Ella Boole, president of the Women's Christian Temperance Union, told Congress in 1928, "I represent the women of America!" Now here was Pauline Sabin—elegant, commanding—leading a delegation before the House Judiciary Committee, saying just the opposite. "Mrs. Sabin spoke bluntly," said *The New York Times* of February 14, 1930, "and her emerald ring glittered as she waved her hand. . . ." She also spoke with chilling eloquence.

". . . women played a large part in the enactment of the Eighteenth Amendment. Many were women who had unhappy experiences as a result of drunkenness among those close to them. They are now realizing with heart burning and heart aching that if the spirit is not within, legislation can be of no avail. They thought they could make prohibition as strong as the Constitution, but instead have made the Constitution as weak as prohibition. . . ." Before the Volstead Act, said Mrs. Sabin, her children had no access to alcohol. Now they could get it anywhere.[15]

Applause interrupted her testimony several times—an explosion of relief, no doubt, from congressmen who finally saw a glimmer of light at the end of the tunnel. Many of these law-makers had known for years that Prohibition was unenforceable, but under the thumb of the Anti-Saloon League, they dared not open their mouths. The League had helped elect many in this chamber, and they were still convinced the League spoke for the woman voter. Mrs. Sabin put the lie to that myth, and the legislators began to breathe again.

In the campaign of 1928, Herbert Hoover's ambiguous platform gave hope to both wets and drys, but once in office the new president came down heavily on the side of Prohibition. Partly to placate the offended wets, he named a panel of experts to study the problem under the guidance of former attorney general George Wickersham. It was clear from the outset that Hoover expected the Wickersham Commission to support the law, and when the report came out in January of 1931, it looked at first glance like a triumph for the drys. On closer reading, however, it turned out only one of the eleven members actually believed Prohibition had a chance. The statements of the other ten ranged from skepticism to outright demand for repeal. More important, the body of the report was loaded with scientific data and expert testimony detailing the devastation—the overwhelming flow of cash, the corruption, the gunplay, the judicial paralysis, the bursting prisons—and the unstoppable, ever-flowing tide of booze. "As an account of what had gone wrong and why, the whole report has not been surpassed," says historian Sean Dennis Cashman.[16] With these facts on record, the politically correct conclusions at the end of the report made the administration look ridiculous. This ditty from the *New York World* summed it up.

> *Prohibition is an awful flop.*
>   *We like it.*
> *It can't stop what it's meant to stop.*
>   *We like it.*

> *It's left a trail of graft and slime,*
> *It don't prohibit worth a dime,*
> *It's filled our land with vice and crime,*
>   *Nevertheless, we're for it.*[17]

But the cat was out of the bag. The wild claims of the prohibitionists—unquestioned in the past—were now confronted with official facts and figures that left no doubt the "Noble Experiment" had been a disaster.

The drys had one last ace in the hole. Prohibition wasn't just a law, it was embedded in the Constitution. Most authorities thought it would be impossible to reverse the process. No amendment had ever been repealed. It takes two thirds of both Houses and three fourths of the states. Senator Morris Sheppard, the wily old Texan who helped install Prohibition, said, "There is as much chance of repealing the Eighteenth Amendment as there is for a humming-bird to fly to the planet Mars with the Washington Monument tied to its tail."[18] But with the Crash of 1929, the country's attention had shifted from morality to survival, and when Franklin Roosevelt swept into office in 1932, it was with the active help of former Republicans Pauline Sabin and Henry Joy. Less than a month after the Democratic landslide, the hummingbird took off for Mars.

Back in the closing days of 1919, just before Prohibition became law, the bar at the Yale Club, with uncanny foresight, had laid in a fourteen-year supply of liquor. On December 5, 1933, when Utah became the thirty-sixth state to ratify repeal, the prescient Yalies had good reason to clink their glasses. They had timed it almost to the bottle.[19]

Harry J. Anslinger had given it his all. A muscular, bullnecked, former railroad cop who could handle himself on any terrain,

Anslinger was one of the men who had tried to make Prohibition work. As U.S. consul to the Bahamas in 1926, he had browbeaten the British into clamping down on the rampant liquor traffic across the Straits of Florida. As head of the Prohibition Unit's foreign control division, he had forced similar treaties down the throats of the Canadians and Cubans. And he had created a vast intelligence network aimed at stopping liquor at the border—all for nothing. He was determined this wouldn't happen to him again.

When the ax finally fell on the Prohibition Unit, it missed Anslinger completely. He had already moved on. Three years earlier his bosses at Treasury had reassigned him to the Narcotics Division, a separate compartment within the Prohibition Unit. The Narcotics Division was supposed to be the enforcement muscle behind the Harrison Narcotics Act, but the agency had been awash in corruption almost from the beginning. When the son of Commissioner Levi Nutt turned up on the payroll of New York mobster Arnold Rothstein, it finally pinned the scandal meter. Nutt was relieved of command and Harry Anslinger was given the job of cleaning up the mess.[20] But this time Congress felt the situation called for more than a reshuffling of the deck, and they decided to pull narcotics enforcement out of the tainted Prohibition Unit altogether. With the Porter Act of 1930, they created the Federal Bureau of Narcotics, a brand-new arm of the Treasury Department. Harry J. Anslinger was given the job of acting commissioner on July 1, 1930, and everybody but Anslinger thought it was a temporary assignment. In fact it was a seat he would hang on to with an iron grip for the next thirty years, and like his colleague J. Edgar Hoover over at the FBI, he would routinely confound and outmaneuver his enemies through five presidential administrations.

The impact of this appointment would ripple through history for half a century and more because Harry Anslinger was no ordinary bureaucrat. He was a law-and-order evangelist—"a cross between William Jennings Bryan and Reverend Jerry Falwell," said biographer John McWilliams—and he brought to the new job a puritanical conviction that alcohol prohibition could have succeeded. It failed, he maintained, not because it was a bad idea, but because law enforcement wasn't tough enough. Anslinger himself beat the drum for years trying to get more draconian penalties—not just for sellers but for drinkers as well—and they wouldn't listen. Now he would get a chance to test his theories in the field of narcotics, and the country would be transformed in the process.

Anslinger's first problem was to clean up the rampant corruption among the agents he inherited from Levi Nutt, but he was sandbagged almost immediately by a couple of fresh scandals in the New York office. Once again, agents were fronting for dealers and protecting mobsters—this time, "Legs" Diamond. Then came the Democratic landslide of 1932, and suddenly Harry Anslinger began to look like a temporary employee. At this delicate moment, he almost cut his own throat. In a memo to the field offices, Anslinger warned his men to be on the lookout for an informant he described as "a ginger-colored nigger."[21] The White House exploded, and even the senator from Anslinger's home state demanded his resignation. Any other third-level bureaucrat would have been on the next train out of Union Station, but somehow Anslinger survived. How was this possible?

There's no doubt the man could be charming and persuasive. Even his fiercest detractors give him that. And he was macho in the gunslinger style that has always appealed to Washington insiders. But it turns out the secret to his longevity was actually buried in the text of the law that set up the Bureau. Before Anslinger, if you wanted to market narcotic painkillers, you had to take your case to a Cabinet-level tribunal consisting of the secretary of state, the secretary of the Treasury, and the secretary of commerce. But when Congress created the Bureau of Narcotics, it eliminated this board and gave the job, whole and entire, to the new Bureau's commissioner—Harry J. Anslinger.[22] So if, say, you wanted to manufacture narcotic pharmaceuticals, you had to check with Harry. It was as if he had been accidentally positioned at the wheel of a gate valve that could direct the flow of money. He and he alone could decide who would gain entry to the narcotics Monopoly game, and by 1936 he had admitted only eight players—Merck, Mallinckrodt, Hoffman LaRoche, New York Quinine, Parke-Davis, Sharpe & Dohme, Eli Lilly, and Squibb—almost all destined to become household names. The arrangement was perfect for Anslinger, since it was obviously easier to police a small group of large manufacturers than a large group of small ones. It was also perfect for the insiders in this oligopoly, and their spectacular financial growth reflected it. This corporate cartel became Anslinger's steadfast ally, and throughout his career, whenever the commissioner needed help on Capitol Hill, the pharmaceutical industry would come running. When he was pushing legislation, they would testify in favor. When he was under attack, they would move behind the scenes twisting arms. This powerful lobby combined with Anslinger's natural constituency—the frustrated drys and law-and-order conservatives—ultimately rendered him unassailable.[23]

Contrary to pop history, Harry Anslinger did not start America's legendary campaign against marijuana. In fact he tried to keep the Bureau out of cannabis enforcement in the beginning because he thought eradication would be impossible. The stuff grows, he said, "like dandelions."[24] But after the curtain came down on Prohibition, the nation's moral focus moved on to the next available villain, and the marijuana issue was waiting in the wings. By 1933 several states had already outlawed the Devil Weed and some officials were calling for a national ban. Anslinger realized he might be able to use this issue as a weapon—a club to whip the states into line. He needed to get local law enforcement more involved in the battle against narcotics because his tiny force of 250 agents could barely keep track of the major traffickers.[25] For months Anslinger had been on the road trying to convince the states to adopt some kind of uniform narcotics enforcement, and he was getting nowhere. The state governments were as strapped as Washington. So sometime in 1935 he decided to build a little fire, and he suddenly upgraded marijuana from a low-priority nuisance to an evil "as hellish as heroin."[26]

Outside of the temperance organizations and a handful of lawmen, most Americans had never heard of marijuana, but along the Mexican border it was a different story. Before the Depression, cheap Mexican labor had given the West its muscle. But with eighteen million unemployed gringos in the breadlines, the brown-skinned guest workers were now looked on as thieves. Just as the people of San Francisco began to notice the menace of opium smokers when the Chinese were done building the Central Pacific, border state lawmen now began to notice alarming behavior among the indolent Mexicans. They would smoke this weed and it would make them crazy. Wild, fearless, they would chop people up with axes and not remember a thing. It took four lawmen, they said, to subdue one of them.[27]

The district attorney of New Orleans added the other essential ingredient when he claimed that marijuana was a sexual stimulant. He said it caused addicts to abandon their civilized inhibitions. Once again the specter of superhuman, sex-crazed savages sent a ripple of fear through the South, and once again it proved irresistible to politicians and the press. The Hearst news syndicate had always been fascinated with drug addicts, and when his editors discovered the menace of marijuana, Hearst himself fell on it with a vengeance. Led by the flagship *New York Journal-American*, the "Marihuana-Crazed Madman" became a staple fixture in Hearst's fifty newspapers, magazines, and radio stations, and very shortly his worst fears were realized.[28] Reports began coming in about young people experimenting with this deadly new drug—hardly surprising given the publicity.

At the head of the parade throughout this campaign, the man beating the bass drum was the indefatigable Spanish-American War hero Captain Richmond Hobson. Now in his late sixties,

Hobson had been completely reinvigorated by the anti-marijuana campaign. And though Harry Anslinger despised the man (a dilettante, said Anslinger, who lived off his wealthy female financial backers),[29] Hobson could still ignite Middle America like a prairie fire. Dispatches from the western States to *The New York Times* headlined: "STATE FINDS MANY CHILDREN ARE ADDICTED TO WEED," "POISONOUS WEED SOLD FREELY IN POOL HALLS AND BEER GARDENS," "USE OF MARIJUANA SPREADING IN WEST," "CHILDREN SAID TO BUY IT."[30]

Now a very real sense of fear welled up in the heartland. Young people were involved. Harry Anslinger found himself in demand as a speaker before women's clubs and parent-teacher associations all over the country, and he painted a horrifying picture. "Take all of the good in Dr. Jekyll and the worst in Mr. Hyde—the result is opium. Marihuana may be considered more harmful. . . . It is Mr. Hyde alone."[31] Within a couple of years, his campaign overwhelmed the state governments, and by 1936 most of them had signed off on the uniform narcotics law, which now included cannabis. The argument was compelling. As one Montana lawmaker put it: "When some beet-field peon takes a few puffs of this stuff, he thinks he has just been elected president of Mexico, so he starts out to execute all his political enemies."[32]

Anslinger's campaign may have been just a tool in the beginning, but fueled with this kind of racial tinder, it quickly got out of hand. The Treasury Department was barraged with cries for help from civic leaders: "I wish I could show you what a small marijuana cigarette can do to one of our degenerate Spanish-speaking residents. . . ."[33]; ". . . a direct by-product of unrestricted Mexican immigration . . ."; "Mexican peddlers have been caught distributing sample marijuana cigarettes to school children."[34] Anslinger's boss, Treasury Secretary Morgenthau, was starting to get pressure from police, mayors, and western governors to do something about the dreaded plant on a national scale. All of a sudden Anslinger, a victim of his own success, was given the unenviable assignment of controlling the use of an indigenous weed that was growing wild alongside gravel roads in all forty-eight states. But there was no turning back now.

At first, the enforcers assumed cannabis could just be wedged into the existing anti-narcotics regulations, but Treasury Department lawyers warned them not to tinker with the Harrison Act. It was in enough trouble with the Constitution already. What they recommended was a separate treaty altogether. And so in the summer of 1936, Harry Anslinger followed the footsteps of Hamilton Wright to the League of Nations forum in Geneva. He made a valiant pitch for a global ban on marijuana and got an emphatic thumbs-down from all twenty-six nations present. They, too, were aware that the stuff grew "like dandelions" and that any attempt at global eradication would be Sisyphean. When Anslinger came home empty-handed, the Treasury lawyers decided to take another look at the tax law. Encouraged by the success of their latest effort, a prohibitive tax on machine guns, they proposed a tax on buyers and sellers of marijuana so onerous the trade would be completely discouraged.[35] Anslinger swallowed his doubts and went up the Hill to try to shove the bill through Congress, and he found such a level of willful ignorance on the subject that it turned out to be a pushover.

The transcript of the 1937 congressional hearings on H.R. 6385, "The Taxation of Marijuana," is a legendary chronicle that was destined to become a source of embarrassment to almost everybody involved. As University of Virginia law professor Charles Whitebread said, "The hearings before the House Ways and Means Committee and the floor debate on the bill are near comic examples of dereliction of legislative responsibility."[36] The professor was referring to this sort of thing on the day of the House vote:

MR. SNELL: What is the bill?

MR. RAYBURN: It has something to do with something that is called marihuana. I believe it is a narcotic of some kind.

MR. VINSON: Marihuana is the same as hashish.

MR. SNELL: Mr. Speaker, I am not going to object but I think it is wrong to consider legislation of this character at this time of night.

The hearings that led up to this vote were no more enlightening. The principal witness before the House Committee was Commissioner Anslinger, and the evidence he presented consisted of newspaper clippings. As for scientific authority, he quoted a pharmacist from Tunisia named Dr. Bouquet, "the greatest authority on cannabis in the world today." And he read from his drug-crime file, sheets of paper with the word "Crime" at the top, followed by handwritten notes; for example:

> *Colored students at the Univ. of Minn. partying with female students (white) smoking and getting their sympathy with stories of racial persecution. Result pregnancy.*[37]

He told the congressmen about two boys in Chicago who murdered a policeman while under the influence of marijuana, and about a fifteen-year-old who went insane. And he mentioned the one crime that horrified him most, the grisly story of Victor Licata, a twenty-one-year-old boy from Florida who slaughtered his whole family with an ax. "The evidence showed that he had smoked marihuana," said Anslinger. He didn't bother to mention that Victor Licata had been diagnosed as mentally unstable long before he took that hit of marijuana.[38]

In any transcript of a congressional hearing on drug legislation, you would normally expect to run across some sort of scientific data, but here you find nothing. There was only one expert medical witness on the whole roster, and when he finally got a chance to speak, it immediately became clear why Anslinger preferred to get his evidence from newspaper clippings. In his opening statement, Dr. William C. Woodward of the AMA debased Anslinger's testimony by pointing out that the

facts and figures in most of these newspaper clippings had originated with the commissioner himself. Then the doctor started
making some embarrassing observations. "We are told that the
use of marihuana causes crime. But yet no one has been produced from the Bureau of Prisons to show the number of prisoners who have been found addicted to the marihuana habit."
Woodward, in fact, had checked with the Bureau of Prisons himself, and they told him they had no such evidence. The same
with the crisis among young people: "You have been told that
school children are great users of marihuana cigarettes. No one
has been summoned from the Children's Bureau to show the nature and extent of the habit among children." When Woodward
himself checked with the Children's Bureau and the Office of
Education, they hadn't heard anything about it. Finally, Woodward asked, why is there nobody here from the Public Health
Service? This question hit a nerve. The Public Health Service
experts were the last people Anslinger wanted in the room. A few
months earlier he had sent the assistant surgeon general a series
of questions about marijuana and got this reply: "*Cannabis in-
dica* does not produce dependence . . . it probably belongs in the
same category as alcohol."[39]

When Woodward completed his testimony, the congressmen
ate him alive. They accused him of obstruction, evasion, and bad
faith, and when he finished they didn't even bother to thank
him. "If you want to advise us on legislation," said the chairman,
"you ought to come here with some constructive proposals
rather than criticism, rather than trying to throw obstacles in the
way of something that the Federal Government is trying to do."
But this remarkable display of hostility to the sole scientific witness had nothing to do with marijuana. This was strictly a political kick in the teeth. The majority in this room were New Deal
Democrats, and they had been slugging it out with Woodward
and the AMA in one hearing after another on the issue of Social
Security and health care. This was their little way of getting
even.[40]

The bill reached the floor of the House on a hot summer afternoon in an age before air-conditioning. The handful of lawmakers still in the chamber were understandably interested in keeping things moving, and in this case they managed to wrap up the whole debate in a little under two minutes. Mr. Snell, the Republican from upstate New York, had a final question: "Mr. Speaker, does the American Medical Association support this bill?"

Committee member Fred Vinson of Kentucky leaped to his feet, "Their Doctor Wentworth came down here. They support this bill 100 percent."[41] Vinson was talking about Dr. *Woodward*, of course, and this was a flat-out lie—all the more remarkable since Fred Vinson later went on to become chief justice of the Supreme Court. But the hour was late and it was time to move on. In a vote they didn't bother to record, on a matter of little interest, a handful of congressmen forwarded a bill that would one day help fill the nation's prisons to the roof beams.

Three years earlier Anslinger had declared the marijuana situation to be a national crisis. Now he declared it to be under control. The lay organizations that were spreading the alarm about cannabis were told to shut up, and the company that created the antimarijuana propaganda posters was put out of business.[42] There was no longer any need to frighten people. The Bureau of Narcotics was on the case. Anslinger could point to the soaring arrest rates as evidence of his success. And though there was never any credible evidence to back any of his charges, he prevailed simply because he controlled the pulpit. In the same way that he wielded his licensing authority to keep the pharmaceutical industry in line, he used his law-and-order credentials to confer endorsements on friendly legislators like a prince dispensing boons of knighthood. And when he was testifying before a congressional subcommittee and needed some impressive numbers, he just made them up. Throughout the 1930s, for example, Anslinger claimed that his sledgehammer approach to enforcement had cut the number of addicts in America from a quarter of a million at the turn of the century down to 60,000 or less. His figures were remarkably precise—9,458 addicts in New York, 7,172 in Illinois, and so on—and one reporter wanted to know how he could be so sure, since there's no way to take a census of illegal activity.

"Because within two years every addict will come to the attention of the authorities whether he's poor or rich," said Anslinger. "You mention the name of any addict and you'll find him in our files. . . . We get reports from the local authorities, we check on our inspection records . . . any excess purchases immediately shows up in our cards and we find out who the addicts are."[43] Since the Bureau of Narcotics was the government's official source on drug statistics, Anslinger could say just about anything he wanted and get away with it.[44] But the gossamer quality of his numbers is revealed by sudden unexplained shifts that hint of manipulation. White addicts, for example, greatly outnumbered nonwhites in the Bureau's reports for a generation, then suddenly one day the official majority was black.[45] When the Bureau went up to Capitol Hill, the size of the addict problem would often depend on whether Anslinger was looking for a budget increase or a pat on the back.

The first serious assault on the Bureau's information monopoly came from the mayor of New York. Fiorello La Guardia had suspected all along that the commissioner of narcotics didn't know what he was talking about, and in 1939 he assembled a blue-ribbon panel under the auspices of the prestigious New York Academy of Medicine—eminent physicians, psychiatrists, pharmacologists, chemists, sociologists, and public health officials, with the full support of the NYPD and the entire medical staff of Rikers Island prison hospital. As biographer John McWilliams observed, "Obviously this was more than a half-hearted attempt to score political points in an election year. Never before or since has such a thorough and extensive study been conducted on marijuana." For the next five years they bent to the task, and when the final report came out just after World War II, it blew away virtually every statement Harry Anslinger and the Bureau of Narcotics had made on the subject. To begin with, they found that marijuana smoking did not lead to addiction in the medical sense of the term, nor was it a gateway to harder drugs. There was no evidence whatsoever that it was widespread in school yards or being used by children. And contrary to the belief that marijuana smokers were aggressive and belligerent, the investigators found the opposite. When one of the committee members visited a Harlem smoking den, he said the people seemed relaxed and "free from the anxieties and cares of the realities of life." And finally, they found no significant relationship between marijuana and juvenile delinquency, and interviews with the police debased the idea that major crimes were inspired by smoking the weed. In summary, "the publicity concerning the catastrophic effects of marijuana in New York City is unfounded."[46]

The clinical section of the report was equally revealing. Seventy-seven volunteer prisoners at Rikers Island were subjected to a series of experiments that showed no alterations in personality or behavior and not a speck of evidence to back Anslinger's claims that marijuana led to insanity or violence.

But anyone who imagined that this stunning indictment might alter the nation's drug policy had seriously underestimated Harry Anslinger. When details of the report began to leak out, Anslinger went after the authors like a pit bull. A full three years before the report was released, he launched a series of preemptive strikes openly attacking members of the committee as "dangerous" and "strange" people, questioning everything but their parentage.[47] His arguments contained no scientific data, no new evidence, just dark accusations and name-calling, but that was good enough. Anslinger understood one thing these other fellows didn't. If the issue is complex, you don't have to win the debate, you just have to raise enough dust. His oppo-

nents—scientists, jurists, academics—never grasped the fact
that the commissioner was not playing by the rules. They were
on a quest for truth and justice. Harry Anslinger was on a mission from God. If he had to cut a few throats to accomplish the
Lord's work, so be it. He managed to get his adversaries fighting
among themselves, and by the time the La Guardia report was finally released in 1945, the profusion of charges and counter-
charges had taken the edge off the issue and the astounding end
product was virtually ignored by the press.

The United States behaves best in a crisis. For a nation so vast
and diverse, there is nothing to unify the citizens like the call to
arms. In the face of an appropriately monstrous foe, the races,
creeds, and colors who are normally at one another's throats
somehow manage to weld themselves into a single-minded, all-
powerful engine of war. Peace, therefore, brings a curious sense
of loss as people turn back to their private lives. The Second
World War, like the First, was followed by a period of disillu-
sionment and suspicion, and when China fell to the Communists in 1949, the United States went through a convulsion of
fear and recrimination that made the Red Scare of the 1920s
look civilized.

Harry Anslinger, once again, was a victim of his own success.
The legions of addicted GIs he predicted after the war had failed
to materialize, and the country was more interested in demobi-
lization than narcotics. "Our funds are so low," wrote Anslinger,
"that we couldn't even send an agent across the border from El
Paso unless he walks. . . ."[48] He needed some way to reinvigorate
his supporters, and the anticommunist firestorm that would
come to be known as the McCarthy era meshed perfectly with
Anslinger's own hatred of the Bolsheviks. Anslinger declared
that the real menace to America was not communist troops but
communist opium. In a precise echo of the postwar propaganda
of the 1920s, he warned that the Red conspiracy was out to destroy the West not with force, but with needles. By the end of the

decade he had succeeded in fixing the idea in the public mind that narcotics and communism were simply two faces of the same monster.[49]

The payoff was immediate. Congress opened the vaults, and the Bureau's budget was doubled over the next five years.[50] But since drug use continued unabated—and was said to be flowering in the black and Puerto Rican ghettos of the North—it was clear that cash alone wouldn't be enough.[51] Anslinger had been lobbying for tougher laws all along, and now he added to the mix an explosive new charge, this time against the judicial system itself. Here again, there was no study, no survey, no evidence other than newspaper clippings and Anslinger's gut-level feelings. But he convinced himself—and would shortly convince Congress—that the problem could be laid at the feet of lenient judges.[52]

As it happened, one of Anslinger's allies, Louisiana congressman Hale Boggs, was in need of a crusade at that moment. The Louisiana State House was in the grip of Governor Earl Long, brother of "Kingfish" Huey Long, but in 1951 Earl was taking some serious hits in a corruption scandal and he was starting to look vulnerable. Boggs saw that if he could position himself as a law-and-order reformer, he might be able to take the governor's mansion in the next race. When he discovered there was a narcotics problem in New Orleans, he thought he'd found the key. In April of 1951, he conducted three days of hearings, and after a catalog of horror stories from Commissioner Anslinger about soft laws and liberal judges, Boggs rammed through the most stringent narcotics penalties in history. This time Congress took judicial discretion out of the hands of judges and handed it to the prosecutors by making the sentences mandatory. The minimum now was two years regardless of the circumstances. Second offenders got at least five years without parole, and the three-time losers, not less than twenty.[53]

Unfortunately, the new law had no noticeable impact on the narcotics trade, but Harry Anslinger was a policeman first and last, and he had absolutely no faith in any approach other than law enforcement. His response was always to tighten the screws. Once again, there was a politician ready at hand—this time it was Senator Price Daniel, a Texas Democrat who was about to make a run for governor. Beginning in 1955, Senator Daniel held hearings all over the country, leading off once again with dramatic testimony from the Commissioner of Narcotics. Anslinger's warnings about heroin and the Yellow Peril were accepted without question, and the Daniel Committee's final report stated flatly: "subversion through drug addiction is an established aim of Communist China."[54] Battling evil on this scale clearly demanded extreme measures, and the resulting Narcotics Control Act of 1956 pulled out all the stops. Police powers were expanded, prosecution simplified, the penalties in the Boggs Act were doubled, and the death penalty was thrown in for good measure. And though this law, like its predecessor, had no impact on the street, it was not a total loss. The following year, Price Daniel was elected governor of Texas.

Inevitably, these unprecedented penalties fell on the heads of small-time dealers and users instead of the major traffickers they were intended for, and the drastic punishment raining down on such minor players struck a lot of people as medieval. One of them was a Washington lawyer named Rufus King who happened to be chairman of the American Bar Association's Criminal Law section. A consummate government insider, the lanky, Lincolnesque attorney was then legislative counsel to the Kefauver Committee on Organized Crime, and while he was writing the committee's final report, he was sucked into the controversy about the Boggs Act and the idea of mandatory minimum sentences. Some of the committee staffers, King included, thought mandatory sentencing was well outside the constitutional fence, since it violated the independence of the judiciary. King wondered what could have prompted this kind of legal extremism, and he decided to look into the whole background of anti-narcotics legislation. What he found there left him reeling.

For openers, he was surprised to discover that the Harrison Narcotics Act was a tax law. "Prohibition"—never mentioned in the legislation—was an after-the-fact bureaucratic achievement of the Treasury Department. From the extensive political maneuvering at the time the law was passed, King could see that the whole concept of narcotics enforcement had been on shaky legal ground right from the beginning. The deeper he dug, the more clearly he could see that it still was. Case by case, he waded through the Supreme Court and appellate decisions—*Jin Fuey Moy, Doremus, Webb*—and then he came to 285 U.S. 280, *U.S. v. Behrman,* and his jaw dropped. "It was a trick," says King. "Dr. Behrman was a flagrant violator who sold four thousand doses of heroin and cocaine to a single addict. But the indictment was drawn as if this were some kind of normal 'treatment.' " The decision against Dr. Behrman essentially ruled out any prescription to an addict under any circumstances. This set the stage for the "reign of terror," as King called it, where the few doctors who were still trying to work with addicts were harassed, destroyed, or thrown in jail.[55]

When King read the next case—*Linder v. U.S.*—he practically leaped out of his chair. In 1924, Charles Linder, a respected doctor in Spokane, Washington, had been set up by an addict on the payroll of the Treasury Department. According to Linder, she told him she was having terrible stomach pains and couldn't reach her regular doctor. She testified that she told him she was an addict. Linder wrote her a prescription for three tablets of cocaine and a tablet of morphine, and the next day Treasury agents stormed into his office and dragged him off to jail. He was convicted and sentenced, he appealed and lost, but he refused to be carried off quietly. When the case reached the Supreme Court in 1925, the justices took one look and tossed out the doctor's conviction in a unanimous vote:

The enactment under consideration levies a tax. . . . It says nothing of "addicts" and does not undertake to prescribe methods for their medical treatment. They are diseased and

proper subjects for such treatment, and we cannot possibly
conclude that a physician acted improperly or un-
wisely . . . solely because he has dispensed to one of
them . . . four small tablets of morphine or cocaine for relief
of conditions incident to addiction.[56]

King was astounded. There it was in black and white—a unanimous decision from the high court pulling the rug out from
under the Treasury Department's whole scheme of enforcement.
And to make sure there was no doubt where they stood, the
judges fired a parting shot:

. . . if the Act had such scope it would certainly encounter
grave constitutional difficulties.

As he read this, King realized that this unequivocal reversal of
the *Behrman* doctrine had made no difference whatsoever to the
Treasury Department. The Narcotics Division had simply ignored the *Linder* decision and continued to enforce the regulations after 1925 as if none of this had ever happened. Apparently
nobody questioned it, because by this time the medical profession was so terrified, it didn't want to have anything to do with
addicts.

King was incredulous. Here were *revenue agents* invading hospitals and waiting rooms, bulldozing through the medical profession, issuing orders about the treatment and care of patients,
and nobody said a word. He was outraged, and as an official of
the American Bar Association, he was in a position to do something about it. As he saw it, the problem was that the legal profession—his profession—had not given the doctors enough
protection when these battles were being waged in the 1920s
and '30s. King decided to try to get the doctors and lawyers together and see if they could get this mess straightened out. First
he got the ABA to adopt a resolution calling for a review of the
federal drug program. Then he went to the American Medical

Association with the same pitch and they signed on. Their mutual creation was called the Joint Committee on Narcotic Drugs of the ABA-AMA, and it consisted of a blue-ribbon group from each organization with Rufus King as chairman. In the fall of 1956 they commissioned a survey of all the available medical and legal data so they could see what new research would be needed.[57]

One thing King was curious about was other countries. How was Europe dealing with the problem? The following spring he headed for the Continent and what he found there surprised him almost as much as the Harrison Act. "I was representing the ABA, so I was able to see top officials in England, Belgium, Holland, France, Italy, and the Scandinavian countries. When I asked about the drug problem, they'd say 'what problem?' I found out that this whole thing was made in America."[58]

But like so many others before him, Rufus King made the mistake of misjudging Harry Anslinger. In the beginning he had invited Anslinger to participate. Anslinger declined, but he asked to be kept informed as the work progressed. Unfortunately, King didn't know about Anslinger's dealings with the La Guardia Committee in 1945, so he agreed. When the preliminary research was done, the Joint Committee put together an interim report and the contents were potentially explosive. They printed a limited number of copies for distribution within the ABA and AMA, but Harry Anslinger had already set up an ambush. To the committee's dismay, the Treasury Department published a document that appeared to be a virtual doppelgänger of the Joint Committee's report—same blue cover, same typeface, even the same title, but with two added words: "*Comments on* NARCOTIC DRUGS: INTERIM REPORT OF THE JOINT COMMITTEE . . ." And where King and his colleagues had printed a few thousand copies, the Bureau of Narcotics flooded the country with its double.

The arguments—and the insults—were a replay of Anslinger's attack on the La Guardia Committee: "When one examines the composition of the Joint Committee of the American Bar Association and the American Medical Association, one finds that the members are, almost without exception, individuals who have identified themselves with one panacea . . . and for all practical purposes, their conclusions preceded the formation of the Committee."[59] Anslinger's blast was followed by a collection of critiques from several old friends—Texas governor Price Daniel, Hale Boggs of Louisiana—a judge, several lawmen, doctors, and a narcotics expert from the Los Angeles College of Medical Evangelists. "Has the Joint Committee given consideration to the ash heaps that lay in the cities of Harbin, Mukden, and Tientsin, during the Japanese invasion of China, bearing mute evidence of the toll of drug addiction?" "Marijuana is a lethal weapon, a killer weed . . . the worst of all narcotics—far worse than the use of morphine or cocaine." "The Interim report is . . . utterly confusing and bereft of basic principles of logic. . . ." Anslinger and his colleagues made it clear that the misguided fools from the AMA and ABA were playing directly into the hands of the nation's communist enemies.[60]

Taken by complete surprise, King was unprepared for the next blow and it proved fatal. The Joint Committee was being funded by a private foundation, and one by one, the trustees were approached by people from the Treasury Department and told that they were sponsoring a "controversial" study. The Treasury Department, of course, held life-and-death power over the fund's tax-exempt status, and according to King the trustees promptly folded.[61] Once again, the commissioner had pulverized his critics before they even got to the starting gate.

Rufus King, however, proved to have more staying power than Anslinger expected. Over the next three years, King forced him into a series of public confrontations, giving him blow for blow in print and on the radio. One day in 1961 shortly after Jack Kennedy's inauguration, King had a visitor. "Dr. Peter Bing came to my office with the aura of the JFK White House. He was Science Advisor Jerome Weisner's assistant. He said, 'Fill me in on Anslinger.' I gave him the tape of a debate that was broadcast on

NBC *Monitor Radio.*[62] He told me later that JFK sat on the corner of his desk in the Oval Office and listened to that tape and he heard Anslinger ranting and raving, and he and Bobby made up their minds he had to go."[63]

Whether the commissioner retired or was pushed, he stepped down a few months later after nearly half a century in the service of his country. It was a much different country from the one he had gone to work for in 1918, and some considerable measure of that change was due to the efforts of Harry J. Anslinger.

Chapter Five

Addiction to Disaster

When Richard Nixon was swept into office in 1968, the United States was on fire in the literal sense of the word. Fractured by the ongoing disaster in Vietnam, the nation was closer to civil war than it had been for a century, and when Martin Luther King was cut down in Memphis that spring, major cities from coast to coast exploded in flames. Within the Halls of Ivy, the flag itself was being torched, and the stunned middle class watched in dismay as their kids burned draft cards, ripped off their bras, grew hair, smoked dope, and joined the Panthers on the barricades. In living rooms across the country the air fairly crackled with fear and rage, and that fall Richard Nixon promised to set it right.

But after demolishing the Democrats as soft on crime, Nixon was faced with an unpleasant reality. It began to dawn on his advisers that there was really not much the White House could do to affect the crime rate directly. The thugs people are really afraid of—burglars, robbers, murderers—are not normally subject to federal law. They're the business of local cops and state courts. That January, as Mitchell and Ehrlichman explored various means of involving the executive branch directly in the fight against crime, they kept running headlong into the Constitution—the first in a series of ultimately fatal collisions with that nettlesome document. Its quaint eighteenth-century sensibilities seemed unsuited to the dangers these men faced. By reserving all this power to the states, the Tenth Amendment hemmed them in, frustrating their best ideas. Then somebody mentioned drugs and everybody looked up. Once again it was the perfect target—exotic imports poisoning the nation's bloodstream—and the federal government already had the authority to bust drug suspects anywhere, anytime.[1]

Many people are under the impression that Richard Nixon started the drug war, but he was simply following the hallowed footsteps of Hamilton Wright, Richmond Hobson, Harry Anslinger, Hale Boggs, and a hundred other political operators over the last half century who have used narcotics to advance their careers. Nixon, however, would shift the process into overdrive. By resurrecting Captain Hobson's image of the Drug User as Vampire, the administration was able to focus public anxiety on junkies and dope smokers in a way that made perfect sense to an America whipsawed by war, riots, and an incomprehensible younger generation. People already suspected that marijuana and LSD were at the root of the youth rebellion, and they read in the papers that heroin was driving inner-city blacks to rape and pillage. On the nightly news, these two images began fusing together as heroin and marijuana merged into a single dreadful scourge in the public mind. Nixon's political genius was to spot these waves of public anxiety before anyone else and to ride them like a surfer. "I believe in civil rights," he said. "But the right of every American is to be free from violence, and we are going to have an administration that restores that right in the United States of America."[2]

In a skillful display of fear management, the White House warned the country that a plague of unimaginable proportions was about to engulf the nation. The numbers were astounding. From a total of 68,088 heroin addicts in 1969, the official count jumped to over 550,000 in two years—an eightfold increase. "The problem has assumed the dimensions of a national emergency," said the president. "I intend to take every step necessary."[3] To fight the drug pushers on their own terms, he would need emergency powers—preventive detention, unorthodox strike forces, more freedom to search, wiretap, and arrest. The Democrats in Congress, impressed with the whip-crack political power of Nixon's law-and-order message, backed him to the hilt.

But it turns out the numbers that launched this spectacular crusade, in the grand tradition of drug wars past, were totally fabricated. The 1971 addict count—559,000—was not arrived at by discovering new junkies, but by taking the 1969 total—68,088—and multiplying it by a factor of eight.[4] The first number, suspiciously precise in itself, was simply a list of all the addicts who had run afoul of the law. Harry Anslinger always maintained every junkie would come to the attention of the cops sooner or later, but by 1970 the record keepers at the Bureau of Narcotics began to suspect this was wishful thinking. After a study of the actual street scene, they concluded that the official count was probably off by about 800 percent. So instead of a dramatic increase in addiction, the new numbers simply reflected a second look at the original data. But nobody at the Bureau bothered to call the White House spokesmen on this flagrant misconstruction of the facts, and the press never bothered to ask.

By 1972, however, the appearance of a growing addict population was becoming an embarrassment. This huge jump had occurred, after all, on Nixon's watch, and this was an election year. So the White House called the head man at the Bureau of Narcotics and told him to cool it. The drug agency, responding instantly to this shift in the wind, arbitrarily cut the number of junkies to 150,000 in the next report, and the administration was able to take credit for the overnight cure of some 400,000 addicts.[5]

After Nixon's landslide reelection, the White House set out to redesign the executive branch, and among the alterations was a new plan for the nation's drug-fighting apparatus. The Bureau of Narcotics and Dangerous Drugs and several other bureaucracies were to be absorbed into a vast new organization called the Drug Enforcement Agency. From its birth in July of 1973, the DEA had awesome powers—as great in many respects as the FBI and Customs combined—and its reach was global. It could detain and interrogate suspects, call for wiretaps and no-knock warrants, and bring in the tax men. And with the influx of several hundred agents picked up from the CIA and Customs, the new superagency now had the talent and ability to conduct black-bag operations and domestic surveillance. But thirteen days before this omnipotent police force was to be turned loose, the D.C. Metro cops arrested five burglars in the Watergate office complex and the administration's secret plans began to come unraveled.

One unexpected benefit of the Watergate debacle was the mountain of evidence, memos, tapes, and diaries, offering a surgical cross section of government operations at the highest level. Author Edward J. Epstein dug through this mountain in the late seventies, and after interviewing the principal players he came to the conclusion that the Nixon War on Drugs was a mask for darker designs. In his book *Agency of Fear: Opiates and Political Power in America*, he makes a persuasive case that the DEA was to have functioned at some level as a private army for the White House. The discovery of the famous Enemies List gave some hint of what they had in mind.

When Richard Nixon's helicopter lifted off the South Lawn for the last time in 1974, he left behind a drug-fighting apparatus that was larger by an order of magnitude than the one he inherited. For half a century, the federal anti-narcotics force had been a tiny sidebar to the country's overall enforcement effort, largely symbolic, never involving more than a few hundred men. Now it was a vast international law enforcement operation with over four thousand agents. And though the agency's operations routinely ran afoul of the Constitution, the public willingly began to surrender bits and pieces of the Bill of Rights because the fear of drugs was now palpable.

In truth, the actual number of heroin addicts throughout the Nixon era remained fairly stable. According to the Pentagon and other government sources, it peaked in 1969 and may have actually been declining when the war on drugs was launched.[6] In any event, the totals were always modest. Even the White House at its most extreme was never talking about more than three people in a thousand.[7] But by blurring the distinction between marijuana and heroin, the prohibitionists effectively added forty million pot smokers to the total, and forty-five million drug users was a frightening epidemic by any measure.[8]

Jimmy Carter, on the other hand, thought jailing people for smoking marijuana was counterproductive.[9] He was not alone. A presidential commission appointed by Nixon himself had recommended decriminalization as early as 1972—a stunning embarrassment for the White House. Nixon had appointed a Republican drug hawk, former Pennsylvania governor Ray Shafer, to head the commission, and his job was to create a scientific foundation for the administration's hard line on marijuana. But after months of digging, the facts overwhelmed the folk tales and the Shafer Commission reversed engines: "Marihuana use, in and of itself, is neither causative of, nor directly associated with crime. . . ."[10] They found no basis for the gateway theory. Alcohol, they said, was probably a greater danger, and they concluded that personal use of marijuana should no longer be a crime.[11] Nixon buried the report, but the facts were on the table nonetheless.

At the same time, a lot of people were disturbed by the way police and prosecutors were using the drug laws as a political sledgehammer. In Texas, Black Panther Otis Lee Johnson got thirty years for passing a joint that wasn't even his, while white college kids doing a lot worse were getting off with a wink and a nod.[12] The blatant hypocrisy was starting to erode respect for the law in general, and that was alarming to bedrock conservatives like William F. Buckley and Milton Friedman.[13] All over the country lawmakers were taking another look at marijuana penalties, and by the time Jimmy Carter got to the White House, eleven states had reduced possession to the equivalent of a traffic ticket.[14]

At this pivotal moment, President Carter turned over the helm of national drug policy to a man who actually knew something about the problem. Stanford-trained psychiatrist Peter Bourne had helped open the Haight-Ashbury Free Clinic, and his observations of the street scene in San Francisco convinced him that prison was the last thing most pot smokers needed. As drug czar, he hammered away at his close friend Jimmy Carter and finally convinced him that the law should be changed. On August 2, 1977, the president told Congress, "Penalties against possession of a drug should not be more damaging to an individual than the use of the drug itself," and for the first time in four decades of criminalization, the White House called for the elimination of penalties for possession of marijuana.[15] It looked, for an instant, like the rules of engagement for the drug war were about to be rewritten.

But while Peter Bourne may have had a clear picture of the medical issues, he was incredibly naive about marijuana politics. An Englishman by birth, he failed to grasp the symbolic connection between reefer and the cultural war that had split the United States since the onset of Vietnam. To at least half the country, marijuana was emblematic of the unpatriotic, long-haired antiwar counterculture—not just a drug, but a flag of anarchy. These citizens had not abandoned the field. They were waiting for a strategic opening and now it was at hand.

By the mid-seventies there were plenty of advance warnings that the country was once again on a collision course with cocaine. *Time* and *Newsweek* were carrying titillating tales about the "smart set" offering coke spoons along with the caviar at fashionable gatherings in Manhattan and Hollywood.[16] But this latest romance with the magic powder would be a replay of the cocaine rush the country experienced earlier in the century, beginning with a rhapsody of praise, followed by assurances that it's nonaddictive, ending with the grim realization that a lot of people couldn't quit if their lives depended on it. But in the opening phase of any drug cycle, people always manage to convince themselves that there is such a thing as a free lunch, and in 1977 cocaine was the miracle energizer that made you witty and charming. In the end, it would devour everything in its path, including Dr. Peter Bourne.

As well-meaning government officials have discovered time and again this century, just talking about reexamining drug policy makes you politically vulnerable. The slightest misstep and you're down like a gut-shot buffalo. In the case of Peter Bourne, the wounds were largely self-inflicted. On a hot summer day in 1978 a young woman on his staff told him she needed a sedative. She was breaking up with her boyfriend and hadn't slept in days. Dr. Bourne wrote a prescription for fifteen tablets of methaqualone. All perfectly legal, but since the woman was a member of the White House staff, he made it out to a fictitious name to protect her identity. She made the terminal mistake of asking a girlfriend to get it filled for her, and the girlfriend happened into a drugstore that was being audited by a state pharmacy inspector. He became suspicious, asked for ID, nothing matched, he called the cops, and the cops called on the doctor who wrote the prescription. Bourne, of course, had a perfectly logical explanation for all this, but as far as the press was concerned, the explanation was coming from an outspoken drug-legalizer who was caught passing a bogus scrip for Quāāludes—a known sex enhancer—to a lovely young female assistant. Within days every mistake Peter Bourne ever made had hit the front page, and one of his mistakes was attending a Christmas party the year before where marijuana and cocaine were used openly. Bourne claimed he never touched the stuff, but his credibility evaporated. With his enemies in full cry, he was run out of town.[17]

A few weeks earlier, a radical change in marijuana policy had been almost a foregone conclusion. Now it was out of the question. The administration itself had become vulnerable on the drug issue and Carter was forced to the right. There would be no more loose talk about legalization from the White House.

Ronald Reagan didn't need any instruction in marijuana politics. Using the drugs-and-crime issue as a battering ram, he flattened the Democrats with a masterful law-and-order campaign, and once in the White House he picked up the ball exactly where Nixon had dropped it.

Reagan promised to get rid of the welfare state and cut big government down to size. To do that he would have to convince everybody that the blame for social problems arose not from inequality, racism, and injustice, as the liberals maintained, but from the immoral acts of bad people—a distinct minority that simply needed to be cut from the body politic like a tumor. The government's role, therefore, was not rehabilitation but vengeance. In June of 1982, Reagan reopened the War on Drugs with a broadside from the Rose Garden. "We're taking down the surrender flag that has flown over so many drug efforts. We're running up a battle flag."[18] This time, there would be no room for the wounded. The federally funded drug-treatment network, begun under Nixon and nourished by three administrations, got the ax.[19] Law enforcement was what the people wanted, and the firepower was about to be escalated dramatically.

As with all previous drug wars, this one began with a list of demands for tougher legislation and fewer restraints on lawmen. Once again, extreme measures would be required. The biggest problem was that the bad guys had more money than the good guys. The staggering profits of the cocaine trade had created a sleek, high-tech underworld with more firepower, better communications, faster cars, planes, and boats than the cops had. To strip the narco-traffickers of this obscene wealth, the administration dusted off a legal strategy that originated in the early days of the republic, when the government fought smugglers by seizing their ships and cargo.[20] The concept, known as forfeiture, was used again during alcohol prohibition to relieve bootleggers of their assets. Now it would be transformed into a sword of Damocles, hanging by a thin judicial thread over every citizen in the country.

The Omnibus Crime Bill of 1984 gave the administration everything it asked for and then some. In addition to the inevitable boost in prison terms, prosecutors could now confiscate cash, cars, boats, homes, bank accounts, stock portfolios—anything *believed* to have been tainted with drugs or drug money—based on nothing more than an accusation. And because drug traffickers are notoriously slippery, the law provided for an element of surprise. It allowed police to take property without notice. In other words, the goods would be seized first, then charges would be filed, then the evidence would be gathered—the exact reverse of due process. While this legal shortcut proved to be a powerful weapon against the guilty, it contained no safeguard for the innocent. And the new law had one additional clause that would subtly alter the relationship between citizens and police. From now on, seized assets would be shared among the law enforcement agencies that made the seizure. The symmetry was appealing—using the trafficker's ill-gotten gains to combat drug trafficking—but in practical terms, the cop on the beat now had a cash incentive to capture property instead of criminals. In an era of belt-tightening, profits from seizures were a way for strapped departments to make ends meet. Very shortly, law-enforcement agencies throughout the country began including seizure projections in their annual budgets. Now there were hard numbers on paper that represented official targets—quotas—that would have to be filled whether there were enough criminals to go around or not. The inevitable consequence of this process was evident in one 1990 Justice Department memo to all U.S. attorneys: "We must significantly increase our forfeiture production to reach our budget target. Every effort must be made to increase forfeiture income in the three remaining months of fiscal year 1990."[21] It was a return to the halcyon days of medieval criminal justice. Generations of property rights going back to the Magna Carta were set aside in the name of legal efficiency. It was now possible for anyone—hostile neighbor or greedy cop—to have you kicked out of your own house. All they had to do was accuse you of buying the place with drug money. No proof would be required. No conviction. No evidence. Suspicion alone would be enough to land you and your family in the street. In case you happened to be innocent and wanted the place back, the burden of proof and the legal fees would be on you. If you couldn't account for every payment, the house could be sold at auction, and if your neighbor was the one who turned you in, he might be eligible to split the take with the police. It was, in fact, this very act—using seizures to finance the king's army—that led Hancock and Jefferson and Adams to pledge their lives, their fortunes, and their sacred honor.[22] If they were with us today, they would surely be at our throats.

Not surprisingly, tales of official chicanery started rolling in almost immediately. The vast majority of cases seldom hit the papers, but every once in a while lawmen would break down the wrong door and the whole country would get a glimpse of asset forfeiture close up. The L.A. County Sheriff's raid that killed reclusive millionaire Don Scott was particularly revealing. The two hundred acres of sagebrush and chaparral that Scott owned may not have been much to look at, but as they say in the real estate business, location, location, location. Trail's End Ranch ran along the spine of the coastal mountains above Malibu, and its rolling crest-line hills were coveted by a number of parties, including the National Park Service. Scott repeatedly refused to sell. In 1992, he married a young Texan named Frances Plante and brought her to Trail's End. About that time it came to the attention of Deputy Sheriff Gary Spencer down in Malibu that Scott's new bride had been busted a year earlier for marijuana possession. And now here she was living up on that isolated mountaintop. A background check revealed that her name had come up in connection with a narcotics investigation. It seemed unlikely to Spencer that she'd be totally clean.

And then, according to the deputy, he got word from an unnamed source that there were three thousand plants growing on the ranch. Convincing his superiors he was onto a major bust, Spencer set out to get some kind of visual corroboration. Over the next four weeks, he organized a surveillance effort that included everybody from the LAPD to the U.S. Forest Service. But despite overflights by the California Air National Guard and extensive ground sweeps by a special Border Patrol mountain unit, nobody spotted anything. Undeterred, Spencer plunged forward, determined to rip the covers off the old eccentric and his junkie bride. The sheriff's office got a search warrant. On the morning of October 2, 1992, with Spencer at the head of the column, thirty officers from half a dozen state and federal agencies wound slowly up the three-mile mountain road from the coast.

The Scotts had been partying all night and were still groggy when the hammering and shouting at the door woke them up. Frances got her jeans on first, and just as she reached the living room, the door collapsed and a sea of armed men crashed in. She screamed. Her husband stepped into the hallway with a gun in his hand. Spencer shouted, "Drop the gun! Drop the gun!" then fired two rounds. Scott recoiled, pitched forward, and his face smashed into the floor. They hustled Frances out of there and proceeded to search the place with—one can imagine—increasing desperation. For days they scoured the rolling hills, choppering along at treetop level and following up on foot, and they did not find a single marijuana seed. A painstaking search of the house failed to turn up the expected coke or heroin stash. All they had to show for their trouble was this body on the living-room floor.[23]

Unfortunately for the L.A. County Sheriff's Office, it turned out Scott had friends in high places. Among them was the district attorney of neighboring Ventura County, and he was not pleased. It seems Trail's End Ranch is not *in* L.A. County in the first place—it is across the line in Ventura. The Ventura D.A. wanted to know why the raid had gone down behind his back. And since the shooting had taken place on his turf, he took over the case. This awkward turn of events led to an unprecedented investigation of one county sheriff by another, and when the report was released five months later it went off like a grenade. The last page was a map taken from Deputy Spencer's files with the note, "80 acres sold for $800,000 in 1991 in same area." At a packed press conference in Ventura, the D.A. said, "Clearly one of the primary purposes was a land grab by the Sheriff's Department."[24]

The Scott case will no doubt see some kind of rough justice at the taxpayers' expense one day, but in the vast majority of forfeitures, the suspect is simply relieved of his assets and sent on his way. Guilt or innocence has nothing to do with it. Eighty percent of the people from whom assets are seized are never even charged with a crime.[25] They just lose their possessions. Minorities are particularly susceptible to this form of institutionalized piracy since everybody knows that a nonwhite with a wad of dough is probably dealing. In the late 1980s, lawmen in Volusia County, Florida, started using the forfeiture law as a toll gate on I-95. A special sheriff's drug squad began stopping Miami-bound drivers for traffic violations, then conducting searches. If one of the people in the car was carrying more than a hundred dollars in cash, it was assumed to be drug money. Of those people from whom the police confiscated money but did not arrest, 90 percent were black or Hispanic. Since fighting to get the money back in court could cost as much as ten grand, few people bothered to try. When public outrage began to attract atten-

tion, the *Orlando Sentinel* discovered that the deputies had re-
sorted to plea-bargaining, offering to take only part of the money
if the travelers promised not to complain.[26] At this point the department was about a step shy of cash registers in the squad
cars.

In time the list of personal tragedies in the drug war would
grow to include hundreds of innocent businessmen, farmers,
home owners, and housewives all over the country who fit some
profile or rented to the wrong person and saw their lives ruined
and their assets vanish. But of all the unintended consequences
of these powerful laws, perhaps the most ominous is to be found
in the small print down at the bottom of the economic spectrum.
One list of asset seizures by the Washington, D.C., police contained items like ". . . Tyrone Payton, $5.00 in United States
Currency . . . Kevin Williams, $5.00 in United States Cur-
rency . . ."[27] These numbers hint at petty shakedowns, and that
bodes ill for the long haul. Try to picture this scene through the
eyes of the teenager with a few bucks in his pocket—quite possibly earned through honest work—who must constantly be on
the lookout for the king's men or lose it all. It would be tough to
come up with a better system for teaching hatred of the law.

Just as police departments became addicted to forfeiture, the
media in the 1980s got hooked on the drug war itself. A survey
of network news during the first five years of the decade showed
the number of cocaine-related stories jumped from 10 a year to
140.[28] Then, in mid-decade, television discovered raid footage—
screaming cops in flak jackets—splintering doors—video images
sizzling with danger and unpredictability. Unfortunately, television has certain technical limitations that determine what it can
and cannot cover. A surveillance van with a hidden camera can
park on a street in Harlem, but it has no access to the Chicago
Yacht Club or the ladies' room at Dan Tana's in West Hollywood.
As a result, the drug-war footage showing up on the nightly news

focused almost exclusively on the urban street scene, and though the vast majority of drug users have always been white, the people doing drugs on TV were now black and Hispanic. When a couple of researchers from the University of Michigan spotted this phenomenon, they started digging through the archives and discovered that from 1985 onward, the number of whites shown using cocaine dropped by 60 percent, and the number of blacks rose by the same amount. "During the Reagan era, the cocaine problem as defined by the network news became increasingly associated with people of color."[29] A lot of people thought this smacked of conspiracy. The picture fit too perfectly with the administration's argument that the inner city was a sinkhole of vice unworthy of assistance. The truth was probably simpler: television likes action and the action was in the streets. It was a good gig for everyone involved. The lawmen looked heroic, and the news crews were into the hottest combat story since Vietnam.[30]

Sixty years earlier, the dawn of commercial radio had given Captain Richmond Hobson a national canvas for his vivid images of the Drug User as Vampire. Now television would provide the country with an eye-popping view of the vampire in action, and he would turn out to be a black teenager.

The media made one other jolting discovery in 1985. That winter, for the first time, crack cocaine hit the front page of *The New York Times*.[31] Although this smokable form of the drug had been around awhile, it didn't become a sensation until somebody realized the stuff was so powerful it could be sold by the toke. A single hit could go for as little as five bucks. This put the drug within reach of the inner-city poor, and in spite of its scary reputation, it was popping up everywhere.

As the politicians fulminated about who was responsible for this disaster, they might well have taken a look in the mirror. Crack cocaine was not so much a creature of pharmacology as a creature of the law—an artifact of prohibition. The government success in making cocaine exhorbitantly expensive simply encouraged the dealers to search for a more attractive way to market the drug. When they cooked up this smokable version, they found you could get very high indeed on a tiny amount. Dealing in contraband always favors the method that puts the most bang in the cheapest package. In the days of alcohol prohibition, this dictum led to the adulterated 190-proof synthetic hooch known as white lightning. It sometimes made you blind, sometimes made you crazy, but always got you high. White lightning was the crack of the 1920s. Then as now, the first-class passengers stayed with the expensive stuff and left the swill for the deckhands.

Since the drug's low cost made it available to the people who could least afford it, crack quickly became the blue-collar drug of choice. Here again, most of the users were white, but the only people who knew this were statisticians.[32] The inner city was the natural Wal-Mart for this new discount drug, and the sudden increase in cash flow ignited violent turf wars. The nightly images of gang shoot-outs, street dealing, and urban chaos helped confirm America's worst fears about the degeneracy of the urban masses.

At this critical juncture, the death of a single individual would take the drug war nuclear. On the night of June 18, 1986, Boston Celtics draft choice Len Bias—a dazzling young black athlete on the brink of fame and fortune—died of heart failure from cocaine poisoning. This tragedy turned out to be larger than life because Bias was no ordinary hoop star. Unlike the dangerous and arrogant young street punks now flavoring the nightly news, here was a clean-cut kid from a religious family in search of the American dream. The fact that the dream was within his grasp when he was cut down made it all the more infuriating. If such a thing could happen to a Len Bias, it could happen to anybody. In the following month the networks aired seventy-four evening news segments about crack and cocaine, and any lingering doubts America had about the drug war evaporated.[33] Congress, equal to the occasion, added another twenty-six mandatory minimum sentences to the books. Now even first-time small-scale street dealers faced ten years without parole.[34]

Thus, the nation's moral searchlight had come to focus squarely on the failings of the inner city. Now it would highlight those failings with a startling new discovery—crack babies, an image so horrifying it seemed to clinch the argument that addicts are indeed vampires. News footage of emaciated preemies—sustained by tubes and electronics at staggering cost—sickened viewers all over the country. Here were the fruits of indulgence, the horrifying issue of women whose moral compasses were so screwed up they had essentially abandoned their babies in the womb. Their pathetic offspring, trembling in the glare of the incubator lights, so grievously damaged by their mothers' weakness, fueled a storm of outrage. Experts said these children were probably beyond salvation. Their IQs would range in the low fifties. They would barely be able to dress themselves, dependent on the taxpayers for life—"a life of certain suffering, of probable deviance, of permanent inferiority."[35] Informed that the bill for a single child might run to a quarter of a million dollars, the president of Boston University questioned spending this kind of money on "crack babies who won't ever achieve the intellectual development to have consciousness of God."[36] In 1987, when Chicago pediatrician Ira Chasnoff surveyed the pregnant women in thirty-six hospitals, his startling discovery created a media frenzy. According to press reports, 10 percent of the women in the survey were on cocaine. Nationwide, that would translate into 375,000 potential cocaine babies *a year*. People began bracing for the arrival of a permanent subhuman biologic underclass.

But when the expected tidal wave of brain-damaged, unteachable monsters failed to materialize, a handful of thoughtful people started looking into some of the original assumptions. They discovered that the crack-baby epidemic, like the Nixon heroin scare, was a total fabrication—a blend of distorted data and sloppy journalism. The tiny infants trembling in their incubators were real enough—no question about that—but they were usually the victims of an older, more established ailment. What the cameras were capturing were the well-documented effects of malnutrition and poverty.

A group of Canadian researchers took a second look at the data from twenty previous cocaine studies and learned that many researchers had lumped the use of cocaine in with other drugs, including alcohol. Reviewing all the data in all twenty studies, they found no link between cocaine use and the so-called crack-baby syndrome.[37] As for the figure of 375,000 crack babies—still gospel to some commentators—it turns out Dr. Chasnoff was simply misquoted. He did not say that 10 percent of the pregnant women he surveyed were crack users. He said that 10 percent of them had, at *some time* in their lives, used *some kind* of drug, which included casual use of marijuana. The jump from there to the crack-baby connection was another leap of pack journalism. The fuzziness of the 375,000 figure itself should have been obvious to any reporter willing to do a quick back-of-the-envelope calculation. If, as the government claimed, one out of ten cocaine users becomes addicted, then every pregnant woman in the country would have to be using cocaine for 10 percent of them to give birth to crack babies.[38]

Nonetheless, the crack baby was such a hit with the media that any expert who got in the way was steamrolled. Claire Coles, a specialist at Emory University Medical School in Atlanta, had been warning reporters all along that a jittery preemie born to a malnourished, abused woman who drinks and smokes could hardly be laid at the feet of cocaine. Women who use cocaine while pregnant also drink more booze, smoke more cigarettes, and dip into more kinds of other drugs. They have poorer nutrition and health and are more often exposed to violence. Rather than cocaine, said Coles, these children were "victims of gross neglect." When she refused to play along with the accepted story line, reporters stopped interviewing her.[39]

Finally, Dr. Chasnoff himself, perhaps in penance for his part in triggering this avalanche, did a follow-up study of infants exposed to cocaine and found that their intelligence fit the normal curve.[40] "They are no different from other children growing up. They are not the retarded imbeciles people talk about." While there are serious health costs to cocaine use, as with any other drug, Chasnoff found the biggest danger these kids faced was the world they were born into. "As I study the problem more and more, I think the placenta does a better job of protecting the child than we do as a society."[41]

The spectacular popularity of the crack baby was a testament to the importance of scapegoats. By blaming these horrifying pictures of quivering infants on an exotic Latin American import, it was possible to ignore the role that poverty played, and to dis-remember the federal cuts that had stripped prenatal care and treatment from Medicaid earlier in the decade. But women of color would pay a disproportionate price for this political expedience. A 1990 study of pregnant drug users found that a black woman was ten times more likely to be reported to the authorities than a white woman.[42] This bias was also reflected in the prosecution of men. Over 90 percent of the drug-trafficking defendants in the nation's courts were now African-American.[43] By the time Ronald Reagan left office, the prison population had not only doubled in size, it had changed complexion. Though only an eighth of the U.S. population was black, blacks now outnumbered white prisoners for the first time. Not even South Africa under apartheid at its worst had a higher percentage of black males in prison.[44] Whether by accident or design, the drug war had evolved into a race war.

The River of Money

When George Herbert Walker Bush took the reins from his former boss in January of 1989, he stood on the flag-draped West Front of the Capitol and assured the country he would deal with the drug problem once and for all. "Take my word," he said. "This scourge will stop." It was a sweeping statement almost foredoomed to failure, but Bush had little choice. He had been badly mauled on the drug issue in the recent campaign. As Reagan's point man in the drug war, he had supervised an eight-year effort that tripled the federal antidrug budget with practically nothing to show for it. Law enforcement officials across the country flatly admitted they were losing ground to a new generation of high-tech smugglers.[1] But Bush not only failed to stem the tide, he was accused of consorting with the enemy. When the Senate's Iran-contra investigators ripped the sheet off covert operations in Central America, they discovered that the CIA had known for some time about contra drug trafficking.[2] They also found evidence of a coke-for-guns cover-up. National Security

aide Ollie North's diaries were riddled with sinister notes—
"wanted aircraft to go to Bolivia to pick up paste, want aircraft to
pick up 1,500 kilos"—and the trail stopped just short of Bush
himself.[3] Then came the revelation that Panamanian strongman
Manuel Noriega had been on the CIA payroll throughout his
brutal career. When Noriega was indicted in the United States
for turning Panama into a free-trade zone for drugs, Bush was
hard-pressed to explain the photos of himself and Noriega chat-
ting it up in Panama at a time when Bush had to have known the
general was up to his ears in the cocaine trade.[4]

Both Dole and Dukakis hammered Bush for his drug war failures throughout the 1988 campaign, and since that turned out
to be one of the few issues that struck a chord, the debate fueled
public anxiety, which in turn animated Congress.[5] When a CBS–
New York Times poll showed half the Americans queried said
drug traffic was the number one international problem, Democrats and Republicans alike tried to outbid each other in an orgy
of breast-beating.[6] By the time of the party conventions in August, Congress had offered up some 250 new antidrug bills.[7]

But as Bush's triumphant motorcade moved up Pennsylvania
Avenue that winter afternoon, the seeds of destruction for his
latest antidrug campaign were already taking root in the Peruvian jungles. Three thousand miles to the south, where the
headwaters of the Amazon spring from the Andean cordillera, an
aging Vietnam-era Huey was choppering through the jungle
haze, and in the doorway, like a haunting snapshot of another
era, a DEA agent in green fatigues cradled an AR-15 automatic
as he scanned the undulating landscape. "Where you see fires
burning," he shouted, "that's where they're going to plant coke."[8]
Ahead, half a dozen plumes of blue smoke rose from the dense
canopy as the *cocaleros* down below slashed and burned fresh
clearings in the jungle. And as far as the eye could see, dappling
mountain slopes and deep ravines, the fields of mature coca
plants stood out like lime-colored pieces of a jigsaw puzzle on a
green felt table. Peruvian officials estimated they were losing

half a million acres of rain forest a year to these ad hoc planta-
tions.[9]

A thousand feet below was the Huallaga River, and on the
slopes above this winding jungle stream grew more than half
the annual supply of leaf for America's ongoing cocaine binge. In
the mid-eighties the Reagan administration had determined to
cut this plant off at the roots in the literal sense, and a massive
coca eradication program was launched with the cooperation of
the Andean nations. Teams of local police and contract workers—armed, financed, and led by American drug agents—were
choppered into the jungles to attack the coca plant with gas-
powered weed cutters. By 1987 the team in Peru was demolishing three thousand acres a month.[10] At this point, unfortunately,
the Maoist Sendero Luminoso guerrilla movement decided to
join with the peasants in return for a piece of the action, and
they were wreaking havoc with the U.S. plans. The helicopter
used to be based at Tingo Maria, a jungle outpost in the heart of
the drug trade. But when the guerrillas wiped out an army patrol
and blew up the power plant a few weeks back, the DEA decided
to fall back to a more defensible position. So at the moment
Bush was promising to end the drug scourge, the U.S. effort in
Peru happened to be in full retreat.

A new encampment was established downriver at the village
of Santa Lucía, but like the Vietnam firebases it was modeled
after, it turned out to be a prison for its occupiers. All supplies
and personnel had to be flown in from the coast because everything outside the barbed-wire perimeter belonged to the enemy.
And since there was no way to protect the workers short of
bringing in the Eighty-second Airborne, the eradication effort
was abandoned. The current strategy called for targeting the
labs where the coca leaves were processed. The idea was that if
all the labs were wiped out, there would be no market for coca
leaves and the farmers would stop growing it.[11] But this theory
had the earmarks of a solution dreamed up by bureaucrats in far-
away Washington. The Huey helicopter, without refueling, has

an operating radius at these mountain altitudes of a little under a hundred miles, and since there was nothing to prevent the traffickers from going deeper into the jungle, the labs were simply moved out of reach.

The underlying problem was the staggering scale of the place, something that few people back in the States could comprehend. In the spring of 1988 Ed Meese had taken a helicopter tour of the Huallaga Valley and he found it a sobering experience. Cresting the Andes at Cerro de Pasco, north of Lima, the attorney general's aircraft descended into an emerald ocean between two monumental ranges of the Andean cordillera and came upon a living carpet undulating to the horizon in all directions. He found it "overpowering." He realized then that trying to stamp out this crop one plant at a time was going to be unrewarding. The Huallaga Valley alone covers an area three times the size of Massachusetts. Clearly, the answer was aerial spraying. What Meese pictured, no doubt, was a squadron of C-130s wingtip to wingtip raining Agent Orange, but that kind of nuclear solution was no longer possible. Even more modest proposals for airborne weed-killing quickly ran into flak from the Peruvians. The predictable outcry from environmentalists was followed by a flat refusal from the government. Lima feared, quite rightly, that massive crop eradication would drive the farmers directly into the arms of the Sendero Luminoso. Beyond that, coca happened to be the country's largest export. One way or another over twenty million Peruvians were making a living off the plant. And since business was booming, there was plenty for everybody—judges, police commanders, politicians, army generals—even the country's top narcotics officer. Dispatches from the State Department were blunt on this point: "Corruption is endemic."[12] It's not hard to understand why. When an army colonel with a base pay of $90 a month could turn a quick $15,000 by ignoring a single drug flight out of the Uchiza airport, anyone with reform on his mind was almost certain to be disappointed.[13]

Peru's newly elected president, Alberto Fujimori, thought the Americans were too hung up on a military solution. He said the only thing that would get the farmers to stop growing coca would be to give them an alternative crop so they could make a living. To the dismay of U.S. officials, Fujimori refused to accept military aid until it was accompanied by economic assistance. Congress finally appropriated some $60 million in farm aid, but any real impact would have called for ten or twenty times that amount, and there was no way Congress was going to drop that kind of cash into the Amazon jungle.[14]

Without meaningful incentives, getting peasants voluntarily to switch crops was a tough sale, even in the face of military force. Put yourself in the place of a farmer who's been asked to pull up his coca fields and plant tomatoes or rice or beans. Most legitimate crops require tillable fields, fertilizer, and insecticides, which all cost money. The crops have to be watered, weeded, and watched over. The coca plant, on the other hand, is almost indestructible. It will grow anywhere, including the sheer face of a cliff, and it will flourish in soil too poor to support anything else. It has built-in resistance to the local bugs, and unlike tomatoes, rice, or beans—which have to be reseeded each season—a single coca plant can last forty years. Instead of one or two crops a year, you can harvest coca leaves every ninety days. As a farmer-friendly shrub, about the only thing that could beat *Erythroxylon coca* would be a money tree.[15]

Even without these natural advantages coca would have been the crop of choice in this remote outback because the Huallaga is simply too far from the coast for anything else to pay off. The road to Lima is a grinding seventy-hour round-trip in second gear. It is cheaper for people in Lima to ship a redwood log four thousand miles from San Francisco than to ship it over the mountain from Tingo Maria. Coca, on the other hand, almost levitates itself out of the jungle. The buyer comes to you, pays cash, he handles the shipping himself, and there's no red tape at customs. On top of that, he pays up to a thousand dollars an acre—ten times what you could get for corn or beans even if you had a road and a truck, which you do not.

In the face of continuing political upheaval and pervasive corruption in Peru, the Bush administration began focusing its hopes on Bolivia, where there were better odds of success. Bolivia had all the same problems, but the country's grinding poverty gave the United States tremendous leverage with its $100 million foreign-aid package. The Bolivians, feet to the fire, were forced to get serious about the drug war, and it was here that the United States finally succeeded in getting a significant number of peasants to substitute other crops for coca. Offering farmers one-time cash payments of eight hundred dollars an acre to pull up their coca fields, Bolivian and U.S. experts arrived in the Chaparé Valley to provide seed, plants, and advice for growing everything from macadamia nuts to passion fruit. Thousands of acres of coca plants were wiped out, and there was a significant and immediate drop in coca production. Unfortunately, nobody seems to have thought beyond the planting season. One typical group of farmers had been talked into planting ginger, and very shortly found themselves up to their asses in ginger. After accumulating forty tons of the stuff, the Bolivian official in charge said, "Now I am trying to stop ginger production because I don't know where I will sell it."[16] The farmers who switched to bananas, grapefruit, and pineapples fared no better. Some of them managed to get crops to market but at a price too low to make a living. Soon, there was smoke rising from the jungle again. "I think coca is here for good," said a local trader. "It's the only product you can grow that you know you can sell the same day and earn enough to stay alive."[17]

In the months before Bush took office, a Cabinet-level document had been circulated that called for the elimination of half the Latin American coca production by 1993.[18] Four years and $2 billion later, the crop was out of control. Constant heat on growers in the Upper Huallaga had sent them into the adjacent jungle, and now coca was being grown in the valley of the

Aguatyía, the Ucali, the Tambo, and the Apurímac. The slopes above the Urubamba were soon expected to rival those of the Huallaga.[19] In all, some two hundred thousand farmers were now growing coca in an area that had been largely rain forest on the day Bush was inaugurated.[20] Beyond that, refining and transportation had spread into neighboring Argentina, Brazil, and Venezuela. The cocaine industry in Latin America now covered an area nearly as large as the continental United States.[21] So to say the eradication program produced no results would be misleading. There were plenty of results, all of them unintended.

And what of the $50 million-base at Santa Lucía? When it was under construction back in 1988 it was lauded as a model for the future of drug eradication—"a package that can be used anywhere, whether it's opium poppy or coca fields."[22] But hopes for this Vietnam-style drug-war bastion were overwhelmed by the reality of the jungle. In a cost-cutting sweep at the end of 1993, the U.S. embassy turned operational control of Santa Lucía over to the Peruvians. The following year a General Accounting Office team dropped in for a look, and their report was bleak: half the helicopters were grounded for maintenance, field operations were paralyzed by an ongoing turf war at the U.S. embassy in Lima, and "the airstrip needed repair because of holes in the runway. . . ."[23]

By the end of the Bush administration total cocaine output in the Andes had increased 15 percent. Some estimates placed it in excess of a thousand tons a year.[24]

The business of turning coca leaves into cocaine is a three-step process. In the first operation, the leaves are sun-dried, then dumped in a plastic-lined pit with a mixture of water and alkali. Then they're trampled into mush by peasants who stomp them like wine grapes. The mix is washed in kerosene, the water and leaves are drained off, alkali is added to the remaining gruel, and the cocaine alkaloids fall to the bottom. The residue is coca paste, which has the consistency and color of putty. It takes about a hundred pounds of leaves to make a pound of paste, so this process usually takes place near the coca fields.

The second step calls for a more sophisticated facility and greater skill. The coca paste is dissolved in water and acid, potassium salt is added to settle out the garbage, and the liquid that's left is dosed with ammonia, which causes the pure cocaine to settle to the bottom. This residue, dried with heat lamps, is cocaine base, which can be smoked but not snorted.

Making snortable cocaine powder from base is the most delicate step of all because it involves volatile chemicals like acetone or ether that can blow up in your face. The cocaine base is dissolved in ether, then dosed with hydrochloric acid, causing the cocaine to crystallize, and it rains to the bottom of the vessel. These crystals—cocaine hydrochloride—are dried in microwave ovens and packaged for shipment to Los Angeles, Houston, Miami, and points north.[25] From farm to lab, it takes about 250 pounds of leaves, worth say $150, to make a pound of cocaine you can sell in the provincial capital for $1,500. But it is in the next step—getting it from the jungle to the streets of Cleveland—that the price takes a spectacular leap from $1,500 a pound to $15,000.[26] This staggering profit reflects the risk involved in moving the product from factory to market, and the handful of fearless killers at the top of this distribution network—the so-called "drug kingpins"—are among the wealthiest men in the world. Geography and history dictated that they would be Colombians. The country's position at the top of the continent made it the natural jumping-off place for United States–bound traffic, and its access to ports on both the Pacific and the Caribbean combined with native hustle to create a hothouse environment for smugglers. By the time Bush reached the Oval Office, one particular gang of traffickers from Medellín was said to be responsible for 80 percent of the cocaine entering the United States.[27]

Here was a target tailor-made for a military solution. The coca eradication effort might be foundering in the jungles of Peru and

Bolivia, but in Colombia, the wide-open network of drug labs and smuggling operations was much more vulnerable. If these outfits could be decapitated—if the men at the top could be neutralized—it would surely do more than anything to stem the flow. This had been the centerpiece of U.S. drug policy under Reagan, and when Bush took over, the man in the crosshairs of Washington's interdiction effort happened to be a thirty-nine-year-old former car thief named Pablo Escobar.

Unlike some of his flashier contemporaries, stocky, hazel-eyed, mustachioed Pablo Escobar Gaviria drove a cheap Renault and dressed simply: rugby shirts, sneakers, chino pants, and a diamond-studded Rolex.[28] Like his idol, Al Capone, he possessed a first-rate criminal mind, voracious ambition, and an unforgiving memory. But Escobar's penchant for violence would have left Big Al agog. The term "ruthless killer" has probably lost some of its impact at the end of the twentieth century, but Escobar would give it new definition. On one occasion when he needed to rub out a couple of suspected informers, he planted a bomb on their flight from Bogotá to Cali, blowing up an Avianca 727 along with a hundred passengers and crew.[29]

But he had a pleasant side. He built more public housing in Medellín than did the government. His showcase project, "Medellín Without Slums," put up hundreds of two-bedroom cement-block houses, new schools, sewers, streetlights, clinics, and sports plazas, capping it off with fifty thousand trees for the city's barrios.[30] He did okay for himself as well. He had sixteen houses in Medellín alone, with heliports, and his country getaway was big enough to sleep a hundred. The swimming pool was flanked by a marble statue of Venus and a mortar emplacement. The surrounding seven thousand acres contained the finest zoo in all Colombia, with camels, lions, giraffes, bison, llamas, and a kangaroo that played soccer.[31]

Escobar was known affectionately as "the Godfather," and *Forbes* magazine listed him as number 69 among the world's 125 non-U.S. billionaires.[32] Anyone with that kind of cash would be above the law almost anywhere, but in Colombia he was a law unto himself. He offered the criminal justice system a simple choice: *plata o plomo*—silver or lead—cash or death. He set the stylistic tone for his MO early in his career when he was arrested with a truckful of cocaine at a roadblock in 1979. After a brief stay in jail, his arrest was mysteriously revoked, the records vanished, and the two cops who busted him were murdered. He hadn't seen the inside of a jail since, even though his rap sheet included the assassination of the Colombian minister of justice, the attorney general, dozens of judges and journalists, scores of innocent civilians, and the machine-gun massacre of thirty peasants.[33]

The Bush administration was obsessed with Escobar because he more than anyone was responsible for industrializing the cocaine trade. Prior to 1980 the business had been dominated by individual operators flying single planeloads or using "mules" to hand carry the stuff through customs. But all that changed dramatically after a bizarre incident in Medellín that had nothing to do with drugs. In the fall of 1981, a Marxist guerrilla group broke into the university and grabbed Marta Nieves Ochoa, the sister of a major local trafficker. Kidnapping the wealthy to finance revolution was a hallowed tradition in Latin America, but this time the guerrillas made a fatal error. These narcotraffickers were not your ordinary capitalists. Instead of paying up, they called a council of war and formed a new organization called Muerto a Secuestradores—Death to Kidnappers—or, alternatively, to "their colleagues or the nearest relatives."[34] The announcement, handed out on street corners and dropped from helicopters, contained a startling revelation. Over *two hundred* organizations had been present at this conclave, and each had agreed to donate ten men to the cause. Over the next ninety days their two-thousand-man hit squad rained horror and destruction on the Marxists. In Medellín, they invaded homes and blew away people merely suspected of involvement with the kidnappers, including union organizers, old ladies, young children, horses, pigs, and chickens. At the university, guerrilla sympathizers were abducted and tortured. On February 17, 1982, Marta Nieves Ochoa was released unharmed. Not a dime had changed hands.[35]

This stunning victory over a well-established guerrilla army impressed the whole country, military and civilians alike, but the people most impressed were the traffickers themselves. All of a sudden Pablo Escobar grasped the potential here. It was time to set old rivalries aside. Early in 1982 he joined with the powerful Ochoa family of Medellín, and Gonzalo Rodriguez Gacha of Bogotá, to form Medellín & Compañía.[36] Since Gacha knew his way around the jungles of Peru, he took charge of raw material, and the Ochoas took over transportation, distribution, and money laundering. Escobar's job was to reorganize manufacturing. He outdid himself. When Tranquilandia, one of his laboratories on the Río Yarí, was raided by the army a couple of years later, they found an industrial complex in the heart of the jungle with air-conditioned executive offices, dormitories, recreational facilities, a pilots' lounge, six runways with hangars, maintenance facilities, and fourteen processing laboratories capable of turning out twenty tons of cocaine a month. The raid also revealed something of Escobar's ability to penetrate the government. Only half a dozen top officials knew about the assault in advance, but the place was nearly deserted when the cops arrived.[37]

It soon became obvious that there was no way Escobar could be brought to justice on his home turf, and the United States was leaning heavily on the Colombian government to extradite him on charges in Miami and Los Angeles. Escobar, of course, hated this idea because he took the U.S. criminal justice system seriously. In Bogotá, you might be able to buy a supreme court justice for as little as $50,000, but judges in the United States were said to be much more expensive. And there were no "Get Out of Jail Free" cards from the federal penitentiary in Marion,

Illinois. So the Godfather set out to terrorize the one institution that had final authority over extradition. In November of 1985, a band of heavily armed guerrillas, now aligned with the traffickers by their mutual hatred of the United States, occupied the Palace of Justice in Bogotá and took three hundred hostages. In the vicious shoot-out that followed, half the Colombian supreme court was slaughtered. By curious coincidence, the eleven judges who died had all voted in favor of extradition. So when the new court convened, its members had a clear sense of mission. They took another look at the U.S.-Colombian Extradition Treaty, found something wrong with one of the signatures, and declared it unconstitutional.

Despite foot-stomping and shouting from Washington, the Colombian court was paralyzed with fear, and there was not a prayer that the equally terrified congress would do anything about it. But in the summer of 1989 there appeared on the horizon a single ray of hope. His name was Carlos Galan, the Liberal party candidate for president in the upcoming elections. By all accounts, one of the most incorruptible public figures in the country, Senator Galan was also a man of extraordinary courage. He alone among the candidates openly favored extradition of Escobar and his compadres. Jubilant U.S. officials were holding their breath. With a Galan victory, they could at last lay hands on some of the most dangerous criminals on the planet. By the week of August 13, the senator was thirty points ahead.

Throughout the campaign, Galan was receiving constant death threats, and he and his phalanx of bodyguards always took extensive precautions. That Friday night as he rose to address the ten thousand cheering supporters at a rally outside Bogotá, he had the sense to wear his bulletproof vest, but it proved no match for the seven hit men who stepped out of the crowd and cut him to ribbons.[38]

Although Pablo Escobar had been correct in identifying the unbuyable Galan as a signal threat to his empire, this time he had apparently stepped over some invisible line. Galan the Martyr would ultimately lead to his downfall anyway. Tens of thousands of outraged mourners surged into the streets demanding justice, and President Virgilio Barco, invoking a state of siege, sidestepped the supreme court and reestablished extradition by decree. That weekend police and military units rounded up nearly ten thousand suspects—all minor players—but while Escobar and his pals were vacationing in Panama, President Barco hit them where they lived. He dispatched the army to impound all the visible ostentation—the ranches and coastal getaways and private islands the traffickers had accumulated over the decade, and the public finally got an eye-popping view inside these baronial fortresses. Along with all the expected stuff— bearskin rugs and marble baths, stables of Thoroughbreds and vintage cars—Gonzalo Rodriguez Gacha had even monogrammed his bullets.[39]

The gauntlet had been thrown. Escobar and his colleagues picked it up. On Monday they issued a press communiqué saying, somewhat redundantly, "Now the fight is with blood"— signed, "The Extraditables." What followed was a war of such stunning savagery that both sides were ultimately brought to their knees. It's probably impossible for most Americans to grasp what the average Colombian went through in this period, but try to imagine a World Trade Center bombing every couple of days. For the next several weeks there were almost continuous explosions throughout the country, with nine banks dynamited in a single day. In September events took an even more horrifying turn when the traffickers began gunning down the wives of police and army officers as they shopped for groceries.[40]

The Bush administration rushed $65 million worth of military aid to Bogotá, including, thoughtfully, five hundred bulletproof vests. But at the same time the United States was cheering the Colombians onward, they were pulling their own people out. By week two of the onslaught, the State Department had evacuated all dependents, and fifty American students were whisked out of the country overnight. The U.S. embassy, surrounded by steel and concrete with marines at the ready, could have been plucked from another era and dropped off here by that last helicopter out of Saigon.[41]

On September 5, 1989, George Bush gave his first prime-time speech to the nation. Speaking from the Oval Office, grim and determined, the president promised the Colombians he would stand with them in their struggle against these "cocaine killers" and he pledged $2 billion in aide to the Andean nations. He demanded the death penalty for kingpins like Escobar and called for the largest budget increase in the history of the drug war. To emphasize the danger America was facing, the president held up a small plastic bag. "This is crack cocaine, seized a few days ago by Drug Enforcement Agents in a park just across the street from the White House."[42] It was a chilling reminder of how this insidious plague touched everyone. But an old-time Chicago newsman like Studs Terkel would note the larger irony. After a seventy-year battle against illegal narcotics, it was now possible to walk out the front door of the White House and do a drug deal across the street.[43]

In Colombia, the Extraditables responded to the Bush speech with a series of explosions, then promised to turn up the heat. A few days later the mayor of Medellín was gunned down after leading an antidrug rally. The following weekend—Colombia's Valentine's Day—was kicked off with three bombs in the nation's capital that wounded scores of shoppers and left two policemen dead. By Sunday the tendrils of fear had reached all the way to Washington, and Secret Service protection was extended to President Bush's five grown children.[44]

Mónica de Greiff, the thirty-two-year-old minister of justice of the Barco regime, happened to be in Washington at the time. She had flown in two weeks earlier asking for a quick $14 million to help protect her country's terrified judges, and she proved to be a hit on Capitol Hill. Whisked around town in a security cordon normally reserved for heads of state, she impressed everybody with her iron resolve. Despite the fact that two of her predecessors had been gunned down in broad daylight, Mónica de Greiff was adamantine. "I am determined that the integrity of our justice system survives this crisis."[45] *The New York Times* lauded "her competence and cool courage,"[46] and drug czar William Bennett put it more eloquently: "Grace under pressure, poise under fire." Then de Greiff got a phone call from the Ex-traditables. They proved to be even more eloquent: "Remember, you are a mother. We can kill your son." As her veins turned to ice, she was given a detailed description of the boy's minute-by-minute movements for the previous day.[47] With a glance at her three-year-old, she decided she'd had enough. On September 21 she resigned her post, requested asylum in the United States, and vanished with her family into a phalanx of federal agents.[48] Her antagonists celebrated by bombing the Bogotá offices of all nine Colombian political parties.[49]

De Greiff's resignation was the first resounding crack in Colombian resolve. And the average citizen, hunkered down behind bolted doors, understood Mónica's fear all too clearly. Why should Colombia be forced to pay this horrible price, when it was the insatiable demand of the gringos that fueled this trade? One surviving presidential candidate—still carrying three bullets in his body from an earlier hit—was openly calling for dialogue with the traffickers.[50] Said Senator Ernesto Samper, "Let's not turn Colombia into the Vietnam of the war on drugs."[51]

At 7:30 on the morning of December 6, with the streets in downtown Bogotá full of people heading for work, a truck loaded with half a ton of dynamite blew the front off the secret police headquarters and heavily damaged two square miles of the city. The concussion shattered windows across from the U.S. embassy, seven miles away. Sixty people were killed outright and nearly a thousand wounded. President Barco, who now rarely ventured outside the walls of his Spanish colonial palace, urged his troops doggedly onward. "We will not allow ourselves to fall to the bloody tyranny of the narco-terrorists." His constituents, on the other hand, were not so sure. By now Escobar had made it plain there were no boundaries. Bombs were going off in su-permarkets, hotels, movie theaters—even schools—and the squads of combat troops racing through the streets after the fact just emphasized their helplessness.[52] Then, a major break came in December of 1989 when Escobar's partner Gonzalo Ro-driguez Gacha was trapped by security forces south of Cartagena near the coastal town of Tolu. In a withering shoot-out, Gacha and his seventeen-year-old son were cut down along with fifteen of his bodyguards.[53]

Five days later, the United States invaded Panama in pursuit of Manuel Noriega. This remarkable act of gunboat diplomacy sent shock waves throughout Latin America, and apparently it got the attention of Pablo Escobar as well. If the gringos could send in the Marines and kidnap a sovereign head of state, what the hell was next? A few days later, as General Noriega was being spirited out of his native land in handcuffs, the Extraditables sent feelers to the Colombian government asking for a deal. Over the next several months, secret peace talks went on in fits and starts, with periods of calm punctuated by waves of may-hem. Politicians who opposed the talks were shot and killed, and journalists who opened their mouths on the subject were kid-napped. With one notable exception, the press had virtually stopped reporting on the drug war. *El Espectador*, the valiant Bo-gotá daily, was still blasting away at the traffickers in spite of hav-ing lost its publisher, several executives, and half a dozen reporters to the guns and bombs of Pablo Escobar. Few other Colombian journalists were willing to put a byline on anything that even mentioned the boys from Medellín.

In May of 1990, in an election run-up punctuated by car bombs, Liberal party candidate Cesar Gaviria won the presiden-tial race walking away. U.S. officials were delighted. Gaviria, like Galan, was an outspoken supporter of extradition, and it looked like the Americans would finally get their way.[54] But once in of-fice, Gaviria immediately began shading his enthusiasm for the drug war. In September he ran up the white flag. Despite howls of outrage from Washington, Gaviria made the traffickers an offer they couldn't refuse: turn yourselves in and you'll be tried in Colombia—not the United States. This move effectively terminated the extradition treaty.

The Bush administration was stunned. In Colombia they were dancing in the streets. After a decade of rush-hour explosions and mind-numbing horror, they had had enough. The three Ochoa brothers—Escobar's surviving partners in Medellín & Compañía—surrendered almost immediately, but Escobar held out for a better deal, bullying the government for another six months. Once again, the Gaviria administration caved in. They were so desperate to get *El Patrón* behind bars they simply agreed to all his demands. When he surrendered on June 19, 1991, he was flown to Envigado, south of Medellín, where a special prison had been built to his specifications. After the press got a look at this "jail," they realized it was not Escobar who had surrendered, but the government. Surrounded by barbed wire, high voltage, and military patrols at the end of a winding mountain road, the comfortable *ranchita* above the Río Cauca was clearly designed not to keep Escobar in but to keep his enemies out. Don Pablo had been allowed to surrender with his entourage intact, and they proceeded to set up shop here with the full protection of the Colombian government. His cell was a three-room suite with an office larger than the warden's. There was a soccer field, a disco, and a bar where the guards served drinks to the hit men and their prostitutes at weekly parties. The media dubbed it "Club Medellín."[55]

The growing fury in the United States was echoed in Europe and in Colombia as well. The headline in *El Espectador* said it all: "TERROR WON."[56] The government's creeping embarrassment was amplified by Escobar's outrageous behavior in prison. He and his pals, it turned out, had not abandoned the drug trade. They had simply relocated their operation to this mountain redoubt. When word got out that Don Pablo had some former employees rounded up and brought to the prison so they could be tortured and executed, Gaviria finally had to act. A military op-eration was mounted to move Escobar to a more secure environ-ment, but of course he was tipped off and vanished into the jungle. He continued to terrorize the country for another year and a half before he was finally brought to earth in December of 1993. At the end of the line, the billionaire who once com-manded an army of ten thousand was trapped with a single body-guard. The two men were shredded in a police fusillade as they tried to escape over the rooftops.

It was three weeks before Christmas when news of Escobar's death was broadcast in Bogotá, and the music that accompanied the announcement was "Joy to the World."[57] This time the wave of euphoria rolled all the way to Washington. The president wired his personal congratulations, and the head of the DEA was exultant. "No matter how powerful they are . . . they are not immune."[58] But for all the joyful high fives, there was a curious note of reserve in the press reports. Yes, the majordomo of the cocaine trade had finally been crushed by the engines of justice, but "his death was not expected to affect the flow of cocaine."[59] It seemed that the Medellín share of the U.S. market had been scooped up by a group of competitors two hundred miles to the south in the provincial capital of Cali. The dreaded Escobar had been replaced by a brand-new set of masterminds—Gilberto Ro-driguez Orejuela and his brother, Miguel.

The leaders of the Cali cartel were as different from their Medellín counterparts as Meyer Lansky from Dutch Schultz. The Rodriguez Orejuela brothers were businessmen, first and foremost—Gilberto was a former banker who owned a chain of drugstores—and they used violence as a surgical instrument rather than a sledgehammer, confining their killing to business and avoiding the slaughter of innocents. While the boisterous Medellín gang was blowing the country to bits, the Rodriguez Orejuelas were quietly buying it up. One U.S. official called their influence unprecedented. "There isn't a politician in the Valle del Cauca who isn't on the payroll or intimidated." When a *New York Times* reporter toured Cali a few days after Escobar's death, he found the genteel four-hundred-year-old city of red-tiled roofs getting an instant face-lift. The skyline, punctuated with construction cranes and garish skyscrapers, framed a jangle of purple neon discos, luxury-car dealerships, and streets full of Land Cruisers with tinted windows. The cabdriver said, "It's starting to look like Miami, isn't it?"[60]

In Washington they expected Gaviria to shift his forces to the new front line in Cali, but the orders never came. The government continued to pretend they were in hot pursuit, and the Rodriguez Orejuelas continued to dine out in public. The truth was, the Colombians no longer had the strength or the courage for another do-or-die confrontation. The horrifying ten-year struggle with Escobar and the Ochoas had damaged the country in ways that would endure for a generation. The best judges, the most incorruptible politicians, the most aggressive journalists, the bravest army officers had all been sacrificed to the war on drugs. Most of the survivors were thoroughly compromised. Given the choice of *plata o plomo,* they had understandably chosen *plata.* But once they took the cash, they found themselves on the payroll, and the resulting moral cancer infected everything in Colombia from the top down. Immediately after Ernesto Samper squeaked by in the 1994 election, tapes of two phone conversations surfaced that linked his campaign to drug money. When Samper's top aide admitted he had indeed picked up $6 million from the Rodriguez Orejuelas of Cali, impeachment was in the air, and TV commentators invoked the term *"Drogagate"* over grainy footage of Richard Nixon. But the subsequent congressional investigation gave Samper a pass, which simply confirmed the widely held fear that the whole country was slipping into a state of narco-paralysis.[61] "President Samper's campaign is not the only campaign to receive drug money," said one Colombian legislator. "Most campaigns over the last fifteen years have."[62]

The dialogue between the two capitals deteriorated to name-calling and the U.S. Senate was about to invoke sanctions when Samper suddenly arrested the leaders of the Cali cartel. Once again there were shouts of joy and backslapping all around, but cynics noted the seizures had a certain stage-managed quality, and subsequent events bore them out.[63] The tender plea bargain offered to the Orejuelas left U.S. officials in such a state of vein-popping rage they yanked the visas of President Ernesto Samper and his top advisers, a diplomatic first for the two countries.[64] And so, after twenty years of bloody conflict, billions of dollars, and tens of thousands of lives, one of the Western Hemisphere's oldest democracies had been transformed into a pariah nation with its leaders on the watch list along with Gadhafi and Saddam Hussein—our own private Afghanistan.

The flow of cocaine, however, continued without a ripple. The endless supply of cartels and kingpins somehow mystified officials in Washington who had convinced themselves that the cartel would collapse without its top men.[65] But the Cali cartel had some five hundred mid-level executives handling the day-to-day business of manufacturing, transportation, finance, and enforcement, and they were unwilling simply to throw up their hands and walk away from a $25 billion-a-year operation.[66] So they divided the work among themselves and continued to operate as independent contractors. Back in Denver the price was still at rock bottom, the quality never better, and 15 percent of the high school seniors said it was "very easy" to get.[67]

Perhaps more ominous for the long haul was the wreckage in Colombia. With millions in cash bubbling up from the sewers every day, narco-dollars were totally distorting the economy, and today property values in parts of Bogotá rival Tokyo. Few middle-class urban Colombians can afford homes anymore. If, say, you inherited an old red-roofed ancestral hacienda, you may find yourself confronted with the familiar choice—*plata o plomo*—a sack of cash worth five times the appraisal or a bullet in the head.[68] Fully one third of Colombia's fertile land now belongs to drug barons who have taken it out of production in favor of show horses and petting zoos. Colombia used to export food, now it imports.[69] And then there is the creeping erosion of regard for the law. "I enjoy driving, but not here," says writer Gabriel García Marquez. "Those same Colombians who run red lights and block intersections in Bogotá are well behaved in Miami."[70]

Despite evidence of failure on a scale unequaled since Vietnam, Washington was still insisting that the Colombians hunker down and get on with it. In the summer of 1996 U.S. ambassador Myles Frichette remained unequivocal. "People sort of bring to the extradition issue a mind-set that existed five years ago—'extradition equals violence'—without any thought to the fact that Colombia has international obligations. Allowing the narcos to say 'we will reimpose violence if you reestablish extradition' is in effect blackmail of the entire Colombian people by these guys."[71] True enough, but the ambassador's courageous position on this issue was probably augmented by the squad of marines who surrounded him in Bogotá.

At that same moment, the three Ochoa brothers—still facing possible life sentences in the United States—were released from prison in Colombia five years after they turned themselves in. They emerged from the ordeal with most of their estate intact. Despite the gnashing of teeth in Washington, they tipped their sombreros and returned to the vast *finca* on the coastal plain south of Cartagena where Don Fabio was roasting forty pigs in honor of his returning sons.[72]

The Ochoas' former partner, Pablo Escobar, had modeled himself after Al Capone and he died a violent death. The Ochoas modeled themselves after old Joe Kennedy, who made a fortune in bootleg whiskey and hung on to all of it. And like Joe Kennedy, the kingpins of Colombia were planning to send their offspring to Harvard and Stanford to prepare them for leadership in the coming century.[73]

Chapter Seven

Montezuma's Revenge

Despite Bob Dole's accusations, George Bush had not been totally ineffectual as commanding general in the Reagan drug war. In the mid-1980s, Bush successfully clamped down on the free-for-all in Florida, where cocaine was pouring in by ship, plane, mule, and diplomatic pouch. Miami was then the port of entry for most of the Colombian product, and as business arrangements shifted from day to day, the murder rate in Dade County skyrocketed. To stem the tide of white powder and violence, Vice President Bush created an interagency strike team called the South Florida Task Force and set out to attack the smugglers by land, sea, and air. Customs and Border Patrol agents were pulled off the Canadian and Mexican frontiers and reassigned to the Sunshine State, and ten Coast Guard cutters fitted for night operation went into action in the Caribbean as AWACS jets circled above the fray directing airborne interceptors in Blackhawk helicopters.[1] All this heat had the desired effect, and once again, the law of unintended consequence crowned success with disaster.

For years there had been a casual relationship between Mexican marijuana smugglers and the Colombian cartels, and with the Florida corridor suddenly awash in lawmen, the cocaine traffic shifted almost overnight to the land route through Mexico. At first the Mexicans were operating strictly as cargo handlers, picking the drug up from the Colombians on one side of the line and handing it back to them on the other for a thousand dollars a kilo. But in the early 1990s, when the cartels were in a death struggle with the Colombian government, cash flow became a problem and they started paying the Mexicans off in cocaine. Since the *muchachos* already had a vast marijuana distribution network in the United States, this new product line—pound for pound ten or twenty times more valuable than marijuana—was like rocket fuel in the gas tank of a lowrider. A laid-back culture imbued with a tradition of *mordida* and skilled at corruption was suddenly supercharged.

Throughout its tormented history, Mexico has been plagued by exemplary economic inequality. Most of the nation's wealth is in the hands of about thirty families, while a fifth of the people live on less than a dollar a day. The ruling Institutional Revolutionary Party has routinely stolen the elections since its inception sixty years ago, creating a fertile climate for under-the-table payoffs. Almost everybody seems to be on the take, from the garbage man to the presidential cabinet, where a suitable gift of cash might get you appointed, say, commandante of the federal judicial police for Baja California Norte. For decades, cabinet officers and presidents routinely left office with unexplained fortunes.[2] In the old days, *mordida*—the "bite"—was accepted as an efficient lubricator, a means of getting things done while sharing the wealth in an otherwise unequal society. But with the arrival of the narco-billions everything shifted gears.

In 1988, after a key official in the previous administration was implicated in the torture-killing of a U.S. drug agent, President Carlos Salinas took office with a promise not to tolerate any more high-level corruption.[3] He came out swinging and immediately landed a stunning blow with the arrest of Angel Felix Gallardo—Mexico's very own "Godfather"—along with his palace guard of some eighty state and local cops. But this impressive strike turned out to be the high point of the Salinas drug war and from here on it was all downhill. And though there were plenty of warning signs—like the runway shoot-out at Veracruz where the army and the police faced off over a planeload of cocaine— the extent of the decay was largely hidden from view.[4]

Then, at a quarter to four on the afternoon of May 24, 1993, Juan Cardinal Posadas Ocampo, archbishop of Guadalajara, arrived at Hidalgo International Airport to meet the papal nuncio. It was an auspicious moment. The Mexican government and the Vatican had been on the outs for most of this century but President Salinas was determined to normalize relations, and the arrival of the pope's personal ambassador would be the capstone of this effort.[5] As the archbishop's driver wheeled into the parking lot across from the terminal, a young man yanked open the door and blasted His Eminence with fourteen slugs, killing him instantly. Half a dozen other gunmen sprayed the scene, killing the driver and five bystanders, including an old woman and her nephew and a startled businessman with a cell phone in his hand.[6]

The hit men stuffed their weapons into carry-on bags and ran to the terminal, flashing police badges, where they boarded Aeromexico flight 110 for Tijuana—which was supposed to have left twenty minutes earlier but was held at the gate for these very important passengers—and during the two-hour flight from Guadalajara to Tijuana, nobody bothered to call ahead with the information that the killers were on board.[7] There was, however, a contingent of Federal Judicial Police waiting in Tijuana, but they were there simply to escort the assassins to the U.S. border, where they vanished into the night.[8]

Like a manhole cover blowing off a sewer, this event got everybody's attention. Even in Sicily, you can't murder a prince of the church without rattling the foundation, and the resulting up-

heaval exposed an ominous specter of moral and political de-
composition. The Catholic hierarchy was convinced that the
archbishop had been targeted by narco-traffickers because of his
outspoken condemnation of the drug trade, but there was another explanation that was almost as revolting. Cardinal
Ocampo may have simply had the bad luck to reach the airport
at the same instant as Joaquin Guzman, head of the Sinaloa cartel. The rival Tijuana gang happened to be lying in wait.[9]

These antagonists were all former protégés of Angel Felix Gallardo, the imprisoned Godfather of Sinaloa, and when Angel
went down he passed control to his blood relatives, the Arellano
Felix brothers of Tijuana. But a splinter group under Guzman
and "Guero" Palma set up shop on their own, and according to
one Mexican official, the Godfather flipped out. "Felix, like the
twisted old man that he is, sends a group of Venezuelan *narcos*
to infiltrate Guero's family." The leader of this squad then ran off
with Guero Palma's wife and two small children, and after per-
suading the woman to withdraw $7 million of Guero's money
from a bank in San Francisco, he cut off her head and mailed it
back to Guero in a hatbox. Then he took the two children to
Venezuela and threw them off a bridge. "After that . . . the Arel-
lanos know it is kill or be killed."[10] The ambush at the airport
was apparently just the latest tit-for-tat, and the ill-starred cardinal happened to have pulled up in a Mercury Grand Marquis, a
favored ride of the drug lords.

No matter which version the public went for, the Mexican
government looked ridiculous. The mortification reverberated
from Rome to Washington and back again—NAFTA was being
debated at the time—and President Salinas dispatched truck-
loads of police to Tijuana to track down the killers. Warrants
were issued for Benjamin and Javier Arellano Felix, who were
said to have personally led the hit squad. Police locked up
dozens of suspects—including Guzman—and seventy police
commanders and prosecutors were arrested or fired. But the
Arellano Felix brothers refused to play the part of the most

wanted men in Mexico. They were repeatedly spotted in shopping malls and restaurants, and everybody seemed to know where they were but the cops.[11] As one investigation after another collapsed, Mexico City finally sent in an elite federal squad of untouchables under the respected commander Alejandro Castaneda. The new man had an immediate impact. In a series of lightning raids, Castaneda arrested two dozen cartel soldiers and seized millions of dollars in Arellano assets.[12] The brothers were still at large but Castaneda was breathing down their necks.

On the evening of March 3, 1994, Castaneda and his team staked out a cartel safe house in upscale Tijuana. Just after eight, the gates opened and a red Chevy Suburban with tinted windows pulled onto the road heading downtown. Castaneda and his crew followed in a pair of blue Suburbans, and as they cruised through traffic along Boulevard Diaz Ordaz, they came alongside the suspects and motioned the driver to pull over. The caravan halted at a busy intersection ringed with shopping centers—*BAM!*—the windows on the red Suburban disintegrated as gunmen inside opened fire with heavy weapons. Somehow all this flying lead missed Castaneda, and he and his men returned fire as screaming pedestrians scattered like chickens.

This time Castaneda had numbers on his side, and his troops quickly overwhelmed the gunmen, killing three and wounding most of the others. As they handcuffed the survivors, Castaneda realized they'd hit the jackpot. The twenty-five-year-old kid he had facedown on the pavement was Javier Arellano Felix. Just then, another squad of lawmen arrived. A carload of Baja state police piled out and one officer walked up to Castaneda and shot him in the back with an AK-47. In the violent gun battle that followed, the federal troops were driven off. Young Javier Arellano Felix was plucked from the sidewalk, hustled away from all this untidiness, and with the assistance of a Baja state attorney general, he was given safe passage back to the Land of Oz.[13]

Naturally there was a wave of public outrage at this grotesque betrayal, but it crashed without effect three weeks later—overwhelmed by the assassination of presidential candidate Donald Luis Colosio at a political rally in Tijuana. If there was any doubt that Mexico was swirling down the same drainpipe as Colombia, the killing of Colosio—a reformer in the mold of Carlos Galan—should have put it to rest.

The traditional "lone deranged gunman" was arrested and he dutifully confessed, and then was hustled offstage when it became clear that nobody would go for this version.[14] For one thing, the candidate was shot from two directions, and videotapes seemed to show at least six men working together to block Colosio's path while deflecting his bodyguards and making way for the killers. President Salinas shipped hundreds of reinforcements to Tijuana, but the pursuit of the killers went nowhere. Shortly after the assassination, the Tijuana chief of police was being interviewed by an American reporter, when he discovered that his secret files on the case had vanished. The next day, he was killed. A few days later the special prosecutor was about to board a government jet to Tijuana, when the police found a bomb on his plane. He decided to reconsider the "lone deranged gunman" theory, and a few days later he handed Salinas his resignation along with a report concluding there was no conspiracy.[15] Salinas appointed another special prosecutor, and he was followed in turn by a parade of senior officials who would unsuccessfully track the braided threads of Colosio, the cardinal, and the Tijuana cartel. One by one these top lawmen would be compromised or eliminated. By 1996 the combat life expectancy for Tijuana prosecutors was about the same as that of a World War II tail gunner. Sergio Armando Silva, chief of the judicial police, was cut down in February. Prosecutor Arturo Ochoa Palacios was killed while jogging at a health club in April. Prosecutor Sergio Moreno Perez was kidnapped and murdered along with his son in May. Former police commander Isaac Sanchez Perez was shot to death in July. Prosecutor Jesus Romero Magana was gunned down in front of his house in August.[16] At this moment Ernesto Ibarra Santes, a close friend of slain police captain Alejandro Castaneda, took over as federal police commander and vowed not only to avenge his fallen comrade but to end corruption in the ranks. He lasted twenty-eight days. On September 14, after flying to Mexico City in secret, he and his aides were blown to bits by machine gunners who pulled alongside on the way in from the airport. Meanwhile, Javier Arellano Felix continued to be spotted from time to time, driving through the beach community of Playas de Tijuana in a white Mercedes.[17]

But by the time Carlos Salinas left office, the thrilling and fruitless pursuit of the Arellano Felix brothers would turn out to be a mere sideshow of the main event. In September of 1994, six months after the Colosio assassination, a senior PRI party official, Francisco Ruiz Massieu, was shot to death in downtown Mexico City. Here was yet another widely respected reformer dropped in his tracks in broad daylight, and an outraged President Salinas vowed to get to the bottom of it. He took the unusual step of naming the dead man's brother, Deputy Attorney General Mario Ruiz Massieu, as special prosecutor. Surely the victim's blood brother could be trusted above all others to pursue the truth wherever it might lead.

Wrong again. After an initial burst of arrests, the investigation quickly ran aground, and U.S. intelligence officials thought they knew why. They suspected that Mario Ruiz Massieu had been bought and paid for. As deputy attorney general, he was chief of the Federal Judicial Police—the country's frontline antinarcotics force—and therefore at the pinnacle of a nationwide pyramid of kickbacks. Mario had one of the most coveted jobs in Mexican law enforcement. "He decided which police chief got which region," said a senior Mexican official. "One of the good regions like Tamaulipas or the other border states can sell for one million to two million dollars." But why would President Salinas have appointed an investigator who was so obviously compromised? One possibility came to light shortly after Salinas left office in December of 1994.[18]

President Ernesto Zedillo came onstage with the standard promise to end high-level corruption once and for all, then shocked everyone by installing a member of the opposition as attorney general. When the new man began digging into the Ruiz Massieu business he discovered that his predecessor had systematically covered up a trail of evidence leading directly to the former president's older brother, Raul. As Mexicans watched in astonishment, Raul Salinas, untouchable member of the ruling class, was hauled away and charged with the murder of Francisco Ruiz Massieu. Suddenly the air was full of feathers. Mario Ruiz Massieu caught the next plane out but was stopped at Newark Airport with $47,000 in his pocket. Shortly thereafter, investigators discovered another $9 million stashed in a Houston bank. But Ruiz Massieu's stash paled in comparison to the $120 million discovered in a Swiss bank account maintained by the former president's brother, Raul.[19] Officials on both sides of the border charged that all this unexplained cash came from drug payoffs.[20]

But these winnings, though impressive, were peanuts compared to the wealth of the man Ruiz Massieu and Raul Salinas were said to be protecting. Juan Garcia Abrego, head of the Gulf cartel, was worth some $15 billion. While all that heat was focused on Tijuana, Abrego had been running a wide-open operation out of Matamoros into Brownsville, Texas, and it was generally understood that he had protection at the highest levels.[21] A police officer who showed up at one of Abrego's fiestas reported that guests were arriving like Arabian princes in a procession of Learjets, and among the bankers, criminals, and off-duty cops was the president's brother. As Raul Salinas stepped off the plane, he received a warm *abrazo* from the host. "When I saw them greet each other, I knew that Abrego was untouchable."[22]

Two years later, as if someone had thrown a switch, Abrego's protection vanished when Salinas left office. Shortly thereafter Abrego was captured and hustled out of the country to face several life sentences in Houston. Subsequently, investigators claimed that Raul Salinas had made a deal to protect Abrego as long as his brother was president.[23] But when Mexican prosecutors suggested calling former president Carlos Salinas in for questioning, he immediately left town. He has since settled in Ireland and has threatened to sue anyone who suggests he or his family had anything to do with the drug trade.[24]

With the nation's law enforcement institutions collapsing around him, President Zedillo finally turned in desperation to the army. By now it was clear that the Federal Judicial Police were so riddled with corruption, it was hard to tell who they were working for. When Zedillo's new police chief took over at the end of 1994, he discovered that most of his men never even bothered to pick up their paychecks since their salary was such a pittance compared to their real income. But just as the new man was about to clean house, he was poisoned in his sleep—left alive, totally paralyzed.[25] Zedillo, surrounded by treachery, decided to put his faith in military discipline. In December of 1996, he named army general José de Jesus Gutierrez Rebollo as Mexico's drug czar, a move that was met with resounding applause in Washington. The United States had been pressuring Zedillo for some time to get the army involved because that was about the only institution left with a shred of integrity. Gutierrez—a tough-minded drug warrior who had personally led the raid on Guero Palma of the Sinaloa cartel—was clearly the man for the job. And since President Clinton's new drug czar was also a three-star general, the two men hit it off immediately. After meeting Gutierrez in Mexico City, General Barry McCaffrey said, "He has a reputation of impeccable integrity. . . . He's a deadly serious guy." McCaffrey predicted a new era in U.S.-Mexican cooperation and promised better sharing of intelligence and fifty new helicopters.[26]

Eleven weeks later the Mexican government announced that General Gutierrez was in a maximum-security prison, charged with taking bribes and protecting the nation's number one drug lord.[27] It seems the general had indeed been tough on traffickers, but selectively. A check of the records revealed one cartel he never touched.

Now yet another archfiend—number fifteen—took center stage in the pantheon of ultimate cocaine kingpins.[28] While the world's attention had been focused on either end of the Mexican border, this operation was apparently hard at work in the middle. Across the river from El Paso, in Juarez, a sophisticated young entrepreneur named Amado Carrillo Fuentes was picking up the pieces of the Abrego and Sinaloa cartels and knitting them into a vast combine. In the cocaine trade, as in any industry, the original rough-and-tumble adventurers are replaced by technocrats as the business matures, and Senor Carrillo was said to be a skilled mediator. "He's more like the Cali people," said a U.S. lawman. "He tries to keep the heat away and not provoke acts of violence."[29] But within his own organization, Carrillo reportedly ran a tight ship. When one of his loads was seized, they said he just killed everybody who knew anything about it, and that way he was certain to get the informant. This kind of ruthless efficiency paid handsome dividends. By syndicating large shipments and assigning different smuggling tasks to different partners, he began to achieve economies of scale his predecessors had never dreamed of.[30] His stronghold in Juarez was peaceful, with gun battles rare, and car bombings unheard of. That quiet, according to U.S. officials, was the sound of business booming.[31] His weekly gross was estimated at $200 million.[32] But Amado Carrillo was more than willing to share. By some accounts, he was laying as much as 60 percent of the proceeds on his close friends in government.[33] Among his many thoughtful gestures was paying the rent on a lavish Mexico City apartment occupied by the nation's drug czar, General José de Jesus Gutierrez Rebollo.[34]

The U.S. Congress erupted at this news. Since Gutierrez had complete access to the most sensitive intelligence, it was likely that the names of agents, witnesses, targets, watch lists, and operational plans were now in Carrillo's hands. But President Clinton chose to look at the bright side. He praised the Mexican government for quick action. "They're obviously saying . . . 'We will not tolerate corruption . . . even if it's at the highest level. . . . And so I'm encouraged by that."[35]

Meanwhile, in Mexico as in Colombia, the brave and honest had all been slaughtered and the compromisers were forced to dance on their graves.

The Reagan-Bush Andean Strategy was intended to stamp out drug production in Latin America by the year 1995. Launched a decade earlier with bands playing and streamers flying, it was now dead in the water and aflame from wheelhouse to engine room. Although the drug warriors in Washington struggled to put the best face on it, the facts on the page were overwhelming. For a view of the global scale of the disaster, it would be hard to beat the State Department's annual *International Narcotics Control Strategy Report.* Despite the always impressive body counts of kingpins and coca fields, the bottom line was unremitting: ". . . Worldwide coca cultivation rose to a new record of 530,000 acres in 1995. . . ." "The discovery that Colombian traffickers were delivering multi-ton shipments of cocaine in jumbo jets underscored Mexico's role. . . ." "The Cali drug mafia has been using Poland as a local hub since the early 1990s, and apparently has been looking for a toehold in Hungary." "Cocaine now moves freely also to Africa." "Cocaine, in short, remains a growth industry in most of the world."[36]

Unfortunately, that wasn't the worst of it. Back in the late 1980s, the market-savvy Colombians spotted an interesting dichotomy. The profit margin on *heroin,* pound for pound, was more than triple the return on cocaine. A kilo of coke worth $2,000 in Bogotá might bring $30,000 in Los Angeles, but the identical block of heroin—only $6,000 in Colombia—could go for $100,000 up north.

With typical Colombian zeal, they decided to cut out the middleman. The high Andes proved perfectly hospitable to opium

poppies, and by 1991 local farmers already had some three thousand acres blossoming in the cloud forests.[37] Meanwhile, the
production wing of the Cali cartel imported the best Asian
chemists money could buy, and within a couple of years they
were flooding the market with heroin so clean and cheap that a
whole new generation of unsuspecting users began walking into
the jaws of addiction. The Colombian product turned out to be
an astonishing 95 percent pure—practically pharmaceutical
grade—and it was dropped into a market that was used to 95
percent garbage. You didn't have to inject this stuff. It was so
powerful you could sprinkle it on cigarette tobacco, and a few
tokes later . . . not a care in the world. Since there were no ugly
needles involved, kids got the impression it wasn't dangerous. Of
course the opposite was true, but once again the well-
intentioned scare tactics of the prohibitionists backfired. Cool
Gen-Xers knew from experience that government claims about
marijuana were exaggerated, so they assumed the grown-ups
were lying about heroin as well. This time, for a change, the
grown-ups were telling the truth. The U.S. addict population—
stable for twenty years—suddenly jumped 20 percent.[38] The
number of heroin-related emergency episodes doubled from
1990 to 1995.[39]

But it is the downstream effect of this tidal wave of catastrophe that is perhaps the most unsettling. The river of money
that has washed away law and order and submerged one Latin
American country after another is still rising, and the crest of the
flood is nowhere in sight. The U.S. border with Mexico is no
more impervious to the tide of corruption than it was to killer
bees. So if the drug lords are spending tens of millions a week[40]
on their friends in government south of the border, how much
are they spending in the North?.

Chapter Eight

Mission Impossible

From the mouth of the Rio Grande at Brownsville on the Texas Gulf, the Mexican border runs a thousand miles upriver to El Paso—"The Pass"—then west for an equal length along five arrow-straight survey lines that slice unbending through the Sonoran desert, across the Continental Divide and a dozen lesser ranges, and down to the surf at San Diego. For much of its vastness, the border is guarded only by the elements—searing heat, howling winds, scorpions, and rattlesnakes. But in those places where humans concentrate, the ebb and flow is funneled through two dozen ports of entry ranging from a hand-powered ferry across the Rio Grande at Los Ebaños, to twenty-four lanes of traffic pouring north from Tijuana into San Ysidro, California.

Supervisory Customs Inspector Tom Isbell can look out the broad windows of his office and see the whole sweep of the line at San Ysidro, two dozen men under his command searching the river of vehicles with rapid eyes, waving the drivers through with a flick of the wrist, stopping one here and there with a raised hand. The average passage takes a few seconds, but when some-thing catches the eye, the dogs are called out, everything is taken apart, and once or twice an hour somebody is led away in hand-cuffs. "It's instinct," says Isbell. "You can't replace that with computers." A twenty-six-year veteran of the force with a repu-tation as a straight shooter, he brags about one of his top men. "Some people look and they don't see. He sees everything. He was having lunch one day and glanced up and through the win-dow he saw a guy driving by who had already cleared primary and was on his way out. And something struck him—the guy was laughing—and he ran out, stopped the guy, and made a seizure."[1]

To the unpracticed eye, the scene outside Tom Isbell's window looks like a model of border-control efficiency, but the supervi-sory inspector sees something else. On a pedestrian bridge a hundred yards to the south is a man wearing a ski mask, watch-ing Isbell with binoculars and talking on a cell phone. "They wait until the traffic is backed up," says Isbell. "Then they call in their shipments from the side streets. We have a mandate not to hold up traffic more than twenty minutes, and they know we've got to open the gates and start waving people through." The man in the mask probably also knows each of the inspectors on sight, knows their habits, and knows which one is least likely to check under the seat of your pickup. So he and Isbell, two professionals in a deadly game, square off on a daily basis in the battle to seal the southern border to the flow of drugs. Ask him who's winning and Isbell will tell you. "We intercept maybe five percent."[2]

In truth it may be a lot less than that. For all of Tom Isbell's considerable diligence, there is mounting evidence that some of the people around him have not been so vigorous. An investiga-tion of corruption at the highest level of the San Diego office has been under way in fits and starts since 1990. The probe was trig-gered quite by accident when a Customs Service dog handler unexpectedly showed up for work a little early one day. His Labrador, Snag, freaked out when they passed an empty tanker truck in the lineup. A supervisor stepped in and said the driver had told him some men were smoking marijuana near the truck down in Mexico. That would account for the dog's reaction, but over the supervisor's objection, the handler insisted on running the truck over the scales anyway. The tanker was more than seven thousand pounds overweight. Over the next several hours, the canine officer's boss tried to get him literally to call off the dogs, but he refused. At this point the supervisor ordered the driver released, and the man took off for Mexico on foot. When the tanker was finally opened up, they found four tons of cocaine—the largest seizure in the history of the port. It was only the tip of the iceberg.[3]

The truck belonged to Hidro Gaz de Juarez, a company that happened to be under surveillance at that moment by a Customs inspector named Mike Horner. What stunned Horner was the fact that the truck got as far as it did. He had already flagged Hidro Gaz on the Customs computer after an informant tipped him that these tankers—and this driver in particular—were involved in the drug trade. But when Horner checked the computer he found his warning had been erased. So had most of his other warnings.[4]

Horner is a Marine Corps veteran of Vietnam vintage and you don't have to explain to him when to cover his ass. There had been a whiff of danger in the air for some time, and he had been secretly copying all of his files. A few months earlier, he had picked up a tip about a group of major traffickers setting up a new operation out of Tijuana, and when he passed it on, the top man in the region demanded the names of his informants. Horner was dismayed. He couldn't imagine why the district director wanted this information, but the man insisted and Horner finally gave in. Four days later one informant was found with a tire iron in one ear and out the other, and the second was stabbed sixteen times. After that, Horner began to look at the larger picture, and all the lines were leading to the top of the pyramid.[5]

When the tanker incident was repeated with another truck, Horner called the inspector general's office, and the Treasury

Department launched an internal investigation. The district director was confronted with a sample of the evidence, and he decided to take early retirement. At this point, the inquiry was dropped. Apparently the inspector general knew as much as he wanted to know about this business.[6] But Mike Horner—*Semper Fi*—was not so easily deflected. Although his files had been confiscated, he had thoughtfully made triplicates, and a copy ultimately fell into the hands of a reporter from the *Los Angeles Times*. A congressional inquiry followed, and the investigators discovered that the situation in San Diego, bad as it may have been, was far from unique. There were charges of cover-ups and corruption at high levels and low from one end of the Mexican border to the other. Over a hundred individuals had been prosecuted or disciplined in the previous thirty-nine months and a hundred more were under investigation.[7] Said Tom Isbell, "As lax as we were in San Diego, we looked like an iron wall compared to the rest of the border."[8]

But anyone who expected this stunning exposé to have an impact on the flow of drugs was ignoring the fundamental equation of the smuggler's art. At a given point in space and time, the only thing that separates Mexico from the United States is the upturned hand of a Customs inspector. He gets paid about $45,000 a year. If he decides to augment his annual income, he can literally double it with a single flick of the wrist. In February of 1995 an inspector at Calexico was booked for looking the other way while traffickers brought in six tons of cocaine, and three months later a couple of inspectors in El Paso were charged with helping to move twenty-two hundred pounds over the line for a reported slice of the pie worth $1 million— peanuts, after all, since the load itself would have gone for fifteen times that much.[9] By 1996 the pace was picking up. The Justice Department reported 110 new investigations into border corruption involving the Immigration and Naturalization Service alone.[10]

Tom Isbell and Mike Horner would be the first to tell you that the vast majority of border agents are honest, hardworking professionals who have never taken a dime in their lives. This is undoubtedly true, but it was also true of the Chicago Police Department in the 1920s. As Al Capone would say, you don't have to corrupt everybody. That's a waste of money. You just corrupt the ones you need. And it's always cheaper in the long run to pay off a handful of people at the top.

The wide-open spaces between the country's official ports of entry are manned by agents of the U.S. Border Patrol and until 1994 they were essentially shoveling sand into the wind. The line of demarcation at San Diego was a rusting chain-link fence so riddled with holes you could see crowds of young men assembling around the gaps every evening at sunset, and down at the shore there was no fence at all. You could simply walk from one country to the other along the beach. But by the end of 1993 the Clinton administration had installed a ten-foot wall of steel sheeting from seaward of the low-tide line running east across the mesa to the base of the San Ysidro Mountains.[11] And there it stopped. Since it was still possible to walk around the end of the fence, the lawmen brought to bear high-tech military weapons like electronic motion sensors, aerial surveillance, and night-vision goggles. Stripping agents away from the Canadian border, they were able to increase their presence on the southern frontier by a third. But as the clamps were tightened around San Diego, the battle lines simply moved east into Imperial County.

"You can see the shift to new routes," says Sheriff Oren Fox. "We're inundated with dope. You can't believe it." Fox is a big man, oversize and rugged like the vast county he has patrolled for the past twenty years. An easygoing grizzly, he never needs to raise his voice. His only symbol of authority is the silver star on his belt buckle. "I've worked narcotics since 'fifty-nine. We've never seen this amount of marijuana seizures. It's amazing. They are just shoving it through in an effort to tie up the Customs, DEA, and the Border Patrol. They're willing to sacrifice loads of drugs, and people, and cars and trucks. And they're getting a lot of it through. Right now they're doing a lot of backpacking of drugs using illegal aliens. The drug delivery is the payment for making the trip—part of the cost of getting to America."[12]

In an attempt to level the playing field, Oren Fox recently managed to pull off something down here that nobody thought was possible. In a remarkable display of political skill and old-fashioned backslapping, he somehow got the Drug Enforcement Agency, Customs, and the Border Patrol to let go of each other's throats for a minute and join with the six southern county sheriffs in a coordinated effort to seal the border. The interagency turf wars were temporarily set aside and the three-week experiment was so successful that the U.S. attorney general singled it out as an example of how the job should be done.[13] But Fox himself has no illusion about having any long-term impact on the drug trade. He's been at this for thirty-five years. "They get more sophisticated all the time—they have our frequencies—we've found them with radios that have the Border Patrol frequencies programmed into them. They have jammers on top of vans to disrupt communications, just like the military. They'll set off a series of ground sensors all over the place and you can't tell where they are. Or sometimes they'll just climb the antenna tower and cut the power cable so the signals from the sensors aren't transmitted at all."

Sitting at his desk beneath a panoramic photo of an old Imperial Valley mining camp, with his legs outstretched and one boot propped on the other, Fox contemplates the mounted head of a longhorn steer on the opposite wall. "There's no way we can compete with the traffickers. They have hundreds of billions of dollars in resources. Every time we do something new, so do they."[14]

In the main channel at the port of Los Angeles, the container ship *Ever Right*, a state-of-the-art steel monolith nearly as long as an aircraft carrier, rides alongside quay 229 at Terminal Island.

The wheelhouse deck is eleven stories above the waterline, and the bridge is so wide the navigator has to communicate with the helmsman by walkie-talkie. The *Ever Right* is not so much a ship as a cargo transfer machine. Operating on a twelve-day turn-around between Los Angeles and the Taiwanese port of Kao-hsiung, she was designed to move the amphora of the modern age—steel containers that fit directly onto the frames of semi-trailers and railroad cars. To maintain this schedule she must be back at sea in less than a day. Hovering over the foredeck, a pair of spiderlike gantry cranes pluck forty-foot containers from the hold and drop them onto the line of waiting trucks at the rate of one every fifteen seconds.[15]

The cargo manifest, a foot-thick computer printout, lists the contents . . . *16 cases, parts for automobiles . . . 847 packages, parts for compact disc players . . . 5432 packages, basketware & rattan furniture. . . .* In most cases, the paperwork reflects the reality. The exceptions are the responsibility of Chief Customs Inspector Wayne Kornmann, but like the other lawmen along the border, Kornmann has no illusions. "We're able to check about ten to twelve containers per shift," he says. "We look at less than two percent."[16]

Sixteen hours after the first dock line coiled down from the foredeck, the *Ever Right* slips her moorings and eases back into the main channel bound for the open sea. On the broad tarmac of the Terminal Island wharf, the cargo she left behind is already on the move—over two thousand containers rolling out through the gates on trucks and railroad cars heading north and east. Not a single container was inspected by U.S. Customs. "This ship is from Taiwan," says the supervisor. "We barely have time to check the cargo coming straight from South America."

The *Ever Right* is only one of a dozen ships to come up this channel in the last twenty-four hours. A dozen more are due to-morrow, and out across the Pacific over a hundred others are making for the port of Los Angeles at this moment. At the great harbors that ring the nation, at Boston, Norfolk, Galveston,

Seattle, and a hundred other ports of entry, two million tons of cargo will cross the dock tomorrow.[17] Los Angeles alone will land 130,000 containers this month. Customs inspectors will examine 400. The other 129,600 will pass through without so much as a tip of the hat. And as this tidal wave of heavy machinery, cameras, car parts, and cuckoo clocks moves off the wharf on endless lines of semitrailers and flatcars, it's worth remembering that the entire annual cocaine supply for the United States would fit in just thirteen of those steel boxes. A year's supply of heroin could be shipped in a single container.[18]

Chapter Nine

Lessons from the Old Country

The rail line from London curves in a great arc northward across the river Mersey, then touches the opposite shore at the working-class suburb of Widnes before sweeping west again for Liverpool. The two-story brick building on Chapel Street in Widnes seems an unlikely testing ground for the great issues of our time, but it was here, according to local officials, that the power and majesty of the United States was brought to bear on a small public health clinic that ran afoul of American drug-war orthodoxy.

Dr. John Marks is an imposing Welshman with fire in his eye and unkind things to say about the Yanks. He traces his problem with the United States to a *60 Minutes* broadcast that aired in 1992 a few days after Christmas.[1] The segment opened with CBS reporter Ed Bradley holding up a vial of pure heroin and asking, "Can Britain teach us anything about dealing with drugs? One thing seems certain: there is little or nothing we can teach them. They tried our hard-line methods back in the seventies and eighties and all they got for their trouble was more drugs, more crime, and more addicts. So they went back to their old way of letting doctors prescribe whatever drug a particular addict was hooked on. Does it work?"

John Marks, interviewed on camera as the psychiatrist in charge of the Chapel Street Clinic, was blunt. "If a drug taker is determined to continue their drug use, treating them is an expensive waste of time."

But what about curing addiction?

"Cure people? Nobody can. Regardless of whether you stick them in prison, give them shock treatment, put them in a nice rehab center away in the country and pat them on the head, give them drugs, give them no drugs—no matter what you do, five percent per annum—one in twenty per year—get off spontaneously. They seem to mature out of addiction regardless of any intervention in the interim. But you can keep them alive and healthy and legal during that ten years if you wish to."

The explosive images that followed—young Liverpudlians getting prescriptions filled for their drug of choice—flew in the face of everything U.S. drug policy stood for, and it didn't take long for the shock wave to rebound. Friends in the Home Office warned Marks that the embassy in Washington was getting heat over the broadcast. They said a high-level meeting had been called and the Americans asked the English to "harmonize" their drug policy with the United States approach.[2] But in spite of all the arm-flapping on the other side of the Atlantic, there was not much anyone could do about Marks. The British government simply had no authority to stop a licensed clinical psychiatrist from prescribing heroin—or anything else—to whomever he chose, in whatever dose, for a day, a week, or a lifetime. Dr. Marks's remarkable invulnerability in this regard was rooted in the bedrock of the British medical establishment. Back in the 1920s, while the American Medical Association was allowing its members to be hounded and jailed by Harry Anslinger, the Royal College of Physicians proved to be of sterner stuff. When the lawmen attempted to get between the British doctor and his patient, they were brushed aside like gnats. A committee of eminent physicians led by Baron Humphrey Rolleston concluded in 1926 that drug addiction was a medical problem and the cops should stay out of it. So the "British System," which the Americans came to abhor, was really no system at all. They simply left it up to individual doctors to deal with addicts as they saw fit.[3]

This single distinction set the two countries down separate paths with starkly different results. While the American addict was being run to ground in a nationwide game of fox and hounds, the Englishman with a habit could go to his family physician, get a prescription for heroin—or morphine, or cocaine, or whatever—and pick it up at the corner pharmacy. In this low-key environment, drugs failed to acquire the kind of underground cachet they enjoyed in the States, and coincidentally the addict population in England remained pretty much as it was—little old ladies, self-medicating doctors, chronic pain sufferers, ne'er-do-wells, "all middle-aged people"—most of them leading otherwise normal lives.[4]

For the next forty years, American medical experts and academics would visit England, note the dramatic difference in crime and addiction rates, then go home and write books calling for a switch to the British system.[5] Commissioner Anslinger would invariably smack down these suggestions, condemning the British numbers as unreliable and questioning the motives of the messengers. Besides, he would point out, Britain was an island. But in 1965, Anslinger could claim he had been vindicated. The numbers, which he now chose to believe, showed that the addiction rate in the United Kingdom had doubled over the previous five years—clear proof that the British system was a failure. Anslinger skipped over the fact that the doubling had been from seven hundred addicts to a total of fourteen hundred in the whole of England. In the United States at that same moment there were probably twenty thousand addicts in Manhattan alone.[6]

Nonetheless, this sudden jump was alarming to the British, and they were equally unnerved by the look of these new addicts. As the upheaval of the sixties washed over England, it brought with it a whole new category of drug user—longhaired rebels with "unsatisfactory work records" who got high for the hell of it. All of a sudden there was a drug subculture in London to rival Greenwich Village. Concentrated in Piccadilly, the scene was so outrageous it became a tourist attraction and the Home Office decided something had to be done. Yet another panel of eminent medics, this time under the guidance of Lord Russell Brain, were commissioned to look into it. They discovered that most of these new users were getting their stash from just six London doctors. One apparently tireless physician wrote scrips for six hundred thousand tablets of heroin in a single year.[7] Clearly this was not sound medical practice.

When the Brain Committee reported back in the summer of 1965, it concluded that the business of maintaining addicts should be taken out of the hands of the general practitioner and turned over to specialists. For the first time in history, the un-limited power of the individual English physician to prescribe drugs was to be circumscribed—but only for addiction. If an or-dinary patient needed pain relief, his doctor could still prescribe anything in the book. If, however, the patient was an addict, he would generally have to go to a treatment center and see a doc-tor who was specifically licensed to prescribe heroin and cocaine on a continuing basis.[8]

Since there were so few addicts in England and so many in America, the people charged with setting up the new treatment centers naturally looked to the United States to see what the ex-perts were doing. In the States, of course, the idea of heroin maintenance was considered the height of madness. Detoxifica-tion was the objective. The typical regimen in New York at that time was a decreasing dose of methadone designed to wean the addict off the drug as rapidly as possible.

Methadone is a synthetic replica of morphine that came out of World War II. A painkiller developed by I. G. Farben when the

Nazi supply of opiates from the Middle East was cut off by the Allies, it came into use as a treatment for addiction in the United States in the late 1940s, apparently proving the theory that Americans will go for anything as long as they can call it something else. Although methadone was originally thought of as a cure for addiction, it didn't actually cure anything. It just substituted one addiction for another, and methadone turned out to be harder to kick. But the new fabricated opiate had certain advantages, mostly for the administrators. Because it was long-lasting, it could be given once a day, it could be taken orally, and it was easier to gauge the dose needed to stabilize an addict. Unfortunately, Congress became directly involved in micromanaging methadone treatment, and its potential as a maintenance drug was thwarted. It came to be used primarily as an agent for detoxing addicts, with or without their compliance, "in a period not to exceed 21 days."[9]

Since the U.S. specialists had dealt with tens of thousands of addicts and their British counterparts had never seen more than a few hundred, they naturally deferred to the American expertise, and the methadone withdrawal approach came to be generally accepted throughout the new English clinic system.

"It was a sledgehammer to crack a very tiny nut," said Bing Spear, former head of the Home Office Drugs Branch. As chief inspector of Britain's principal drug-control agency, Spear had a lofty vantage point for viewing the turmoil of the sixties and seventies, and he believes the Brain Committee overreacted. "If only a handful of doctors were involved, why deal with the whole medical profession?" Spear thought the new policy was a ticking bomb and events would bear him out. "Hardly anybody in the medical profession knew anything about the problem. And the only people who had any experience—the general practitioners—were derided and criticized." The addicts were taken away from the doctors who knew them and handed over to a new bureaucracy that was determined to whip them into shape. Once again, the best intentions were flattened by the law of unintended consequences. The serious drug users left the system and hit the streets, where they found the price of heroin had undergone a 600 percent jump. The black market exploded, and violence exploded along with it. "In the late seventies you began to see the sort of thing, the traffic in heroin, that you had in America," said Spear. "Up until the Brain Committee report, illicit heroin was not something that was ever known in this country."[10]

But away up in the North Country, far from the hurly-burly of Piccadilly, there were occasional heretics who chose to ignore the American advice, and here and there you could still find a clinic that continued the old practice of heroin maintenance. One such backwater was the Chapel Street Clinic in the Liverpool suburb of Widnes, and in the spring of 1982, Dr. John Marks, M.B.Ch.B (Edinburgh), M.R.C. Psych. (London), arrived with his newly framed certificates to take over as consultant psychiatrist. "When I took up my post, I found this old British System clinic that was handing out a ration of drugs, and I was a bit surprised. I thought, 'This is a silly policy.' I was interested in real madmen. Drug takers to me are not mentally ill, and I missed real psychiatry. I thought, 'We'll evaluate it to make sure it doesn't work, close it down, and use the money for a new schizophrenic hospice.' "

But as he began digging through the records, Marks made a series of surprising discoveries. Among the cohort of serious needle-users now in his charge, he expected to find 15 to 20 percent infected with the AIDS virus—Liverpool is a port city, after all—but there was not a single case in the whole roster. When he checked for drug-related deaths he found the same thing. Then he interviewed the patients and was dismayed to find them in good health, most with jobs, and all clean and properly dressed.[11] His next surprise came from the local police. Heroin maintenance, they said, cut crime. In one test, the Cheshire Drug Squad tracked a hundred users before and after they entered the clinic and found a 94 percent drop in theft, burglary, and property crimes.[12] But the most interesting finding was the decline in the number of new users. After the clinic opened, convictions for illegal possession in the area dropped immediately.

"We could explain why the crime rate dropped," said Marks. "We could explain why there were fewer deaths—they were getting clean heroin instead of rubbish. But what we couldn't understand was the reduction in the incidence of new cases. *It seemed to prevent the spread of addiction.* And we just thought we'd done the experiment wrong. But when we consulted official statistics—both American and English and other foreign statistics—we found identical results: that if you loosened up a little bit on drug issues, you actually got a fall in the incidence of addiction. But if you loosened up too much, and made it freely available like we now have with alcohol, it started to rise again."[13]

What Marks realized was that the demand curve for forbidden fruit is not linear—it's U-shaped. If drugs and alcohol are too freely available—or if they're prohibited—you increase consumption. "Free markets promote use; prohibitions pedal use. And I discovered quite by accident the validity of this at the Widnes clinic."

O n a typical Tuesday morning in March, seven drug addicts wind their way up the narrow stairs to the second-floor clinic on Chapel Street. They're here to pick up their weekly prescriptions, but first they'll have to sit in on a group session—not therapy exactly—just a little chat so the staff can eyeball them and see how they're doing. As they pull their chairs into a circle in the cluttered conference room, they are indistinguishable from any other seven citizens on the streets of Liverpool. Nothing in their appearance or behavior would suggest that they are serious addicts. Among them is a round-faced Irish brunette with a wry smile. Well dressed, in her mid-thirties, she could easily be taken for a businesswoman or a teacher, but something about her eyes suggests broader experience. Maureen shoots heroin once a day.

"I've tried most drugs, and heroin is the most physically and mentally addictive drug ever. And I wouldn't advise anybody to get into it. I just think that, anybody who does find themselves in that mess, there should be somewhere, an option to go somewhere to get help."

For the first twenty years of her life Maureen had no idea what trouble was. Growing up in a big house in suburbia, she dreamed of becoming a movie star. But in the early eighties she fell in love with a young guy from a rich family who gave her three kids and a heroin habit. "My husband and I were both taking drugs and he lost his job and I started getting on at him and he's getting on at me, and the marriage just crumbled. So there I was; I was left on my own with three children. And because we spent all the money on drugs, the rent didn't get paid, so I became homeless."

For the next several years, she moved the kids from one bed-and-breakfast to another, supporting herself with prostitution and shoplifting, all the time frantically chasing the dragon. "Everything revolved around heroin. I couldn't plan a weekend away. I had to worry about the next fix. And going out and being frightened that the guy's been busted and it's not gonna be there. You're so channeled into that, you can't think of anything else. It's just heroin, heroin, heroin. The minute you've got spare money for a birthday or Christmas or something, it's gone on the heroin—'I'll put it back in later'—you never do. You're just completely kidding yourself the whole time."

Somehow, she managed to keep all these balls in the air, simultaneously feeding three children and a major habit. Like most addicts, she tried to kick repeatedly without success. "When you're on the drug, you can say, well, I'll do this and I'll do that. But when the drug's wearing off, it's a different story. You'll do anything. And if it means dragging three children around for hours . . . I knew those children were going to be very bored sitting in the back of the car waiting for a dealer to come with drugs, so I'd pacify them with ice cream or make them promises that I knew I wasn't going to keep."

By 1991 the health officials were breathing down her neck and she was in serious danger of losing the kids. Frantically searching for high ground, she heard about John Marks in Chapel Street and went there to see if it was true. Marks and his staff examined her, investigated her background, confirmed that she was indeed a heroin addict, and on her next visit he wrote her a prescription for a week's supply. Almost unbelieving, she took the slip of paper to the chemist up the street and he filled it without batting an eye.

As she stood at the counter staring at the small round container of pure heroin and the packet of new needles, an odd sensation washed over her. The auger of panic that had been twisting her gut every waking moment for a decade was spinning down. For the first time in memory, she had a tiny bit of brain space that wasn't focused on the next fix. It began to dawn on her that it no longer made any difference whether or not her dealer would show up. She didn't have to figure out who to con, how to get the cash, what to do if she got busted, or if the shit was any good. . . .

She slipped the packages into her purse, and as she turned away, she caught a glimpse of her reflection in the glass and for the first time in ten years she stopped to take a serious look. She was stunned.

Then she glanced down at her children, and she said, "Oh, my God."

The morality that had been instilled in her as a child suddenly came flooding back. "I felt so disgusted. . . ." Over the next weeks and months her dose was stabilized at a point that allowed her to function without suffering withdrawal, and within a year her life had been completely turned around. "I've been able to rebuild a home. And I can take the kids out for treats. I can do anything that anybody else does. The only difference is that I'm on a heroin prescription. I can have one injection and I can function normally for the rest of the day." The piece of paper John Marks handed her almost nonchalantly turned out to be a passport out of hell. By 1994, she was again talking about one of the dreams she lost in the haze of the previous decade. "Three years ago, I wouldn't have even considered going to college. Now I've got a much wider scope. I want to do everything." And, as Marks expected, there was even a chance that Maureen might be among the lucky 5 percent every year who escape addiction. Secure in the knowledge that the clinic would be there for her if she relapsed, she was beginning to talk about permanent withdrawal. "Now I'm at the point where I'm thinking . . . I don't get stoned at all, I live a normal life . . . why bother taking it? It's as if it's run its course with me."[14]

Unfortunately, Maureen would never get the chance to find out. Dr. Marks may have been personally invulnerable to his critics, but the Widnes clinic was not, and in 1995 the local health authority simply pulled the plug on Chapel Street and gave the contract for psychiatric services to somebody else. On April 1, some 450 of Dr. Marks's former patients were handed over to the Warrington Community Health Care Trust. The new organization, not surprisingly, was in perfect sync with the American concept of total abstinence, and the addicts were informed that they were to be taken off heroin and cocaine completely. "The idea is to negotiate with clients," said one official, "offering a gradual change to methadone."[15] Unfortunately, a survey of the clients themselves revealed that 60 percent would probably refuse methadone treatment, and when the dust finally settled, most of them were back on the streets.[16] "Two years later," said Marks, "twenty-five of the addicts were dead."[17]

And what of Maureen, the heroin user with three children who planned to go to college? "I saw Maureen the other day," said Marks. "She was desperate, back to criminality, a lot of her friends are back in prison. She's on the streets. She saw me in passing and asked if I could take her back on. Her doctor tried to refer her to me, but the Warrington Health Authority refused to defray the costs."[18] And so the state, in its righteous determination to set everything straight, has managed to teach Maureen and her children a lesson. It's a lesson they won't soon forget.

. . .

One of the most frequent broadsides leveled at the Widnes clinic was that John Marks's startling claims were never verified by independent investigators. In fact, a serious study was undertaken in 1990 to measure the Widnes approach against the results of methadone treatment, and for a minute it looked like there might be a face-to-face scientific shoot-out between the British and the American systems. The one-year survey was already under way when word suddenly came from the regional health authority demanding immediate return within twenty-four hours of the entire research grant. No explanation was given.[19] And though Marks repeatedly invited outsiders to confirm or refute his numbers, there were no takers until 1995. Then the government finally set in motion a major review of all drug-treatment regimes in the United Kingdom. It was set to start on April 1, 1995—the day the Chapel Street Clinic closed down—once again, neatly avoiding any unfortunate comparisons.

But not everybody in Europe was so dazzled by the American experience. Swiss health authorities had been watching the developments in England for some time, and they decided the concept of prescribing drugs to serious addicts was too intriguing to be tossed in the dustbin. So with famous Swiss precision, they engineered a tightly controlled experiment with the intention of putting a measuring stick up against this issue once and for all.

Most Americans are under the mistaken impression that Switzerland tried drug legalization back in the 1980s and that it ended in disaster. The "Needle Park" scene at the Platzspitz in Zurich was often cited by U.S. officials as proof of "the failure of legalization programs tried in other parts of the world such as Zurich."[20] In fact, there was never a legalization experiment in Zurich. The debacle in Platzspitz was nothing more than an unsuccessful attempt at street cleaning. The burghers tried to tidy up the city center by designating a free-trade zone for serious drug users in hopes they would stay out of sight. For a time, they were given free rein over a riverside park called the Platzspitz, but it was soon overrun with addicts from all over Europe. Eighty percent were from out of town. The scene finally spun out of control and had to be shut down, but in no way was this an experiment in anything other than crowd control.[21] Back in the days of alcohol prohibition, an equally disgusting sight could have been created by designating Lafayette Park as a sanctuary for alcoholics.

The first actual large-scale controlled experiment in heroin maintenance—an experiment that had been successfully avoided since the 1920s—got under way in January of 1994 when the Swiss government authorized a three-year research program involving one thousand addicts under the watchful eye of the Swiss Academy of Medical Sciences and the World Health Organization. Eight hundred volunteers were to be given heroin, one hundred would get morphine, and one hundred would be put on methadone, all in seventeen different locations throughout the country.[22] The volunteers had to be daily users with a long history, and they had to have proof of at least two serious attempts to kick. The study included independent evaluation and rigorous controls.

When the Swiss Federal Office of Public Health issued the final report in July of 1997, the conclusions were exactly as John Marks would have predicted. Crime among the addict population dropped by 60 percent, half the unemployed found jobs, a third of those on welfare became self-supporting, nobody was homeless, and the general health of the group improved dramatically. By the end of the experiment, eighty-three patients had decided on their own to give up heroin in favor of abstinence.[23]

A severely marginalised group of long-standing heroin-dependents was able to be reached through the study, and to a high degree (80 percent) be kept in treatment.

No significant side-effects of heroin prescription were noted.

The controlled prescription of heroin is clinically and practically feasible.[24]

For Marks and his colleagues up in Liverpool, the Swiss report must have been vindication of a sort, but he was more concerned with the short range. "What will happen in Widnes? The gangsters will move in and we'll have a situation like the no-go areas in Manchester or the Bronx."

As they say in the lowlands, "God made Heaven and Earth, but the Dutch made Holland." In the lobby of the city hall in Amsterdam, there is a subtle reminder of that tiny nation's ongoing battle with the Atlantic. Rising two stories into the atrium is a slender glass column filled with water. The level rises and falls during the day because the tube is connected to the coast at Ijmuiden, and it shows how far above your head the surface would be if the dike broke.

This water column speaks volumes about the Dutch. When your enemy is the North Sea, it breeds respect for reality, and that has evolved into a national reverence for pragmatism. The Dutch are interested in what works, and that always takes precedence over what would be nice. Among their more interesting departures from less flexible cultures is a legalistic loophole—the "expediency principle"—that might be called the rule of common sense. If a law turns out to be more trouble than it's worth, they don't enforce it. It may remain on the books. It's just ignored.

To the ongoing horror of U.S. officials, one of the laws the Dutch have chosen to ignore is the law against marijuana. And though the Americans have unleashed a twenty-year barrage of invective at The Hague for their deviant behavior, the Dutch have yet to blink. They did not come to this position lightly. It was based on evidence, and given their history, it's not likely that a moral argument will overwhelm their scientific measurements.

The origins of the Dutch heresy go back to the early seventies when governments on both sides of the Atlantic were suddenly confronted with a generation of dope-smoking hippies and anti-war protestors. The global alarm over the clouds of marijuana smoke inspired high-level investigations throughout the free world. In the United States, Richard Nixon created the Shafer Commission, the Dutch assembled a group of experts called the Baan Working Party, the United Kingdom formed a prestigious committee under Baroness Wootten, and in Toronto, law school dean Gerald Le Dain headed the Canadian Government's Commission of Inquiry.[25] While the U.S. group was front-loaded with conservative politicians who were expected to come down heavily against the Devil Weed, their conclusions surprisingly mirrored those of the more scientifically rounded commissions. All four groups found marijuana roughly as intoxicating and dangerous as alcohol, and the English report went a step further: "The evidence of a link with violent crime is far stronger with alcohol than with the smoking of cannabis."[26]

Without exception, these four disparate committees, which included some of the leading legal, medical, and scientific specialists of the Western world, recommended that laws against marijuana be relaxed. President Nixon dealt with this unwelcome news by sweeping it under the rug, and the Canadian government followed suit. But in Holland, where scientists and engineers are taken seriously, they simply followed the recommendations. The Baan group, like the other commissions, noted the significant difference between marijuana and the other drugs on the dealer's shelf. And since they recognized the ritual duty of young people to flirt with danger, the Dutch thought it would be better for the ones who chose to experiment with drugs to experiment with reefer rather than smack. The plan was to erect a wall between the so-called soft drugs—marijuana and hashish—and hard drugs like heroin and cocaine. This meant they would have to set up a quasi-legal distribution system, because if young people had to buy their grass from criminals, they would be exposed to every other conceivable option as well. So the government came up with a utilitarian scheme for "hashish coffee shops" that were allowed to sell small amounts of marijuana to anyone over sixteen. They were tightly controlled—absolutely no hard drugs, no underage customers, no advertising—and the rules turned out to be easily enforceable since the proprietor, like the tavern owner, had an incentive to keep the lid on or lose the farm.

Today in Amsterdam it's still against the law to smoke marijuana. But if you stop a police officer on the street and ask him where to buy it, he'll probably give you a choice of half a dozen modern-day speakeasies within walking distance. Along the Warmoesstraat near the Centraalstation, you'll see an occasional storefront with a potted plant in the window, and at the bar inside might be a college professor or a journalist, a couple of dismayed tourists from Vermont, and seated around tables covered with newspapers, comics, and chessboards you can find college kids, bricklayers, office workers, and visiting Germans. Ask to see the menu and the waiter will pull a three-ring binder from under the bar that looks like a wine list, but the plastic pockets contain samples of everything from Jamaican ganja to Moroccan hashish at bargain prices. At the bar a Dutch insurance salesman splits a cigarette with his thumbs and dumps the tobacco onto an E-Z Wider rolling paper. He crumbles some hashish, sprinkles it on the tobacco, rolls it, lights it, and offers a hit to the total stranger sitting next to him. At a glance, the place looks like any other small-town college hangout, but the laid-back atmosphere contrasts sharply with the noise from the saloon across the street where they're serving alcohol.

There are some twelve hundred of these clubs scattered throughout Holland, over three hundred in Amsterdam alone. And despite continuous international pressure to shut them down, the Dutch have held fast. Their original objective was to keep young people away from hard drugs and by that measure the program has been a smashing success. Today the average age of a heroin addict in Holland is thirty-six. It was ten years younger when the experiment began.[27] This aging cohort means that young recruits are no longer joining the ranks, and the Dutch may have saved themselves from a whole new generation of heroin shooters.

They have also paid a price for this victory with an increase in the use of marijuana, and to American critics, that price is unacceptable. When the latest Dutch drug statistics were released in 1995, U.S. Representative Gerald Solomon of New York rose in the House to lash out in shock and anger: "Mr. Speaker, the test has been conducted and the results are in from the Netherlands. . . . From 1988 to 1992, cannabis use among pupils increased 100 percent. . . ." But the congressman was avoiding the larger picture. Yes, marijuana use among Dutch teenagers had doubled, but in the United States at that moment, despite the most repressive prohibition in history, teenage drug use had also doubled and was still climbing.[28] As the Dutch gently observed, "Soft drug use among young people is on the increase in a large number of Western countries, and in some, more strongly than in the Netherlands."[29]

But perhaps even more galling for strict prohibitionists like Solomon was the fact that Dutch tolerance for soft drug users extended to hard drug users as well. In Holland, people holding small amounts of heroin or cocaine for personal use are ignored, and the police themselves are the strongest supporters of this arrangement. "Nobody in my country is happy with the drug problem," says Bernard Scholten, "but we accept that there are drug users, and then find ways to be realistic." Scholten's office is on the top floor of Police Headquarters in Amsterdam. He's the department's official spokesman and he spends much of his time trying to straighten out misinformation being spread by foreign officials. "This is for us a good system. If you compare this soft drug addiction to the alcohol addiction . . . alcohol addiction is a much bigger problem. We have the figures."

What about hard drugs?

"We have eight thousand registered hard drug users in Amsterdam. About four hundred of this group are the hard core"—

people frequently busted for making a nuisance of themselves. "In case one of this group is arrested for the fourth time in twelve months, that person has to make a decision: treatment or punishment. And there always is capacity in the clinic and there always is capacity in the jail."[30]

This tolerance for drug users, however, does not extend to dealers. The government of the Netherlands, like other signatories of the United Nations Single Convention, is obligated to go after traffickers, and they have to take the obligation seriously. Rotterdam is the largest port in the world and the European gateway for South American and Asian shippers. So the Dutch pursue drug kingpins with a vengeance and overlook the street dealer with a wink and a nod. It's a policy that Bernard Scholten acknowledges as "enlightened schizophrenia."

In spite of all evidence to the contrary, U.S. officials never seem to tire of reporting the collapse and fall of the Dutch system, but from time to time this conceit blows up in somebody's face. Lee Brown, first drug czar of the Clinton administration, was speaking to a Los Angeles town hall meeting about the disaster in Holland when a gentleman in the audience stood up and introduced himself as the consul general of the Netherlands and politely refuted everything Brown had just said.[31] But while the Americans are the most vocal, they are not the only critics of Dutch liberalism. The French are also hopping mad. When President Jacques Chirac took office in June of 1995, he reportedly told the Dutch prime minister, "Either you fight drug trafficking or I close the borders." Chirac was particularly annoyed with the parade of French narco-tourists crossing into Rotterdam on weekends to get high on heroin. The Élysée Palace berated the Dutch for their corrupting influence. And the Dutch, ever courteous, skipped the opportunity to remind Chirac that his addiction rate was nearly double theirs.[32]

In 1994 an American journalist was interviewing Bing Spear, former chief inspector of the Home Office Drugs Branch, and after recounting some three decades of drug-war history in the United Kingdom, Spear was lamenting how it had all gone wrong. The reporter asked if he felt the Americans were the dark force in this scenario, and Spear said, "I'll put it this way. You Yanks have a lot to answer for."[33]

Chapter Ten

Reefer Madness

The high-water mark for drug prohibition in the twentieth century may have been reached on November 5, 1996, when citizens of California and Arizona chose to ignore the warnings of President Clinton, former presidents Bush, Ford, and Carter, the governors of both states, and all their collective law enforcement and drug experts, and voted overwhelmingly in favor of making marijuana legal for medical use. It was a stunning defeat for the prohibitionists. Both Proposition 200 in Arizona and Proposition 215 in California allowed medical patients to use marijuana virtually without limit, but the Arizona voters went further, turning the clock back eighty years to a time when doctors could prescribe any drug they saw fit, including heroin.

Apparently taken by surprise when late-summer polls showed both initiatives leading by wide margins, the antidrug establishment launched a main-force effort to head the measures off. Drug czar Barry McCaffrey made repeated trips to the West Coast, blasting the proponents for their cruel hoax. "How dare they capitalize on the suffering of victims of cancer and AIDS, who deserve the best American medical care?"[1] Six days before the election, McCaffrey arrived in Los Angeles with a letter signed by three former presidents saying the initiatives would send "the erroneous message that dangerous and addictive drugs such as heroin, LSD, marijuana and methamphetamine are safe." Public officials from Washington to Sacramento vilified the proponents and issued dark warnings about their hidden agenda.

The electorate turned a deaf ear. They seemed more impressed by the televised images of fellow citizens in pain. In one spot, a California oncologist tells the camera, "I've been treating cancer patients with chemotherapy for over twenty-five years. But the side effects can be very severe: nausea, vomiting, loss of appetite. . . . There is a medicine that can help. It's marijuana. I've seen it work." In another commercial, a lady you could meet in the checkout line says, "I've been a nurse for over forty years. But when my husband, J.J., was dying of cancer I felt helpless. The nausea from his chemotherapy was so awful, it broke my heart. So I broke the law and got him marijuana. It worked. He could eat. He had an extra year of life." Against these earthly tales, the impassioned doomsday warnings of generals and lawyers proved unequal to the occasion. The two measures won by a wider margin than the President himself in both states: 56 percent in California, and a whopping two-to-one majority in Arizona, where they voted to unfetter not only the doctors but the prisoners as well. Proposition 200 called for releasing nonviolent drug offenders.

The reverberations were tectonic. Here was a fault line no one could paper over, and from Washington to Sacramento, agitated congressmen and federal agents began shooting from the hip. The Senate Judiciary Committee called a hearing, the administration promised to prosecute any doctors foolish enough even to discuss marijuana with a patient, and Dan Lungren, the California attorney general who led the battle against Proposition 215, was apoplectic. "This thing is a disaster. What's going to happen? We're going to have an unprecedented mess."[2]

The only plausible explanation was that the voters had been duped. "It's not the only mistake that was made in November," said former drug czar William Bennett. "That this initiative passed is a scandal. It's also understandable given the promotion and advertising that were used." That was the key. The voters had been seduced by slick advertising. "A moneyed, out-of-state elite mounted a cynical and deceptive campaign to push its hidden agenda to legalize drugs," said former secretary of health Joe Califano, Jr., and *The New York Times*'s A. M. Rosenthal named names. At the top of the list was financier George Soros, whose "gobs of money" Rosenthal likened to "the fortunes manipulated by drug criminals." He accused Soros and his ilk of "preaching the benefits of slavery."[3] For Soros, a self-made Hungarian billionaire who escaped both the Nazis and the Communists before coming to the United States, it must have been a novel experience to be accused of preaching the benefits of slavery, since he had personally donated more cash to the struggle for human rights than probably anybody else on the planet. After the fall of the Soviet Union, while the West equivocated, Soros rushed into Eastern Europe and handed out a billion dollars of his own money to aid the new democracies. But when he dropped $6 million on the Drug Policy Foundation, a group opposed to the drug war, he was transformed from a capitalist Galahad into a carpetbagger with a foreign accent—"the Daddy Warbucks of drug legalization."[4]

But laying this disaster at the feet of an evil genius would prove to be a tough sell. The voters in both states had been extensively surveyed before either of the laws were written, and they had apparently come to the conclusion that jailing sick people was unenlightened. In California, the legislature had in fact already legalized medical marijuana two years in a row but the governor had torpedoed it. In Arizona, the initiative was backed by civic beacons from left, right, and center, and the honorary chairman was Republican icon Barry Goldwater.[5] But probably even more decisive, the opponents of the law were unable to explain their own failure. In spite of DARE, Zero Tolerance, Drug-

Free America, and the full weight of the criminal justice system, drug use in Arizona elementary schools had gone up 1,000 percent in four years.[6]

On the other hand, the explosive reaction to the two initiatives was evidence that the decisive hour had come. Strategists on both sides know this could be the El Alamein of the war on drugs. After this, everything changes. If marijuana turns out to be a medical miracle instead of the Devil's handmaiden, public support for confiscating houses and sending nonmedical users to prison will quickly erode. And marijuana is the linchpin. Take reefer out of the equation and the number of illegal drug users instantly drops from thirteen million to three million, and the drug war shrinks from a national crusade to a sideshow.[7] To maintain the present $16 billion-a-year federal effort, the concept of medical marijuana must be defeated at all costs. In Arizona, the state legislature was subjected to intense pressure to gut the law. After a four-month high-level blitz from Washington, with the President himself reportedly standing by to lean on the holdouts, the Arizona lawmakers rode to the rescue and passed a bill demanding federal approval of marijuana before it's prescribed.[8] This put the ball safely back on Washington's side of the net, but there was nervousness at the statehouse in Phoenix. You don't slap down 65 percent of the voters without paying some kind of price on down the line.[9] In any event, this particular genie was already out of the bottle. The debate over marijuana that the government has successfully suppressed for twenty-five years was under way.

Back in the old days when Harry Anslinger had his back to the wall and he needed some impressive numbers, he just made them up. So far there's no indication that modern drug enforcers have given up the practice, but in the age of digital information, fact-alteration can produce unpredictable results. When General McCaffrey was asked on CNN whether there was any evidence that marijuana was medically useful, he was emphatic. "No, none at all. There are hundreds of studies that indicate that it isn't."[10] Yet any eighth-grader with access to the Internet could find evidence to the contrary just a mouse-click away on the World Wide Web. There you could read of reports like "Inhalation Marijuana as an Antiemetic for Cancer Chemotherapy," from the *New York State Journal of Medicine*,[11] and discover that the general didn't know what he was talking about. McCaffrey, an exemplary soldier, was undoubtedly just repeating information he'd been given, but one wonders how he would have reacted in Vietnam if he'd discovered his staff officers were producing phony maps.

If you had just arrived from Mars and were trying to make some sense out of the furor surrounding the medical usefulness of a local herb, you would probably wonder why nobody had bothered to do a definitive test. The problem is that marijuana is not just a controlled substance, it is totally illegal—not even available to qualified medical researchers. Investigators could always buy a stash from their students, but that's not how scientific research is done. You must apply instead for special dispensation from the government, and for the last twenty years, the government has said no. Anyone who challenged this position was invited onto a labyrinthian bureaucratic game board with constantly moving goalposts.

The Controlled Substances Act of 1970 labeled marijuana a drug of maximum danger and no redeeming value. This classification was immediately challenged by the National Organization for the Reform of Marijuana Laws, but the government simply refused to discuss it. In 1986 the DEA finally decided to hold the public hearings that the U.S. Court of Appeals had ordered seven years earlier, and the resulting parade of doctors, patients, professors, and lawmen left a two-year court record that is the most thorough review of the evidence in our time. In 1988, twelve years after the case first hit the docket, the DEA's administrative law judge stunned the agency by ruling for the plaintiffs: "Marijuana in its natural form is one of the safest therapeutically active substances known to man. . . . One must reasonably conclude that there is accepted safety for use of marijuana under medical supervision. To conclude otherwise, on the record, would be unreasonable, arbitrary, and capricious."[12]

The DEA concluded otherwise. The administrator brushed aside the ruling and ridiculed the very idea of medical marijuana as a "dangerous and cruel hoax." Besides, researchers had finally figured out how to synthesize marijuana's psychoactive ingredient, THC, and it was now available in pill form as Marinol. Since there was obviously no longer any need for the crude natural product, DEA officials slammed the door on cannabis with finality in 1992.

Anyone who tried to approach the issue from the other flank—setting up a scientifically controlled test to see if the stuff actually worked—hit the same wall. In 1992, Donald Abrams, a professor of medicine at the University of California, designed a pilot study to compare the effectiveness of smoking marijuana with the synthetic Marinol as a treatment for AIDS-related weight loss. The plan for the study made it past each hurdle in turn—the University of California's Institutional Review board, the state examiners, the Food and Drug Administration—and in 1994 Abrams applied to the National Institute for Drug Abuse, the country's sole source of legal marijuana, requesting a supply from the government's plot in Mississippi. NIDA deftly moved him back to square one. They questioned the basic design of his study, and each answer he gave just provoked another question. Years later the project was still in limbo.

On the flip side of this issue, any researchers who were willing to delve into the dangers of cannabis and search for its harmful effects found funds and assistance raining down from government and private institutions. But even this kind of enforced academic tilt did not always produce the desired results.

A classic illustration was the 1975 study by Robert Heath of Tulane that proved marijuana smoke causes brain damage. Since rhesus monkeys don't normally smoke, Dr. Heath had to force it on them through a gas mask, but he was unable to precisely measure the amount of dope that was pumped in. One fellow scientist claimed that Heath's doses were in the range of ninety joints a day, and he wondered whether the brain damage could have been caused by these large amounts. A subsequent study of rhesus monkeys at the National Center for Toxicological Research effectively repudiated all of Heath's findings.[13]

Unfortunately, the Heath study fits a pattern that characterizes much of official marijuana research. What separates these projects from normal science is that they usually hit the evening news before they've been debated in the halls of academe. Typically, a research group funded by the U.S. government will find a smoking gun proving that marijuana causes serious physical or mental damage. In time, other researchers discover the claims are flawed, and the study is discredited within the scientific community, but the average citizen is stuck with the original headlines. As a result, most Americans believe to one degree or another that marijuana damages the brain, that it lowers testosterone, that it weakens the immune system, and that it breaks chromosomes, when in fact there's no accepted evidence for any of this.

One surefire way to hit the front page is to come up with a test result that proves marijuana is a stepping-stone to harder drugs—the "gateway" theory. In 1994, the Center on Addiction and Substance Abuse at Columbia University made the shocking announcement that marijuana smokers were eighty-five times more likely to go on to cocaine than nonsmokers.[14] They discovered this by taking the estimated number of cocaine users who had smoked reefer first, and dividing it by the estimated number who hadn't (almost nobody). Using the same quasi-scientific procedure, you can establish that coffee, alcohol, tobacco, and cherry pie are also precursors. Another headline in this vein hit the front pages in the summer of 1997—"STUDIES BACK GATEWAY ROLE OF POT"—when a group of Italian scientists announced they had discovered that marijuana and heroin stimulate the same pleasure centers in rat brains.[15] While this was scientifically interesting, the authors leaped from this tiny fact to the more thrilling conclusion that marijuana use may prime the brain for other drugs. But here again, these same principals could be used to demonstrate that sex and cheese will turn rats into junkies.[16] Another group came up with evidence that marijuana withdrawal causes the same chemical changes in rats as do hard drugs. "This blurs the distinction between a hard drug and a soft drug."[17] But long-term students of the battle point out that all attempts to prove the addiction thesis using real human beings have failed completely.[18]

Currently, one of the leading scientific lights of the marijuana prohibition movement is Dr. Gabriel Nahas, a hero of the French Resistance in World War II and a sworn enemy of the cannabis plant. As consultant to the U.N. Commission on Narcotics, Dr. Nahas has been an adviser to the White House and to most of America's major antidrug organizations. Over the last quarter century he has endeavored to supply a scientific rationale for the drug war, and while his efforts have been lauded by the prohibitionists, his colleagues in the medical profession seem less impressed. As one observer put it, "No drug-abuse scholar in recent history has been the subject of such scathing commentaries in the scientific journals."[19] A review of his work in the *New England Journal of Medicine* called it "psychopharmacologic McCarthyism" peppered with "half-truths, innuendo and unverifiable assertions." *JAMA*, the journal of the American Medical Association, noted that "examples of biased selection and . . . omissions of facts abound in every chapter." *Contemporary Drug Problems* was even less charitable: "meretricious trash."[20] When Nahas recently published a paper in the *Medical Journal of Australia*[21] claiming that new research proved marijuana was toxic, he was immediately attacked by pharmacologists from the University of Sydney who discovered that he was largely quoting himself, and that 80 percent of his references were misleading or distorted.[22] Nonetheless, his work is still a primary source of scientific justification for the war on marijuana.

On a blustery winter morning in 1990, Harvard psychiatrist Lester Grinspoon was in his Cambridge office listening to the windows rattle when he got a call from a desperate woman on the other side of the country. She had read some of Grinspoon's work—he literally wrote the book on medical marijuana—and she needed help. Her son had been arrested in Malaysia for possession of half a pound of cannabis. She wanted to take a chapter from one of Grinspoon's works—"Medical Uses of Illicit Drugs"—and rewrite it in the form of an affidavit. When her son was twelve, she said, he had fallen off a sixty-foot cliff while hiking. The newspapers called his survival a "Christmas Miracle," but his left shoulder was permanently deformed and subject to excruciating muscle spasms. The young man later discovered that cannabis controlled the pain better than anything the doctors had given him and it had fewer side effects. So when he went to Malaysia on a yearlong sabbatical, he had foolishly mailed himself a package of marijuana.

Grinspoon was shaken. He told the woman she needed a hell of a lot more than an affidavit. Malaysian law doesn't differentiate between marijuana or heroin or cocaine. To them all drugs are encompassed within the catch-all term "dadah." The penalty in Kuala Lumpur for possession of half a pound of dadah is death by hanging and they aren't kidding. More than a hundred drug users and traffickers have seen their last sunrise from a Malaysian gallows. Grinspoon put her in touch with former attorney general Ramsey Clark, a man who knows something about traveling to the boondocks in defense of human rights, and Clark flew to Kuala Lumpur to get the lay of the land. On his return, he and Grinspoon mapped out a medical-necessity defense that seemed ironclad. Then Grinspoon assembled his supporting documents and took off for Asia.

His first stop was the grim fortresslike Pudu Prison, where he examined the young man and found him, not surprisingly, terrified, depressed, and subject to muscle spasms in his arm and shoulder. Over the next several days, Grinspoon worked with the defendant's Malaysian attorney, giving him an education in the medical-necessity defense. After Grinspoon had walked the man through the three-thousand-year history of cannabis, recounting its widespread medical use from the beginning of the written word up through 1937, the lawyer was openmouthed. He immediately began making phone calls to influential Malaysian doctors and lawyers and arranged for them to hear the same lecture the next night. They, too, were amazed. Grinspoon told them that a groundbreaking study of the medicinal uses of cannabis was based on observations made right there in Malaysia and India in 1839.[23]

But when the legal team reached the courthouse the next morning, they were almost blown out of the water before Grinspoon could open his mouth. The lawyer introduced his American expert, and the judge exploded. "Why have you brought this man halfway around the globe to testify when it has been established that the defendant possessed 265.7 grams of cannabis and the punishment is prescribed?"

Reluctantly, since Grinspoon had already made the trip, the judge agreed to let him speak, even though it was obviously pointless. But as with the audience of the night before, the judge's skepticism melted, he became intrigued, and finally brushed the lawyer aside and began questioning the witness himself. Grinspoon told him the defendant was one of thousands of people who claim that marijuana is the best thing they can find for controlling the kind of painful spasms associated with quadriplegia, multiple sclerosis, and traumatic nerve injury.

After lunch, it was the prosecutor's turn. Grinspoon had been warned that the state was anxious to swing this young American from the yardarm and they did not look kindly on this intervention. In his opening volley, the prosecutor threatened to have Grinspoon himself arrested and thrown in prison for not following procedures, then waded into him with a withering barrage of questions. Unfortunately, the questions turned out to be based on misinformation, and each response from the professor steamrolled the prosecutor with a roll call of references to the scientific literature. After an hour of this, the infuriated official said, "Dr. Grinspoon, all that you have reported here about the capacity of cannabis to relieve suffering of one type or another comes from papers and journals! What has been your experience in observing this for yourself?"

Wrong question. To a courtroom now packed with late arrivals who had heard of the furious duel, Grinspoon traced his experience back to that day in 1967 when his ten-year-old son was diagnosed with acute lymphatic leukemia. At first, he said, Danny was good-natured about the treatments, but by 1971, he was involved in major chemotherapy and Grinspoon and his wife found themselves subjected to heart-wrenching scenes at the hospital. "He would start to vomit shortly after treatment and continue retching for up to eight hours. He vomited in the car as we drove home, and when we got there he had to lie in bed with his head over a bucket on the floor."

Then one day Grinspoon arrived at the hospital and found his wife and son already there. They were uncommonly relaxed and it was obvious something was up. He was shocked to see his son take the medicine without a fight, and after it was over there was no sign of nausea. Instead of throwing up in the car, Danny asked if they could stop off for a submarine sandwich. When they got home, Grinspoon pulled his wife aside. She admitted she had stopped by the school yard on the way to the hospital and one of Danny's pals had given them a marijuana cigarette. She and Danny had smoked it together before the session.

Grinspoon was stupefied. They could have been arrested! What about the law? What about the risk of embarrassment to the hospital staff and the university?

Their son, meanwhile, rather than going straight to bed as in the past, went out to play. And at that point the shaken professor began to reexamine his position. Dr. Grinspoon would ultimately write two major books on the subject—*Marijuana Reconsidered* in 1971, and *Marihuana, The Forbidden Medicine* in 1993.[24] And in the last year of his son's life, thanks to the infamous weed, they were able to have a few more submarine sandwiches and a few more laughs.

According to a U.S. embassy official, when Grinspoon finished "you could hear a pin drop in that courtroom." Thirty days later the judge ruled: ". . . there was enough evidence adduced from the accused to show that the cannabis was for his own consumption . . . to relieve pain from injuries he suffered in a fall off a mountain." The death penalty would be set aside. The defendant would be released in twenty-six months.[25]

On his last visit to the impregnable colonial fortress where his client was to spend the next two years, Grinspoon examined the young man one final time and asked how he was managing to control his muscle spasms in jail.

"Marijuana."

Grinspoon looked at him, incredulous.

"I buy it from the guards."

Chapter Eleven

Prescription for Sanity

Thirty days after the earthshaking vote from the western frontier, Americans were treated to another unsettling dispatch from the front lines of the drug war. Once again it was Ed Bradley in the trenches, reporting from Virginia for CBS.

"Imagine living every day in excruciating pain. Then imagine there was a simple treatment to relieve that pain, but your doctor wouldn't give it to you."[1]

Bradley was focusing the *60 Minutes* spotlight on one of the saddest by-products of the drug war—people who legitimately need narcotic painkillers and find it almost impossible to get them. Since the early 1920s the medical profession in the United States has been so terrorized by federal drug agents that it has virtually abandoned patients with chronic pain. These people—victims of accidents, botched surgery, degenerative disease—sometimes require massive doses of drugs like morphine just to get out of bed. Patients who take narcotics for pain generally don't get high. The opiates just put the pain at a distance and cancel the fear that often accompanies this kind of ongoing agony. With the right dose, consistently maintained, the victim can sometimes lead a reasonably normal life.[2]

But chronic-pain patients, by definition, don't get better and they sometimes get worse. That's the problem. The drug enforcers may be willing to let doctors prescribe a reasonable amount of pain medicine for, say, a lung removal, but they expect these prescriptions to taper off quickly. Anyone who gets an ongoing dose of narcotics—let alone an increase—gets the attention of state and federal officials, and hardly a day goes by that they don't lift some doctor's license.[3] So the medical profession, not surprisingly, has largely abandoned the field, and most doctors actively avoid treating any of these tortured souls. For the past half century, they have been left to their own devices, screaming in a vacuum.

But there's always someone whose compassion gets ahead of his sense of self-preservation, and in this case it was a D.C. physician named William Hurwitz. It was the trial of Dr. Hurwitz that brought Ed Bradley to Virginia. The state board of medical examiners was in the process of pulling his license, and the hearing room was full of patients who had come from all over the country begging the officials not to sanction him. Hurwitz, they said, was the one doctor with the courage to help, and between them they represented an awesome collection of physical agony.

Jim Klimek came from Tennessee. His car had run off the road on a long-ago winter night and when he was discovered the next morning his legs were frozen. Gangrene set in and a series of amputations followed that ultimately cut away everything below his navel. Only his torso, head, and arms remain. But the nerve endings they sliced through are still active, and he claims he needs morphine to deal with the sensation that his lower half is still in the process of being sawed off. In Virginia, however, narcotics agents are trained to see through this kind of clever ruse. They know that many times people like Klimek are simply faking their symptoms to feed a drug habit. As the Virginia state police manual warns, "Physicians should be alert for 'Professional Patients' showing up in wheelchairs missing various limbs."[4]

But one of these professional patients, a former cop from up-state New York who had been pulverized by a school bus, upped the ante. He warned the board that if they lifted Hurwitz's license and cut off his prescription, he would kill himself.

The board was sympathetic but there were larger issues involved. Dr. Hurwitz was clearly prescribing narcotics in amounts that far exceeded the norm. If this was sound medical practice, then why was he the only one doing it? The board had a statutory duty to protect society at large from this kind of recklessness, and they found Hurwitz guilty of overprescribing and revoked his license. Four weeks later, as promised, the former police officer committed suicide, but first he made a video and Ed Bradley ran it on the air.

"It's pretty damn stupid that the only person I can get to help me, they turn around and take his license away from him.

"Suicide was not what I wanted. Pain treatment and control is what I wanted."

When Bradley played this tape for the medical examiners, they were unmoved. "Tragic as this is," said one, "the Virginia Board of Medicine may have saved other lives by this action."[5] In other words, a greater good may have been served by making sure these powerful narcotics did not somehow fall into the hands of young people. But as is so often the case in this conflict, the message sent was not necessarily the one received. Any teenager watching the *60 Minutes* broadcast would probably have come away with the clear understanding that this was a society willing to torture its citizens to prove a point.

Regardless of what else may happen in the drug war, pain control is one front that is almost certainly headed for a change. The baby boomers are coming up on sixty, and as members of this enormous wave of humanity start getting liver cancer, they will dramatically alter pain treatment as they have transformed everything else in their path.

And this may be the central problem for the prohibitionists in the coming debate. The seamless propaganda campaign that has blanketed the drug war for eighty years has always had as its central focus the image of the Drug User as Vampire. As long as these wretched monsters could be completely stigmatized—like the Jews in Nazi Germany—anything was possible.[6] You could confiscate their property without due process, put them in concentration camps, and conduct medical experiments on them against their will. And since they never numbered more than a tiny fraction of the population, they could be fearlessly blamed for everything.

But by demanding that cannabis be included in the sweep of absolute prohibition, the drug enforcers may have overreached their grasp. They are now confronted with a huge segment of the electorate that has had direct experience with marijuana. Over seventy million Americans have taken at least a few drags, and while some of them may not have inhaled, most of them did. When they failed to experience the instant insanity that the authorities had promised, it was for many an epiphany more powerful than the drug itself—the realization that the government makes things up.

No doubt the Anslinger-inspired exaggerations about marijuana sprang from the highest motives, but when you're caught red-handed in a total fabrication, it dents your credibility. What's more, the Woodstock generation was also the generation of The Wall, citizens who came to know firsthand that the noble crusades of the government can be grounded in illusion. To bring these skeptics on board the war on drugs, it was necessary to convince them that the basic facts about marijuana had changed dramatically. Drug czar William Bennett was among the first to break the bad news: the children of the boomers were facing a far more powerful form of cannabis than the stuff their parents experimented with in the sixties. The amount of psychoactive THC in the new plants was said to be *forty times* greater.

But once again, close inspection revealed a flaw in the official tale. It seems the baseline samples from the 1970s were not properly preserved, so there's really no way to tell what their original THC content was. On top of that, the government's own long-term study of marijuana potency at the University of Mississippi undermined Bennett's argument. The official numbers showed an average THC content in marijuana seized by the police since 1981 ranging between 2.3 and 3.8 percent. In the 1970s on the other hand, independent analysts found THC averaging 2 to 5 percent with some samples as high as 14 percent.[7] As one authority put it, "If parents want to know what their kids are smoking today, they need only recall their own experience."[8]

The fallback line for cannabis prohibition, the moat around the castle, has always been the idea that marijuana is a stepping-stone to harder drugs. But here again the actual experience of the boomers did not mesh properly with the official line. Of the seventy million Americans who smoked the weed, 98 percent didn't wind up on anything harder than martinis. Only a tiny fraction went on to become heroin or cocaine addicts, and the cause-effect connection to reefer for this group was no more evident than was the connection to coffee.[9] As these scientific counterclaims began to surface, the prohibitionists found themselves in the same boat as the CIA, whose operatives always insisted on a right to lie in the interest of national security and then seemed genuinely dismayed when nobody believed them.

When Dr. Hamilton Wright almost single-handedly launched America on the voyage of drug prohibition at the beginning of this century, he believed that opium and cocaine addiction could be cured by simply passing a law. From 1914 onward, with growing dedication and expanding armies, his successors labored to bring the dream to fruition, but the light at the end of the tunnel always turned out to be an oncoming train loaded with exotic new chemicals. After eighty years of brutal combat, the official dispatches from the front lines are harsh and unequivocal:

> *During the last two decades, the world has witnessed the "globalization" of the drug abuse problem and the situation has worsened drastically.*
>
> —UNITED NATIONS NARCOTICS CONTROL BOARD, 1993[10]

The migration of gang and posse members to smaller U.S. cities and rural areas resulted in increases in drug-related homicides, armed robberies, and assaults. . . .

Crack continued to be used in epidemic or near-epidemic proportions in most major cities. . . .

Worldwide opium production was 4,157 metric tons [an increase of 20 percent in a single year].

—DRUG ENFORCEMENT ADMINISTRATION, AUGUST 1996[11]

Despite some successes, United States and host countries' efforts have not materially reduced the availability of drugs. . . .

. . . international drug-trafficking organizations have become sophisticated, multibillion dollar industries that quickly adapt to new U.S. drug control efforts.

—U.S. GENERAL ACCOUNTING OFFICE, MARCH 1997[12]

This tragic defeat did not rise from a lack of will or resources. In the attempt to make America drug-free, the taxpayers laid out over $300 billion in the last fifteen years alone. To put that in perspective, we went to the moon for less than a third of that amount.[13]

The underlying problem has always been the basic concept. In retrospect, a drug-free America had no more chance of success than an alcohol-free America. As Mark Thornton of Tulane University points out in *The Economics of Prohibition*, the black market is the purest form of unfettered free-market capitalism. The rules are Darwinian—survival of the fittest—and no matter what you do, the pirates will always be a step ahead. With each failure to stamp out the traffic, the authorities will respond by tightening the screws—the only option available—and the increasing risk will increase the payoff. And the violence. Which will succeed only in eliminating the timid players, leaving the market ultimately in the hands of barbarians like Capone and

Escobar who will stop at nothing. And as Professor Thornton makes clear, these are structural forces, like gravity, that cannot be altered by moral arguments.[14]

Not only has America nothing to show for this monumental effort, but the failed attempt has clearly made everything worse. After blowing hundreds of billions of dollars and tens of thousands of lives, the drugs on the street today are stronger, cheaper, more pure, and more widely available than at any time in history. Everything from crack cocaine to Dilaudid is just a phone call away and chances are they'll deliver. You can buy it in the school yard, in the alley, and you can buy it in small Indiana farm towns that just a few years ago had never even heard of the stuff.[15]

The fallout from this misadventure cannot be looked upon simply as one of our many problems. It rains down on everything, blanketing the nation in a smog of delusion so pervasive nobody can see it, even as it warps U.S. foreign policy, corrodes the Bill of Rights, and successfully reverses years of progress in race relations. One of the most shocking things about the O. J. Simpson trial was the gulf it revealed between black and white perceptions of the criminal justice system. White people instinctively believe the cops—"Why would they lie?" Black America, more accustomed to being spread-eagled on the pavement, has an entirely different perspective of the officer on the witness stand. With one black man in four now behind bars or under supervision by the state, it's hard to find an African-American family that has not had a direct, personal, unpleasant experience with law enforcement—more often than not, something to do with the drug war.

This is the arena where the fault lines of American justice are clearly visible. In a drug bust, the complaining witness is the cop, who can decide on the spot whether to prosecute or not. This absolute power is inevitably subject to political pressure and favoritism. The white kid in the Mercedes gets a pass and the black kid in the car behind him gets five years without parole. When Indiana congressman Dan Burton's son was caught with eight pounds of marijuana in his trunk and thirty plants in his apartment, he got probation.[16] It would be hard to imagine a black teenager from the South Side of Indianapolis getting the same deal.

Unfortunately, that's not the worst of it. Far and away the most ominous by-product is the corrosive flood of illegal cash that is lapping at the country's foundations. Honest cops everywhere are watching in dismay as their departments are sucked under by payoffs at every level. Former San Jose police chief Joseph McNamara says it's eating us alive: "Every week, somewhere across the country, there is another police scandal related to the drug war—corruption, brutality—even armed robbery by cops in uniform."[17]

But as our friends from south of the border warn us, we ain't seen nothin' yet. At a drug-policy conference in 1993, former Colombian high court judge Gomez Hurtado told the Americans, "Forget about drug deaths, and acquisitive crime, and addiction, and AIDS. All this pales into insignificance before the prospect facing the liberal societies of the West. *The income of the drug barons is greater than the American defense budget.* With this financial power they can suborn the institutions of the State and, if the State resists . . . they can purchase the firepower to outgun it. We are threatened with a return to the Dark Ages."[18]

As Western civilization stands transfixed, paralyzed by the specter of twentieth-century Vandals devouring one country after another, it's important to remember that this particular impending catastrophe can be avoided with the stroke of a pen. The criminal enterprises that now encircle us from the Golden Triangle to Tingo Maria and Tijuana, from Watts and Bronxville to Bel-Air and Sutton Place—the powerful, ruthless combines that threaten to overwhelm the rule of law itself—all could be cut off by simply closing the black market money tap.

The prohibitionists have never been called to account for their part in this disaster, but they are quick to demand a full accounting from their critics. People like George Soros and Lester Grinspoon are accused of advancing some dark agenda without regard for the consequences. Says the DEA's Thomas Constantine, "Those who advocate legalization have many motives. But they frequently do not have answers to a lot of the questions we are asking."[19] Questions like: How many new drug addicts will you create under legalization? Who's going to give them their drugs? How will they be handed out? Who's going to pay all the social and criminal costs? And finally, what drugs would you legalize? Heroin? LSD? *Crack?* These queries are assumed to be argument-terminators for which no acceptable answers exist.

But lately answers have been coming anyway. Independent scientists, swimming upstream against the flow of government largesse, have been digging into these issues in detail and they're coming up with interesting information. For one thing, they point to a University of Maryland survey of high school students, which contains an amazing revelation. The hardest drug to get, say the kids, is not reefer, but *alcohol.*[20] And if you think about it for a second, it's not so amazing after all. Alcohol distribution is controlled by the government. Drug distribution is controlled by the mob.

Ethan Nadelmann—sometimes referred to as the Johnny Appleseed of the drug reform movement—is a former Princeton professor who now heads the Lindesmith Center, a New York think tank that is at work on the problem. For Nadelmann and his colleagues, the central objective of any drug policy should be harm reduction—cut the damage caused by both drug addiction and drug prohibition. To get there, he says, marijuana must be available to adults under tight controls, and some form of drug maintenance has to be established for the incorrigible. Any solution that leaves gangsters in control of the market will not cure the cancer, and no matter what short-range problems may be solved, the corruption will only be fertilized. The only way to destroy the black market is to underbid it. If that means drugs have to be given away to serious addicts, so be it. Anyone who's determined to use heroin regardless of the consequences must be able to get the stuff from a legitimate source at a price that doesn't require stealing car radios. A tightly controlled legal market, offering clean, unadulterated pharmaceuticals, would instantly terminate the cash flow to the street bazaar, and the river of money that has fueled the most brutal collection of criminal combines in the history of the planet would dry up like a Mojave arroyo on Independence Day.

The prohibitionists insist that the black market would still exist because drugs would obviously be illegal for children, but the experience with alcohol after Prohibition suggests otherwise. While it's possible for a marginal operator to make a few bucks selling booze to kids, there's not much money in it and the risk is substantial. There are no beer pushers hanging around the playground. You can't make a living at it.

Crack cocaine, of course, is an unparalleled menace, but the prohibitionists hardly have clean hands on this issue. Crack is a creation of the black market. The only reason for its existence is economic. It's cheap. Unfortunately, you get what you pay for. The high lasts only seconds before the bottom drops out, but low cost makes it available to the blue-collar market. There are few crack addicts on Wall Street. The traders prefer the smoother ride of the pure powder, and they can afford it. If a range of treatment and maintenance options were available to serious addicts, there is every likelihood the demand for crack would begin to disintegrate. In Liverpool, where John Marks gave addicts cocaine by prescription, nobody asked for crack.

As for who would supply these drugs to the addicts, it would be better for all concerned if they got their stash from a pharmacist instead of a fourteen-year-old.

The overarching case against drug-policy reform has always been the number of new users that would be created if criminal sanctions were set aside. When Prohibition ended in 1933, say the drug warriors, there was a significant jump in alcohol consumption. If a comparable jump followed repeal of narcotics prohibition, there would be a horde of new addicts. They insist that Prohibition, despite its flaws, actually cut alcohol consumption dramatically.

"The truth," says historian Harry G. Levine, "is more complex and more interesting. Prohibition knocked out beer, which is smelly, bulky, and had to be brewed locally. Hard liquor, on the other hand, does not spoil, it's more compact, and it's easy to ship. So during Prohibition, ironically, Americans drank more hard liquor than ever. When repeal came, beer consumption rebounded and liquor went down, mainly because of the new liquor laws. There was a conscious policy on the part of the states to discourage hard liquor consumption. It was taxed more heavily, some states sold it only in government liquor stores, and they made it as hard to get as possible. It's still prohibited in some counties. But for the next ten years the total amount of *alcohol* consumed stayed about the same." So it turns out that state liquor laws held down consumption about as well as Prohibition, but without all the gunplay.[21]

The experience in Europe also suggests there is less to fear from regulated narcotics sales than some people imagine. When narcotics were made available to serious addicts in England and Switzerland, the street trade diminished along with the crime rate.[22] And in the only test of limited decriminalization within the United States, the results did not support the prohibitionists. Between 1973 and 1978, possession of marijuana was reduced to a misdemeanor in twelve states, but the predicted explosion in cannabis use failed to materialize. The University of Michigan's annual high school survey, *Monitoring the Future,* showed the seniors in these dozen states reported no more marijuana use than their counterparts in the other states.[23] Among adults, marijuana use did go up slightly but alcohol consumption went down. While that may have been alarming to the liquor industry, it was a net plus for public health since booze can kill you and cannabis can't. In addition, there were significant financial benefits. The individual states saved hundreds of millions of dollars apiece in prosecution and police costs alone.[24]

One of the major success stories the prohibitionists take credit for—the dramatic decrease in cocaine use among the middle class in the 1980s—had a number of causes, and law enforcement may have been least among them. A study of some two hundred heavy cocaine users in northern California from 1985 to 1987 revealed that fear of arrest was number six on the list of reasons for quitting. Far more important were health problems, financial difficulties, problems at work, and pressure from a spouse or lover. "What keeps many heavy users from falling into the abyss of abuse, and what helps pull back those who do fall, is a stake in conventional life." Jobs, families, friends—the ingredients of normal identity—turned out to be the ballast that allowed these people to pull back from the edge.[25] It seems the real reason most people stay away from drugs—alcohol and tobacco included—is not criminal sanctions but common sense.

And this points to a path out of the swamp. Apparently the one surefire way to cut down on drug use is to give people the facts and let them use their own judgment. In 1914, just before drug and alcohol prohibition began, both drugs and alcohol were in general disfavor and their use was declining among all segments of the population.[26] The Pure Food and Drug Act of 1906 forced manufacturers to list ingredients on product labels, and when people found out what was in some of those home remedies, the use of narcotics dropped by a third—the largest single decrease ever—and that was before Prohibition.[27] The most successful antidrug crusade in history was the one waged against tobacco over the last thirty years, a campaign that avoided prohibition altogether. The tool was education, and it proved far more formidable than coercion. California cut smoking 40 percent in a single decade by using cigarette taxes to finance antismoking ads.[28]

• • •

The conservative wings of both major political parties have been urging Americans to take charge of their lives and become less dependent on government, and drug-policy reform is one area where the American people will indeed have to do it themselves because they can expect no help from Washington. As in the 1920s, the political establishment is paralyzed on this issue, like a jackrabbit frozen in the headlights of an oncoming locomotive. Anybody who questions the idea of jailing our way to abstinence is labeled soft on crime, and that is still a career-ender of the first order. Surgeon General Joycelyn Elders was hounded out of office not for suggesting legalization, but for suggesting a *study* of legalization.

Clearly it's time for such a study, whether Congress likes it or not, but the legislators will likely have to be jolted into motion. Incapable of leadership on anything this loaded, they will respond like bellboys to whatever the people ultimately decide. Franklin Roosevelt and the New Deal Congress of 1932 got credit for repealing Prohibition, but it was private citizens like Pauline Sabin, Henry Joy, and the du Pont brothers who led them to it by the nose.

Professor Arnold Trebach of the American University was one of those academics who traveled to England in the late seventies and came home to write a book about it. *The Heroin Solution,* published in 1982, highlighted the superiority of the old British system and put Trebach at the center of the reform movement.[29] He began attracting like-minded thinkers, and with Washington attorney Kevin Zeese, he created the Drug Policy Foundation, whose board of directors quickly grew to include financiers, lawyers, doctors, scientists, police chiefs, a federal judge, and Baltimore mayor Kurt Schmoke. The foundation's national conferences brought the leading drug-policy reformers from all over the world under one roof for the first time, creating a critical mass that ignited the current push for reform.

The Drug Policy Foundation is doing essentially the same job that Pauline Sabin's group performed during the closing hours of Prohibition. It was obvious by the late 1920s that the Noble Experiment wasn't working, but since the prohibitionists controlled the numbers, people had no idea of the depth of the disaster. Sabin's organization and others like it funded the research that gave the public its first dose of the unadulterated facts.

Sixty years later it's equally clear the war on drugs has gone belly-up, and the intellectual heirs of Pauline Sabin are making sure this information gets into the hands of the public. For decades Americans have been assured that if they would "stay the course"—tighten the screws, hire more agents, bring in the military, seal the border, crack down on the source countries, arrest Carlos, or Pablo, or De-De—this vast underworld mechanism could be brought to a halt. Success was always just over the next rise. But with the arrival of serious reformers on the scene, the prohibitionists no longer have control of the dialogue. Now the public at large is starting to ask questions. The op-ed and letters-to-the-editor pages are peppered with demands for another look at the drug war as people across the political spectrum begin to realize that, despite the most monumental prison-building program in history, despite a skyrocketing commitment of money and manpower, despite the arrest of a million people a year for drug offenses, everything is going downhill. The bad guys are getting richer and whole governments are dissolving in the acid-bath of corruption. The U.S. Constitution is now so riddled with drug-emergency exceptions it looks like the flag over Fort Sumter.

The parting knell for the Eighteenth Amendment was the 1931 report of the Wickersham Commission, a panel of experts assembled by President Hoover to see how Prohibition could be salvaged. Instead they produced an official catalog of failure so damning it set the stage for Repeal. If Wickersham and his colleagues were around today, they would no doubt be astounded at how little we've learned. For one thing, the murder rate is back to where it was in 1933, and the country is once again awash in corruption. Unfortunately, there is no chance Washington would risk empaneling a group like this today, because the results are too predictable. Every scientific inquiry into marijuana since the Indian Hemp Commission of 1894 has found the weed relatively harmless, and while Richard Nixon was able to bury the Shafer report in 1972, that would be hard to pull off in the age of the Internet.[30]

With the federal government quick-frozen on this issue, the battleground has shifted to the states, and this opening is ripe with possibilities. The individual states have always been the testing ground for new ideas. When Prohibition was repealed, it was state legislators who stepped into the breach with a menu of regulatory schemes, and over time the country hammered out a system for controlling alcohol sales that reflected regional concerns.

At this moment, history is repeating itself in California. When the Golden State voted to allow medical use of marijuana, there were hysterical predictions from Washington and Sacramento. But California did not fall into the sea, and after the name-calling subsided, the combatants had to start dealing with reality. The public was then treated to the spectacle of sheriffs, prosecutors, doctors, and pot growers sitting down together to hammer out regulations for controlling the distribution of marijuana to legitimate patients.

If California survives this apostasy, other states will follow. Some will enact stringent rules while others may experiment once again with broader decriminalization. When a national consensus finally forms on this issue, it's almost certain to come down in favor of the sick and dying because they make much more convincing TV commercials than men in suits. At that point, the majority of U.S. citizens will be in opposition to their own government's policy and something will have to give.

The coming engagement promises to be bloody because the outcome of the whole war is at stake. Prohibition, as policy, can only ratchet in one direction. Each failure must be met with more repression. Any step backward calls into question the fundamental assumption that repression is the solution. Ultimately, every available gun will be brought to bear because marijuana is the pawl on the ratchet, the little catch that keeps the drum from unwinding. For sixty years, Harry Anslinger and his successors have put their backs to this wheel, laboring to hoist drug prohibition to the level of a national crusade. But if somebody jiggles that pawl and the drum slips, support for the current policy will plummet like a loose cage in a mineshaft, because it cannot sustain a serious evaluation.

With the future of the republic at stake, there is growing consensus that it's time at last to put the prohibitionists in the dock, time to demand some justification for a brutal eighty-year conflict that has produced the opposite of what was intended. If there was one thing all sides agreed on, it was the necessity to keep drugs out of the hands of children. How, then, do the drug warriors justify a policy that has not only given children ready access to drugs, but has guaranteed them employment as frontline runners in a marketplace so dangerous they have to be armed? Why, after nearly a century of the most stringent prohibition in history, was the nation's drug czar forced to admit that the latest jump in heroin use was among eighth-graders?

Prior to the Harrison Narcotics Act, if people wanted drugs they at least had to go to a drugstore. Now they can get anything they want from the neighbor's kid. It would seem that if Americans are to have any say at all in what their teenagers are exposed to, they will have to take the drug market out of the hands of the Tijuana Cartel and the Gangster Disciples, and put it back in the hands of doctors and pharmacists where it was before 1914.

Appendix A

U.S. MURDER RATE
HOMICIDES PER 100,000

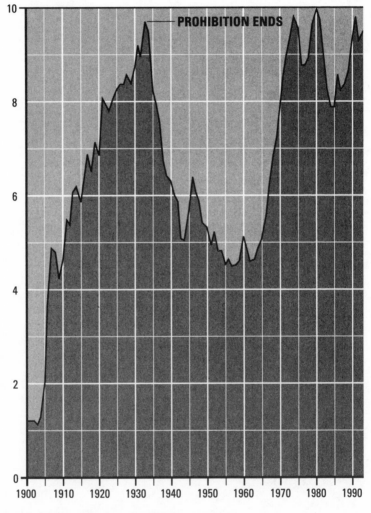

SOURCE: CENSUS BUREAU, FEDERAL BUREAU OF INVESTIGATION

FEDERAL DRUG WAR BUDGET
1981 – 1993

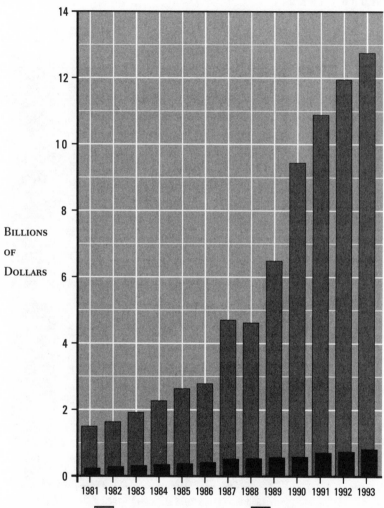

LEGEND : ▩ FEDERAL DRUG BUDGET ■ DEA SHARE

SOURCE: U.S. DEPARTMENT OF JUSTICE, DEA BRIEFING BOOK—
SEPTEMBER 1993

STATE AND FEDERAL PRISON POPULATION

1966–1996

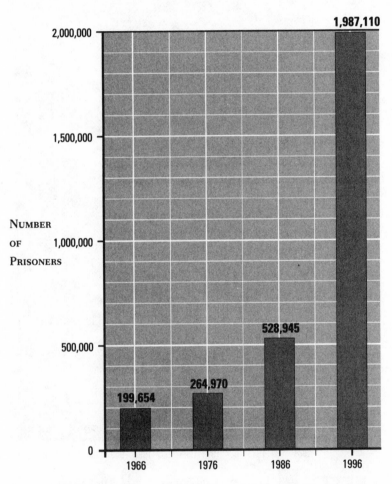

Source: U.S. Department of Justice, Bureau of Judicial Statistics

AN ACTIVIST'S GUIDE

When Surgeon General Joycelyn Elders was run out of town for raising questions about the drug war, Dave Borden decided it was time to get involved. A Princeton graduate with a degree from the New England Conservatory of Music, Borden had no interest in drugs, but he was appalled by the social havoc the drug laws were wreaking. Skillfully working the Internet, he developed a network of local activists, students, and drug-policy critics who began exchanging ideas and action alerts with a rapidly growing membership list. Borden's Drug Reform Coordination Network (DRCNet) quickly became an international clearinghouse.

One of his earliest supporters was Clifford Schaffer, a California businessman who felt the nexus of the problem was information. If people knew the facts, said Schaffer, they would demand a change in course. Schaffer's contribution was a burgeoning electronic library, a searchable database of original drug-war documents and statistics where you could find links to the House Hearings on the Marijuana Tax Act of 1937 or the Swiss report *Medical Prescription of Narcotics*. It would be impossible to estimate the impact of DRCNet, but these days when a politician makes a wild statement about the drug war, he's likely to be called out in print by a well-informed letter writer who probably got his or her facts from the Internet. This easy access to scientific and historic data is beginning to have an impact on the press as well.

For those who agree with Borden that it's time to join the fray, here's a list of organizations on all sides of this issue, from the Drug Enforcement Administration to the National Organization for the Reform of Marijuana Laws.

DRUG-POLICY LIBRARIES

http://www.drcnet.org/
Web site of the Drug Reform Coordination Network (DRC-Net). Includes articles on prohibition, harm reduction, needle exchange, sentencing, asset forfeiture, medical marijuana, chronic pain treatment, international drug policies, and methadone maintenance, as well a calendar of events, action alerts, and a weekly news bulletin.

http://www.druglibrary.org/
World's largest online drug-policy library, sponsored by DRC-Net. Information on a wide range of drug-policy topics, including the full text of major reports. Front page includes links to a number of substantial online collections.

http://www.drugtext.nl/
Drugtext Europe, web site of the International Foundation for Drug Policy and Human Rights. One of the largest online library collections on drug policy. U.S. mirror site at http://www.drugtext.org/.

http://www.lindesmith.org/
The Lindesmith Center is a Manhattan-based drug-policy research institute. Its site features full-text articles from the academic and popular press focusing on drug policy from economic, criminal justice, and public health perspectives. Recent "focal point" topics include drug maintenance programs and medical marijuana.

http://www.drugsense.org/
Web site of DrugSense. Includes a searchable library of news articles related to all aspects of drug policy. Provides a weekly newsletter and a daily news reporting service, both for no charge over the Internet.

GOVERNMENT SITES

http://www.ncjrs.org/
National Criminal Justice Reference Service.

http://www.usdoj.gov/dea/
Drug Enforcement Administration (DEA).

http://www.ncjrs.org/drgshome.htm
NCJRS Drugs & Crime Clearinghouse.

http://www.state.gov/www/global/narcotics_law/
Bureau of International Narcotics and Law Enforcement Affairs.

http://www.ojp.usdoj.gov/bjs/
Bureau of Justice Statistics.

http://www.fedstats.gov/
Fedstats.

http://www.health.org/
National Clearinghouse for Alcohol and Drug Information.

http://www.nida.nih.gov/
National Institute on Drug Abuse.

http://www.niaaa.nih.gov/
National Institute on Alcohol Abuse and Alcoholism.

http://www.fda.gov/
Food and Drug Administration.

http://inet.ed.gov/offices/OESE/SDFS/
Safe and Drug-Free Schools Program.

OTHER DRUG-POLICY INFORMATION SITES

http://www.prdi.org/
The Partnership for Responsible Drug Information holds public forums on drug policy and provides extensive informational resources for parents and the media.

http://www.vcl.org/
Named after an organization of attorneys that played a critical role in bringing about the repeal of alcohol prohibition, the Voluntary Committee of Lawyers works with lawyers, law professors, law students, and others associated with the legal profession to foster an open, honest, and constructive discussion about the drug war and what it is doing for and to our nation and legal system.

THINK TANKS

http://www.rand.org/centers/dprc/DPRCpubindex.html
The RAND Corporation's Drug Policy Research Center includes a subject index and abstracts for all publications on their site. Topics include drug policy and trends, state and local drug policy, national drug policy, international drug policy, prevention, treatment, enforcement, data systems and analysis, and modeling and policy gaming. Reports can be ordered online.

http://www.sproject.com/
The Sentencing Project, a think tank that researches the impact of criminal justice policies and advocates alternatives.

http://www.ncianet.org/ncia/
National Center on Institutions and Alternatives (NCIA) web site.

http://www.cato.org/
Well-known libertarian think tank.

Asset Forfeiture

http://www.fear.org/
Forfeiture Endangers American Rights (FEAR), national organization opposing the rampant abuses of asset forfeiture. Site features victims' stories and federal and state forfeiture legislation.

Chronic Pain

http://www.actiononpain.org/
American Society for Action on Pain (ASAP), organization advocating for adequate pain treatment for all who need it.

Harm Reduction/Needle Exchange

http://www.harmreduction.org/
Web site of the Harm Reduction Coalition (HRC), a national organization promoting strategies for reducing the harm related to substance abuse and sexual behavior.

http://www.lindesmith.org/tlcintro.html#harmred
The Lindesmith Center's index of harm reduction–related documents on its site.

http://www.drcnet.org/needle-exchange/
"Needle Exchange: A Form of Harm Reduction," DRCNet's "topics in depth" page on needle exchange.

http://www.nasen.org/
North American Syringe Exchange Network (NASEN) home page.

http://www.safeworks.org/safeprograms.html
The Safeworks AIDS Project in Minneapolis, Minnesota, maintains a directory of needle exchange program web sites.

http://www.safeworks.org/savelivesnow/
State-by-state data on drug-related AIDS from the Health Emergency reports of the Dogwood Center.

LAW ENFORCEMENT PERSPECTIVES

http://www.usdoj.gov/dea/
Drug Enforcement Administration web site.

http://members.aol.com/deawatch/
"The Voice of America's Front-line Drug Warriors" is sponsored by the American Law Enforcement Electronic Library rather than the Drug Enforcement Administration (DEA).

http://www.drcnet.org/cops/cops.html
"Cops Against the Drug War," from DRCNet's "Topics in Depth" section, contains materials on the Hoover Law Enforcement Summit written by Dr. Joseph McNamara, a former police chief of San Jose and Kansas City.

MANDATORY MINIMUMS AND SENTENCING

http://www.famm.org/
Web site of Families Against Mandatory Minimums (FAMM), a national organization advocating repeal of mandatory minimum sentencing and reform of the federal sentencing guidelines. Features victims' cases and links to further information.

http://www.november.org/
The November Coalition, an organization focusing on drug-war prisoners.

http://www.pkdata.com/cure/
Citizens United for the Rehabilitation of Errants (CURE) home page, national organization advocating for rehabilitation and alternatives to incarceration.

http://www.ussc.gov/
United States Sentencing Commission (USSC) web site.

http://www.fjc.gov/
The Federal Judicial Center (FJC) web site.

MEDICAL MARIJUANA

http://www.calyx.com/~olsen/MEDICAL/YOUNG/young.html
DEA judge Francis L. Young's ruling (September 6, 1988) on medical marijuana—the ruling of the chief administrative law judge of the DEA after hearing two years of testimony, pro and con, on the issue of the medical use of marijuana.

http://www.druglibrary.org/schaffer/medical_mj.htm
Medical marijuana master reference, an extensive directory of medical marijuana information available on the net.

http://www.marijuana.org/
Web site of the San Francisco Cannabis Cultivators' Club (formerly the Cannabis Buyers' Club).

http://www.marijuanamagazine.com/
"The Medical Marijuana Magazine," a medical marijuana magazine by former NORML (National Organization for the Re-

form of Marijuana Laws) director Dick Cowan and author
Peter McWilliams.

METHADONE MAINTENANCE

http://www.lindesmith.org/methmain.html
The Lindesmith Center's "focal point" on methadone, featuring
nearly twenty scholarly articles on methadone maintenance
and a directory of methadone information.

http://www.methadone.org/
Home page of the National Alliance of Methadone Advocates
(NAMA).

HUMAN RIGHTS/LATIN AMERICA

http://www.wola.org/
Washington Office on Latin America.

http://www.igc.apc.org/csn/
Colombia Support Network.

http://www.hrw.org/about/initiatives/drugs.html
Human Rights Watch Drugs and Human Rights project (international and domestic).

NEWS ABOUT DRUG ISSUES

http://www.mapinc.org/
The Media Awareness Project publishes a daily digest of drug-
war news items from around the world with links to the full
text.

http://www.ndsn.org/
"News Briefs," the monthly newsletter of the National Drug
Strategy Network (NDSN). News about all aspects of the drug

problem—American and international—with detailed coverage
going back to 1993. Nonadvocacy.

http://www.drcnet.org/rapid/
DRCNet bulletins, including "The Week Online" news service.

PREVENTION AND DRUG EDUCATION

http://www.arf.org/
The Addiction Resources Foundation (ARF) is a reputable
source of accurate information on drugs and addiction.

http://www.drugfreeamerica.org/
The Partnership for a Drug-Free America (PDFA) is a nonprofit
coalition of media and advertising agencies using national television and print advertising to stigmatize drug users and warn
against drug abuse.

http://www.dare-america.com/
"How to Raise Drug-Free Kids" is sponsored by *Reader's Digest.*

http://www.drcnet.org/DARE/
"A Different Look at DARE" is featured in DRCNet's "Topics in
Depth" section.

http://www.druglibrary.org/schaffer/library/daremenu.html
Multiple documents on the controversial Drug Abuse Resistance Education (DARE) program, from the DRCNet online
drug-policy library.

http://www.jointogether.org/
Join Together, a national network of prevention organizations.
Includes an extensive directory of links to sites on prevention,
treatment, self-help, and education.

Prohibition Advocacy

http://www.casacolumbia.org/
The National Center on Addiction and Substance Abuse
(CASA) is a nonprofit advocacy organization that produces reports on the harm to individuals and society caused by drug
abuse.

http://www.drugwatch.org/
Drug Watch International (DWI) is a nonprofit coalition advocating much stronger law enforcement.

http://www.emory.edu/NFIA/
National Families in Action (NFIA) is a nonprofit grassroots
antidrug organization that works to set up community drug
abuse prevention programs.

Reform Advocacy Groups

http://www.dpf.org/
The Drug Policy Foundation (DPF) is the largest drug-policy
reform organization, with a major annual conference, grants
program, newsletter, and a wide array of services to policy mak-
ers and the media who are interested in drug-policy issues.

http://www.cjpf.org/
The Criminal Justice Policy Foundation (CJPF) assists public
health, criminal justice, and other public officials in finding in-
novative solutions to criminal justice and drug-policy problems.

http://www.aclu.org/
The American Civil Liberties Union (ACLU) is heavily involved
in Constitutional law aspects of drug-policy reform.

http://www.wps.com.au/druglawreform/
Families and Friends for Drug Law Reform, Australian organization for people who have lost loved ones to drug abuse.

http://www.maps.org/
The Multidisciplinary Association for Psychedelic Studies
(MAPS) focuses on research into medical uses of marijuana
and psychedelics. Raises funds and helps researchers overcome
regulatory obstacles.

http://www.mpp.org/
The Marijuana Policy Project (MPP) lobbies for reform of the
marijuana laws and is currently focusing on medical marijuana.

http://www.norml.org/
The National Organization for the Reform of Marijuana Laws
(NORML) is the oldest and largest marijuana reform organiza-
tion and advocates the legalization of marijuana for adults.

http://www.drugsense.org/
Web site of DrugSense. DrugSense and its Media Awareness
Project get reform volunteers working together toward a common objective of influencing the media through weekly focus
alerts and Internet reports on drug-related news.

TREATMENT AND SELF-HELP

http://www.alcoholics-anonymous.org/
Alcoholics Anonymous (AA) pioneered the "twelve-step" self-
treatment program for people with severe drinking problems.

http://www.ca.org/
Cocaine Anonymous (CA) is a self-treatment program for people with cocaine problems, modeled after Alcoholics Anonymous.

http://comnet.org/mm/
Moderation Management (MM) is a moderation-oriented treatment program that emphasizes self-management, moderation,

and a balanced lifestyle. It is "not intended for alcoholics or those severely dependent on alcohol."

http://www.frw.uva.nl/cedro/peele/
The Stanton Peele Addiction Web Site contains a library of materials on the addiction experience.

http://www.ncadd.org/
National Center of Alcoholism and Drug Dependence (NCADD) is a federal drug abuse treatment and prevention advocacy agency that focuses largely on alcoholism.

http://www.samhsa.gov/csat/csat.htm
The Center for Substance Abuse Treatment (CSAT) of the Substance Abuse and Mental Health Services Administration (SAMHSA) works to expand federal drug abuse treatment efforts.

http://www.wsoinc.com/
Narcotics Anonymous (NA) is a self-treatment program for people with narcotics problems, modeled after Alcoholics Anonymous.

Notes

CHAPTER 1: A TALE OF TWO CITIES—CHICAGO 1995/1925

1. *Los Angeles Times*, September 29, 1993, p. A12: "Many of these officers were so brazen that they hung out in an East Village store with drug dealers and snorted cocaine while on duty"; *Los Angeles Times*, December 8, 1994, p. A4; *The New York Times*, December 16, 1993, p. A18; *Los Angeles Times*, March 15, 1990, p. A1.

2. "12 Police Officers Charged in Drug Corruption Sweep," *The New York Times*, April 16, 1994, p. A1; "11 More Officers Removed in Investigation," *The New York Times*, May 5, 1994, p. B8.

3. "Tape Provides Inside Look at Sheriff's Drug Scandal," *Los Angeles Times*, April 26, 1990, p. A1; "Key Witness . . . Says He Saw a Fellow Officer Dump Hundreds of Thousands of Dollars on a Bed and Then Divide the Cash," October 18, 1990, p. B1; "Widespread Corruption in Narcotics Squad Told," March 20, 1992, p. B3.

4. Frank Goff, Chicago Police Department, interviews, November 13, 1993; August 29, November 22, and December 10, 1994.

5. "Influence of Chicago Gang Boss compared to Capone's," *Los Angeles Times*, March 24, 1994, p. A1.

6. Ibid.

7. Robert J. Schoenberg, *Mr. Capone* (New York: William Morrow and Co., 1992), p. 57.

8. David Kyvig, ed., *Law, Alcohol, and Order: Perspectives on National Prohibition* (Westport, Conn.: Greenwood Press, 1985), p. 125.

9. Andrew Sinclair, *Prohibition: The Era of Excess* (Boston: Little, Brown and Co., 1962), p. 222.

10. Ibid., p. 124.

11. Ibid., p. 125.

12. Ibid., p. 126.

13. Schoenberg, *Mr. Capone*, p. 110.

14. Sean Dennis Cashman, *Prohibition in America: The Lie of the Land* (New York: Macmillan, 1981), p. 36.

15. Steven Duke and Albert C. Gross, *America's Longest War* (New York: G. P. Putnam's Sons, 1993), p. 87.

16. Ray R. Cowdry, *Capone's Chicago* (Lakeville, Minn.: Northstar Books, 1987), p. 35; Chicago Police Dept., "Street Gang Turfs 1991," *Street Gang-Motivated Homicide, Violence, and Drug Crime, 1987–1990*, Exhibit 4, p. 5.

CHAPTER 2: MAY IT PLEASE THE COURT

1. Randolph N. Stone, Cook County Public Defender, "The War on Drugs: The Wrong Enemy and the Wrong Battlefield," Statement to the Congressional Black Caucus, Longworth House Office Building, September 15, 1989.

2. Ibid.

3. U.S. Dept. of Justice monograph, *Drug Night Courts: The Cook County Experience*, NCJ 14185, August 1994.

4. Tim Lohraff, Cook County Public Defender, interview, November 11, 1993; Criminal Court appearance, November 10, 1993.

5. "Dwayne Thomas" is not his real name.

6. U.S. Dept. of Justice monograph, *Assessment of the Feasibility of Drug Night Courts*, NCJ 142415, June 1993, p. 10.

7. Ibid., p. 18.

8. "War on Crack Targets Minorities Over Whites," *Los Angeles Times*, May 21, 1995, p. A1.

9. Ibid. Although the percentage of crack smokers is higher among blacks than whites, the government numbers show 2.19 million whites versus .9 million blacks. *The National Household Survey on Drug Abuse: Main Findings 1990*, National Institute on Drug Abuse (ADM) 91–1788, 1991, p. 59.

10. Jimmie L. Reeves and Richard Campbell, *Cracked Coverage: Television News, the Anti-Cocaine Crusade, and the Reagan Legacy* (Durham, N.C.: Duke University Press, 1994), pp. 162–83; James Inciardi, Dorothy Lockwood, and Anne E. Pottieger, *Women and Crack Cocaine* (New York: Macmillan, 1993), p. 8.

11. "War on Crack Targets Minorities Over Whites," op. cit.

12. U.S. Dept. of Justice, Bureau of Justice Statistics, *Sourcebook of Criminal Justice Statistics—1993*, NCJ 148211, p. 457.

13. Sgt. Joe Kosala, Chicago Police Dept., ride-along, November 10–13, 1993.

14. U.S. Constitution, Fourth Amendment. Though Jefferson was in Paris at the time, he lobbied mightily for the Bill of Rights.

15. William Pitt, Earl of Chatham, speech to Parliament on the Excise Bill, 1777.

CHAPTER 3: LONG DAY'S JOURNEY INTO NIGHT

1. *Encyclopaedia Britannica*, 15th Edition, 1982, Macropaedia, vol. 15, p. 1142.

2. Andrew Sinclair, *Prohibition: The Era of Excess* (Boston: Little, Brown and Co., 1962), p. 19.

3. David F. Musto, *The American Disease: Origins of Narcotic Control* (New York: Oxford University Press, 1987), p. 31.

4. Ibid., pp. 4 and 292, n. 31.

5. Arnold H. Taylor, *American Diplomacy and the Narcotics Traffic* (Durham, N.C.: Duke University Press, 1969), p. 55: "To [Hamilton Wright], more than to any other single individual, must go the greatest share of the credit for the success of American efforts in the antiopium drive in the first two decades of the twentieth century. . . ."

6. *The New York Times*, March 12, 1911, supplement p. 12.

7. David T. Courtwright, *Dark Paradise: Opiate Addiction in America Before 1940* (Cambridge, Mass.: Harvard Unviversity Press, 1982), p. 1: "During the nineteenth century the typical opiate addict was a middle-aged white woman in the middle of the upper class. Mary Tyrone in Eugene O'Neill's autobigraphical play, *Long Day's Journey Into Night*, exemplifies the characteristics of the generation of addicts: female, outwardly respectable, long suffering—and thoroughly addicted to morphine."

8. Musto, *The American Disease*, pp. 5 and 281, n. 13: "By 1900 America had developed a comparatively large addict population, perhaps 250,000. . . ." The U.S. population was then 76.2 million.

9. David Musto, "Opium, Cocaine, and Marijuana in American History," *Scientific American*, July 1991, p. 41.

10. Musto, *The American Disease*, p. 281, n. 13.

11. Taylor, *American Diplomacy and the Narcotics Traffic*, p. 60, n. 33.

12. Dr. Lawrence Kolb, Sr., U.S. Public Health Service, quoted in Musto, *The American Disease*, p. 303, n. 36.

13. Musto, *The American Disease*, p. 295, n. 72.

14. *Felsenheld v. U.S.*, 186 U.S. 126 (1902), quoted in Benjamin F. Wright, *The Growth of American Constitutional Law* (Chicago: University of Chicago Press, 1942), p. 16.

15. Musto, *The American Disease*, p. 65: "Cocaine raised the specter of the wild Negro, opium the devious Chinese. . . ." *The New York Times*, February 8, 1914, p. 1: "Those cocaine niggers sure are hard to kill. . . ."—a southern sheriff.

16. Musto, *The American Disease*, p. 8: "The claim of widespread use of cocaine by Negroes is called into question by the report in 1914 of 2,100 consecutive Negro admissions to a Georgia asylum over the previous five years. The medical director acknowledged the newspaper reports of 'cocainomania' among Negroes but was surprised to discover that only two cocaine users . . . were hospitalized between 1909 and 1914."

17. Ibid., p. 7.

18. Richard H. Blum et al., *Society and Drugs: Drugs I: Social and Cultural Observations* (San Francisco: Jossey-Bass, Inc., 1969), p. 12.

19. Edward M. Brecher, *Licit and Illicit Drugs: Consumers Union Report* (Boston: Little, Brown and Co., 1972), p. 43.

20. "The 'White Hope' of Drug Victims," *Colliers*, November 25, 1913, p. 16. The quoted conversation is as Towns reported it. He never did identify his partner.

21. Musto, *The American Disease*, p. 80.

22. Ibid., p. 88.

23. Ibid., p. 89.

24. Taylor, *American Diplomacy and the Narcotics Traffic*, p. 90.

25. Brecher, *Licit and Illicit Drugs*, p. 49.

26. Musto, *The American Disease*, p. 64.

27. Brecher, *Licit and Illicit Drugs*, p. 50.

28. Charles E. Terry, "Narcotic Drug Addiction and Rational Administration," *American Medicine* 26 (January 1920), pp. 29–35, quoted in Alfred Lindesmith, *The Addict and the Law* (New York: Vintage Books, 1965), p. 21.

29. Ibid.

30. Brecher, *Licit and Illicit Drugs*, p. 33.

31. Ibid., pp. 33–35.

32. Annual federal appropriations for the drug war had reached $16 billion by 1996; total expenditures, including court costs, incarceration, and state and local police, are estimated at $30 billion.

33. Rufus King, *The Drug Hang-Up: America's Fifty-Year Folly,* 2nd ed. (Springfield, Ill.: Charles C. Thomas, 1972), p. 27.

34. Edward J. Epstein, *Agency of Fear: Opiates and Political Power in America* (New York: G. P. Putnam's Sons, 1977), p. 27.

35. Musto, *The American Disease,* pp. 190–94, 349, n. 32.

36. NBC network, March 1, 1928, quoted in Musto, *The American Disease,* p. 191.

37. Alphonso Alva Hopkins, quoted in Sinclair, *Prohibition,* p. 19.

38. Sinclair, *Prohibition,* p. 20.

39. Editorial, *The New York Times,* December 18, 1918, p. 14.

40. *Webb et al. v. U.S.,* 249 U.S. 96.

41. King, *The Drug Hang-Up,* p. 41.

42. Arnold S. Trebach, *The Heroin Solution* (New Haven, Conn.: Yale University Press, 1982), p. 149.

43. Lindesmith, *The Addict and the Law,* pp. 149, 160; Trebach, *The Heroin Solution,* p. 149.

44. A. G. DuMez, "Treatment of Drug Addiction," memo to the surgeon general, February 28, 1919, quoted in Musto, *The American Disease,* p. 145.

45. Musto, *The American Disease,* p. 148.

46. Ibid., p. 173.

47. Shreveport *Journal,* June 7 and 9, 1923, quoted in Ibid., p. 174.

48. *Encyclopaedia Britannica,* 15th Edition, 1982, Propaedia, vol. 8, p. 945.

49. Sources: Census Bureau, Federal Bureau of Investigation, U.S. Department of Justice Statistics, quoted in *The New York Times,* January 28, 1996, p. E5. Though many causes contributed to the dramatic rise in the U.S. murder rate, the percentage that could be ascribed to Prohibition was revealed on repeal in 1933, when the murder rate took a precipitous plunge for the next eleven years. (See graph, page 200.)

CHAPTER 4: THE DEVIL AND HARRY ANSLINGER

1. Andrew Sinclair, *Prohibition: The Era of Excess* (Boston: Little, Brown and Co., 1962), p. 248.

2. David E. Kyvig, *Repealing National Prohibition* (Chicago: University of Chicago Press, 1979), p. 74.

3. Charles Hanson Towne, *The Rise and Fall of Prohibition* (New York: Macmillan, 1923), p. 61, quoted in Mark Thornton, Cato Institute Policy Analysis, no. 157, July 1991 (Washington, D.C.), p. 9.

4. Sinclair, *Prohibition*, pp. 211, 212.

5. John C. McWilliams, *The Protectors: Harry J. Anslinger and the Federal Bureau of Narcotics, 1930–1962* (Newark: University of Delaware Press, 1990), p. 34.

6. Sinclair, *Prohibition*, p. 198.

7. Ibid., p. 233.

8. Harry Philips, a reporter for the *New York Evening Sun*, quoted in Sean Dennis Cashman, *Prohibition: The Lie of the Land* (New York: Macmillan, 1981), p. 18.

9. Clark Warburton, *The Economic Results of Prohibition* (New York: Columbia University Press, 1932), pp. 70, 72, quoted in Mark Thornton, Cato Institute Policy Analysis, no. 157, July 1991 (Washington, D.C.) p. 5.

10. Sinclair, *Prohibition*, p. 234.

11. Kyvig, *Repealing National Prohibition*, p. 32.

12. Sinclair, *Prohibition*, p. 208.

13. Cashman, *Prohibition*, p. 212.

14. Kyvig, *Repealing National Prohibition*, pp. 119–23.

15. *The New York Times*, February 14, 1930, p. 18.

16. Cashman, *Prohibition*, p. 209.

17. Franklin P. Adams, *New York World*, quoted in Sinclair, *Prohibition*, p. 366.

18. Speech in Denver, Colorado, June 25, 1923, quoted in Kyvig, *Repealing National Prohibition*, p. 2.

19. Cashman, *Prohibition*, p. 28.

20. McWilliams, *The Protectors*, p. 41.

21. Circular Letter No. 324 from H. J. Anslinger, December 4, 1934, Franklin D. Roosevelt Presidential Library, box 19, file OF 21-X, quoted in McWilliams, *The Protectors*, p. 84.

22. H.R. 11143, Sec. 3a, March 26, 1930, 71st Cong. 2d Sess., and McWilliams, *The Protectors*, p. 46.

23. McWilliams, *The Protectors*, p. 86.

24. David F. Musto, *The American Disease: Origins of Narcotic Control* (New York: Oxford University Press, 1987) p. 222.

25. McWilliams, *The Protectors*, p. 46.

26. Ibid., pp. 56, 57.

27. Ibid., p. 48.

28. Edward M. Brecher, *Licit and Illicit Drugs: Consumers Union Report* (Boston: Little, Brown and Co., 1972), p. 414; McWilliams, *The Protectors*, pp. 36, 37.

29. David Musto, interview, September 14, 1995.

30. *The New York Times*, September 16, 1934, sec. 4, p. 6; September 15, 1935, sec. 4, p. 9.

31. McWilliams, *The Protectors*, p. 51.

32. Charles H. Whitebread II, "The History of Non-Medical Use of Drugs in the U.S.," speech to the California Judges Association, 1995 annual conference.

33. Floyd K. Baskette to FBN, September 4, 1936, quoted in Musto, *The American Disease*, p. 223.

34. *The New York Times*, September 15, 1935, sec. 4, p. 4.

35. Musto, *The American Disease*, p. 223, 225.

36. Charles H. Whitebread II and Richard J. Bonnie, "An Inquiry Into the Legal History of American Marijuana Prohibition," *Virginia Law Review*, vol. 56, no. 6, October 1970, Ch 5B.

37. McWilliams, *The Protectors*, p. 53.

38. Ibid., p. 59.

39. Dr. Walter Treadway, head of the Mental Hygiene Division, quoted in Musto, *The American Disease*, p. 225.

40. *Taxation of Marihuana*, U.S. House of Representatives, Committee on Ways and Means, Hearings, May 4, 1937, pp. 102–103, and Musto, *The American Disease*, p. 228.

41. Whitebread, "The History of Non-Medical Use of Drugs in the U.S.," op. cit.

42. Musto, *The American Disease*, p. 228.

43. NBC *Monitor Radio*, July 1959.

44. McWilliams, *The Protectors*, p. 58.

45. Rufus King, *The Drug Hang-Up: America's Fifty-Year Folly*, 2nd ed. (Springfield, Ill.: Charles C. Thomas, 1972), p. 108.

46. *Sociological, Medical, Psychological and Pharmacological Studies by the Mayor's Committee on Marijuana* (The La Guardia Report), reprinted in David Soloman, *The Marijuana Papers* (New York: Signet, 1968), pp. 297, 307.

47. McWilliams, *The Protectors*, p. 104.

48. Ibid., p. 97.

49. Ibid., p. 98.

50. Ibid., p. 107.

51. Musto, *The American Disease,* p. 230.

52. Alfred R. Lindesmith, *The Addict and the Law* (Bloomington: Indiana University Press, 1965), p. 26.

53. *Public Law No. 255,* 82nd Cong., approved November 2, 1951; McWilliams, *The Protectors,* p. 108.

54. *The Illicit Narcotics Traffic* (Senate Report no. 1440, 84th Cong., 2nd Sess., 1956), quoted in Musto, *The American Disease,* p. 359, n. 6.

55. King, *The Drug Hang-Up,* pp. 41–43.

56. *Linder v. U.S.,* 286 U.S. 5, April 13, 1925.

57. King, *The Drug Hang-Up,* p. 163.

58. Rufus King, interview, May 4, 1996.

59. *Comments on Narcotic Drugs: Interim Report of the Joint Committee of the ABA-AMA on Narcotic Drugs; by the Advisory Committee to the Federal Bureau of Narcotics* (U.S. Treasury Dept., Bureau of Narcotics, 1958), introduction.

60. King, *The Drug Hang-Up,* pp. 165–75.

61. Ibid., p. 170: "Directly and indirectly Russell Sage Trustees were approched from the Treasury Department . . . and given to understand that they were sponsoring a 'controversial' study, that the ABA and AMA spokesmen were irresponsible if nothing worse, and that it would be discreet to drop the project."

62. NBC *Monitor Radio,* July, 1959.

63. Rufus King, interview, May 4, 1996.

Chapter 5: Addiction to Disaster

1. Dan Baum, *Smoke and Mirrors: The War on Drugs and the Politics of Failure* (Boston: Little, Brown and Co., 1996), p. 15.

2. Ibid., p. 12. Richard M. Nixon speech at Disneyland, September 1968.

3. Richard M. Nixon, message to Congress, June 17, 1971, quoted in Edward J. Epstein, *Agency of Fear: Opiates and Political Power in America* (New York: G. P. Putnam's Sons, 1977), p. 77.

4. Epstein, *Agency of Fear,* pp. 174–77.

5. Ibid., p. 177.

6. Ibid., p. 176.

7. The U.S. population in 1970 was 203,302,000, and the official numbers show the apparent heroin epidemic peaked at 559,000 addicts, or 0.27 percent.

8. Baum, *Smoke and Mirrors*, p. 258.

9. Ibid., p. 87.

10. *Report of the National Commission on Marijuana and Drug Abuse*, Chapter 3: "Evaluating the Social Impact of Drug Dependence."

11. *Marijuana: A Signal of Misunderstanding*, National Commission on Marijuana and Drug Abuse, March 22, 1972, quoted in Baum, *Smoke and Mirrors*, p. 71.

12. "Grass Grows More Acceptable," *Time*, September 10, 1973, p. 67.

13. Brecher, *Licit and Illicit Drugs*, p. 421.

14. Baum, *Smoke and Mirrors*, p. 93.

15. President Jimmy Carter, message to Congress, August 2, 1977, quoted in Baum, *Smoke and Mirrors*, p. 95.

16. "Freud's Cocaine Capers," *Time*, January 6, 1975, p. 76; "Cocaine: the Champagne of Drugs," *The New York Times Magazine*, January 6, 1975, p. 14; "In Showbiz, the Celebs with a Nose for What's New Say the New High Is Cocaine," *People* magazine, January 6, 1978, p. 16.

17. Arnold S. Trebach, *The Heroin Solution* (New Haven, Conn.: Yale University Press, 1982), p. 240; Baum, *Smoke and Mirrors*, pp. 112–115.

18. Ronald Reagan, *Remarks on Signing Executive Order 12368, Concerning Drug Abuse Policy Functions*, June 24, 1982; quoted in Baum, *Smoke and Mirrors*, p. 165.

19. Baum, *Smoke and Mirrors*, pp. 144–45.

20. Susan Adams, "Forfeiting Rights," *Forbes*, May 20, 1996, p. 96.

21. Executive Office for U.S. Attorneys, Department of Justice, *U.S. Attorneys Bulletin* 38, p. 180, quoted in Congressman Henry Hyde, *Forfeiting Our Property Rights: Is Your Property Safe from Seizure?* (Washington, D.C.: Cato Institute, 1995), p. 35.

22. Hyde, *Forfeiting Our Property Rights*, p. 20.

23. Office of the District Attorney, County of Ventura, State of California, Michael D. Bradbury, D.A., *Report on the Death of Donald Scott*, March 30, 1993.

24. Ventura County District Attorney Michael D. Bradbury, *Los Angeles Times*, March 31, 1993, p. A3.

25. Hyde, *Forfeiting Our Property Rights*, p. 6.

26. Ibid., pp. 38, 39; Jeff Brazil and Steve Barry, "Tainted Cash or Easy Money?," *Orlando Sentinel*, June 14–17, 1992.

27. "Take the Money and Run," *Washington City Paper*, November 20, 1992, p. 8.

28. Jimmie L. Reeves and Richard Campbell, *Cracked Coverage: Television News, the Anti-Cocaine Crusade, and the Reagan Legacy* (Durham, N.C.: Duke University Press, 1994), p. 16.

29. Ibid., pp. 18, 66.

30. Baum, *Smoke and Mirrors*, p. 226.

31. Jane Gross, "A New Purified Form of Cocaine Causes Alarm as Abuse Increases," *The New York Times*, November 29, 1985, p. 1.

32. National Institute on Drug Abuse, *National Household Survey on Drug Abuse*, 1990, p. 59. Over two million whites have used crack and less than a million blacks.

33. Baum, *Smoke and Mirrors*, p. 226.

34. Ibid., p. 228.

35. Columnist Charles Krauthammer, quoted in Jane Greider, "Crackpot Ideas," *Mother Jones*, July/August 1995, p. 52.

36. Greider, "Crackpot Ideas," op. cit.

37. G. Koren et al., "Relationship Between Gestational Cocaine Use and Pregnancy Outcome: a Meta-Analysis," *Teratology* 44(4) (October 1991), pp. 405–14.

38. David F. Duncan, "Uses and Misuses of Epidemiology in Shaping and Assessing Drug Policy," Brown University Center for Alcohol and Addiction Studies, Providence, R.I., 1994.

39. Ellen Goodman, "The Myth of 'Crack Babies,'" *The Boston Sunday Globe*, January 12, 1992, p. 69; Dan Baum, *Smoke and Mirrors*, pp. 217–18.

40. I. J. Chasnoff, "Polydrug Use in Pregnancy: Two-Year Follow-up," *Pediatrics* 89(2) (February 1992), pp. 284–89.

41. Arnold S. Trebach and James A. Inciardi, *Legalize It?* (Washington, D.C.: The American University Press, 1993), pp. 117–19; see also Katharine Greider, "Quieting the Crack-Kid Alarm," *The Drug Policy Letter* #27, Drug Policy Foundation, Washington, D.C. (Summer 1995), p. 16.

42. I. J. Chasnoff, "The Prevalence of Illicit Drug or Alcohol Use During Pregnancy and Discrepancies in Mandatory Reporting in Pinellas County, Florida," *New England Journal of Medicine* 17(322) (April 26, 1990), p. 1202.

43. Reported in Michael Tackett, "Minor Drug Players Are Paying Big Prices," *Chicago Tribune*, October 15, 1990, from a RAND Corporation study; quoted in Baum, *Smoke and Mirrors*, p. 249.

44. Baum, *Smoke and Mirrors*, p. 259.

CHAPTER 6: THE RIVER OF MONEY

1. "The Traffic in Drugs," *The New York Times,* April 10, 1988, sec. 1, p. 1.

2. *Los Angeles Times,* December 30, 1996, p. A10. A 1987 congressional investigation led by Senator John Kerry (D-Mass.) found that two of the contras' main air-cargo contractors were owned or operated by known drug traffickers who reportedly used the planes for smuggling. Several witnesses told the Kerry subcommittee that the Cali traffickers gave about $10 million to the contras, perhaps in hope of using rebel airfields for cocaine flights. At the peak of the contra war, the CIA had as many as four hundred people in the field, many of them former military personnel on short-term contract.

3. North Diaries, *Drugs, Law Enforcement, and Foreign Policy: A Report Prepared by the Subcommittee on Terrorism, Narcotics, and International Operations of the U.S. Senate, Committee on Foreign Relations* (The Kerry Committee) GPO, Washington, D.C., 1989, pp. 145–47; Warren Fiske, "North's Notes Suggest He Knew of Drug-Running by Contras," Knight-Ridder Tribune News Service, October 23, 1994: Oliver North jotted down a series of notes in the mid-1980s that indicate knowledge of possible drug-running into the United States while directing the White House's covert effort to arm the contras. On July 9, 1984, North wrote that contra leader Frederico Vaughan "wanted aircraft to go to Bolivia to pick up paste, want aircraft to pick up 1,500 kilos." August 9, 1985: "DC-6 which is being used for runs [to supply the contras] out of New Orleans is probably being used for drug runs into the U.S." July 12, 1985: "$14 million to finance Supermarket [a weapons storehouse in Honduras] came from drugs."

4. *The New York Times,* September 28, 1988, sec. 1, p. 1: Bush-Noriega contacts detailed; 1983 photo of Bush and Noriega.

5. "Drug Issue Gives Democrats Major Lift in Campaign; Poll Says Voters Are Upset with Reagan Administration's Focus on Other Priorities in Central America," *The New York Times,* April 13, 1988, sec. 1, p. 25. "Drug Problem Is Becoming Key Issue in '88 Campaign," May 24, 1988, sec. 4, p. 26; "Dukakis Attacks Bush's War Record on Drugs," September 17, 1988, sec. 1, p. 9; "Aides to Vice Pres Bush Move Swiftly to Combat Report That Prompted New Round of Questions About When Bush First Learned of Noriega's Alleged Involvement in Drug Trafficking," September 23, 1988, sec. 1, p. 23.

6. *The New York Times,* April 10, 1988, sec. 1, p. 10.

7. Ibid., July 10, 1988, sec. 4, p. 5.

8. Ibid., October 31, 1989, sec. A, p. 1.

9. "New Coca Cultivation Destroys 500,000 Acres of Peru's Amazon Rain Forest Every Year According to Peru's National Institute of Natural Resources," *The New York Times*, November 21, 1993, sec. 1, p. 10.

10. *The New York Times*, June 13, 1989, sec. A, p. 9.

11. Ibid., March 4, 1990, sec. 4, p. 26.

12. *International Narcotics Control Strategy Report*, U.S. Dept. of State, April 1994, p. 120: "Corruption is endemic in all GOP [Government of Peru] institutions, fueled by very low salaries. . . . Some officials have been subjected to judicial or disciplinary action for drug-related corruption. The highest ranking official to face such proceedings was the director of the PNP [Peruvian National Police] Antidrug Directorate."

13. *The New York Times*, November 11, 1991, p. A6: Army officers make ninety dollars a month. "When a typical colonel has to drive a taxi to make ends meet, you know you have problems," a Western diplomat said. *The New York Times*, March 4, 1990, sec. 4, p. 88; Stephen G. Trujillo, op-ed, "Corruption and Cocaine in Peru," *The New York Times*, April 7, 1992.

14. Trujillo, op-ed, "Corruption and Cocaine in Peru," op. cit.

15. Michael Massing, "Cocaine War . . . The Jungle Is Winning," *The New York Times*, March 4, 1990, sec. 4, p. 88.

16. *Los Angeles Times*, May 21, 1990, p. A1.

17. "On the Drug Battlefields of Bolivia, U.S. Sows Dollars and Reaps Hate," *The New York Times*, March 13, 1992, p. A4.

18. "Ambitious Eradication Goals and Withering Obstacles," *The New York Times*, April 10, 1988, p. A10.

19. "Coca Growers Prove Tenacious and Elusive," *Los Angeles Times*, July 7, 1992; World Report, p. 1.

20. "U.S. Aid Hasn't Stopped Drug Flow," *The New York Times*, November 21, 1993, p. A10.

21. Michael Massing, "Drug War: Wrong Forces, Wrong Front," *Los Angeles Times*, January 21, 1990, p. M3.

22. *The New York Times*, March 4, 1990, sec. 4, p. 88: "The Upper Huallaga Valley is going to be the model for the world," said an American official helping to implement the program.

23. "Drug Control: U.S. Antidrug Efforts in Peru's Upper Huallaga Valley," December 7, 1994, General Accounting Office, GAO/NSIAD-95-11.

24. Michael Massing, "Drug War: Wrong Forces, Wrong Front," *Los Angeles Times*, January 21, 1990, p. M3; "U.S. Aid Hasn't Stopped Drug Flow," *The New York Times*, November 21, 1993, p. A10.

25. Drug Enforcement Administration, *Coca Cultivation and Cocaine Processing: An Overview*, Executive Summary, September 1993.

26. James A. Inciardi, *The War on Drugs II* (Mountain View, Calif.: Mayfield, 1992), p. 88; *Los Angeles Times*, May 21, 1990, p. A1; *National Narcotics Intelligence Consumers Committee Report, 1992*, DEA, September 1993, p. 2.

27. *The New York Times*, August 20, 1989, p. A14.

28. *The Miami Herald*, February 9, 1987, p. A1.

29. Ibid., November 28, 1989, p. A1.

30. Rensselaer W. Lee III, *The White Labyrinth: Cocaine and Political Power* (New Brunswick, N.J.: Transaction Press, 1989), pp. 5, 134.

31. *The Miami Herald*, February 9, 1987, p. A1.

32. *Forbes* magazine, list of 125 non-U.S. billionaires, July 1988.

33. *The New York Times*, December 3, 1993, p. A1.

34. Paul Eddy, Hugo Sabogal, and Sara Walden, *The Cocaine Wars* (New York: W. W. Norton, 1988), p. 287.

35. Ibid., p. 289.

36. Lee, *The White Labyrinth*, p. 289.

37. Ibid., p. 170; Eddy, Sabogal, and Walden, *The Cocaine Wars*, pp. 290–99.

38. *The New York Times*, August 21, 1989, p. A3.

39. Ibid., August 30, 1989, p. A10.

40. Ibid., September 6, 1989, sec. 2, p. 7.

41. "U.S. Officials' Families to Quit Bogota," *The New York Times*, August 31, 1989, sec. 2, p. 8.

42. "Text of President's Speech on National Drug Control Strategy," *The New York Times*, September 6, 1989, p. B6.

43. Dan Baum, *Smoke and Mirrors: The War on Drugs and the Politics of Failure* (Boston: Little, Brown and Co., 1996), pp. 286–89. It was later revealed that the dealer had been enticed away from his normal base of operations some five blocks away so the agents could bust him in Lafayette Park.

44. *The New York Times*, September 18, 1989, sec. 1, p. 13.

45. "Bogota's Justice Aide Impresses Washington," *The New York Times*, September 2, 1989, sec. 1, p. 4.

46. Editorial, "Courage in Colombia," *The New York Times*, September 9, 1989, sec. 1, p. 22.

47. *The New York Times,* September 29, 1989, sec. 1, p. 3.

48. Ibid.

49. Ibid., September 24, 1989, p. A20.

50. Ibid., August 28, 1989, p. A10.

51. Ibid., September 24, 1989, p. A20.

52. Ibid., October 2, 1989, sec. 1, p. 1.

53. Ibid., December 16, 1989, sec. 1, p. 1.

54. "Drug War at Stake in Colombia Vote," *The New York Times,* May 26, 1989; May 28, 1989, sec. 1, p. 1.

55. *Los Angeles Times,* June 14, 1991, p. A1.

56. Ibid., July 2, 1991, p. A3.

57. "Crowd Mobs Escobar's Funeral," *The Miami Herald,* December 4, 1993, p. A8.

58. DEA Acting Administrator Stephen Greene, *Los Angeles Times,* December 3, 1993, p. A1.

59. *The New York Times,* December 3, 1993, p. A1.

60. "Drug Spotlight Falls on an Unblinking Cali Cartel," *The New York Times,* December 17, 1993, p. A8.

61. Editorial, "A Great Gift Lies in Samper's Hands," *Los Angeles Times,* June 17, 1996.

62. Representative Martinez Guerra, *The Washington Post,* August 23, 1995, p. A29.

63. *Time,* July 17, 1995, p. 31.

64. *Los Angeles Times,* July 12, 1996, p. A6.

65. *The New York Times,* August 13, 1995, p. E3.

66. Ibid. "Simply put, there are able lieutenants who are perfectly capable of keeping the system going," said Rensselaer W. Lee, a drug-trafficking and organized-crime expert at the Foreign Policy Research Institute in Philadelphia. "There may be 500 or 600 people who do the day-to-day work, managing the laboratories and moving the money around"; Eddy, Sabogal, and Warden, *The Cocaine Wars,* p. 288. In 1981 when the drug lords first met to form Muerto a Sequestradores, there were 223 trafficking organizations present.

67. U.S. Dept. of Justice, *Bureau of Justice Statistics Sourcebook, 1995,* NCJ-158900, p. 202.

68. "Could Colombia Survive Without This Plant?" *Los Angeles Times Magazine,* September 24, 1995, p. 36.

69. Gustavo de Greiff, Jr., Colombian Trade Ministry, Los Angeles, interview, January 23, 1997.

70. Gabriel García Marquez, "Cocaine's Reality," *The New York Times,* March 11, 1995, p. A3.

71. Ambassador Myles Frichette, interview, National Public Radio, *All Things Considered,* August 27, 1996.

72. "Short Prison Terms of Freed Drug Lords Rile Colombians," *Los Angeles Times,* September 21, 1996, p. A11.

73. "Drug Spotlight Falls on an Unblinking Cali Cartel," *The New York Times,* December 17, 1993, p. A8.

CHAPTER 7: MONTEZUMA'S REVENGE

1. *The New York Times,* May 5, 1991, sec. 1, p. 11.

2. *Fortune,* September 4, 1995, p. 100.

3. *The Washington Post,* National Weekly Edition, March 20–26, 1995, p. 10. His predecessor, Miguel de la Madrid, enabled major drug-trafficking cartels to escape prosecution for the 1985 torture-killing of DEA agent Enrique Camarena. The killing of Camarena by members of the Guadalajara drug cartel, with the complicity of high-ranking Mexican government officials, created a firestorm in bilateral relations.

4. *The New York Times,* November 29, 1991, p. A1.

5. Ibid., May 25, 1993, p. A1.

6. Ibid., May 26, 1993, p. A1.

7. Governor Ernesto Ruffo Appel, *Los Angeles Times,* October 4, 1996, p. A30.

8. *The Nation,* July 10, 1995, p. 50.

9. *The New York Times,* May 26, 1993, p. A1.

10. *Los Angeles Times,* June 16, 1995, p. A1.

11. Ibid., January 11, 1996, p. A18; June 16, 1995, p. A21.

12. Ibid., March 7, 1994, p. A1.

13. Ibid., March 5, 1994, p. A1; March 7, 1994, p. A1; June 16, 1995, p. A21; "Crusade to Avenge Friend Perished with Baja Official," September 16, 1996, p. A1; October 4, 1996, p. A1.

14. *The Wall Street Journal,* February 27, 1995, p. A9.

15. *The Washington Post,* National Weekly Edition, March 20–26, 1995, p. 10.

16. "Another Mexican Official Is Slain," *Los Angeles Times,* August 20, 1996; August 21, 1996, p. A10.

17. "Baja Police Chief Slain After Vowing Shake-Up," *Los Angeles Times,* September 15, 1996, p. A1.

18. *The Washington Post,* National Weekly Edition, March 20–26, 1995, p. 10; *The New York Times,* March 11, 1995, sec. 1, p. 3.

19. "Mexican Aide's Millions: U.S. Charges Drug Link," *The New York Times,* November 12, 1996, p. A10; March 11, 1995, sec. 1, p. 3: "Mexican officials charged deputy attorney general Mario Ruiz Massieu with trying to thwart an investigation into his brother's assassination last year, and also engaged in the embezzlement of more than $750,000 in government money. They say he hid about $10 million. Ruiz Massieu was charged on Monday with intimidating witnesses and falsifying evidence in the investigation he led last fall into his brother's death in order to protect Raul Salinas de Gortari. Salinas was arrested last week and has been charged with ordering the killing and paying of governing party congressman Manuel Munoz Rocha to have it carried out."

20. "Ex-Officials in Mexico Tied to Drug Lord, Report Asserts," *Los Angeles Times,* February 17, 1997, p. A17; "Testimony Ties Former Top Mexican Officials to Cartels," March 13, 1997, p. A1.

21. "Juan Garcia Abrego Boasts a Net Worth of Some $15 Billion from His Control of the Northeastern Mexican Cocaine Routes," *Fortune,* September 4, 1995, p. 100.

22. *Newsweek,* June 12, 1995, p. 37.

23. *Los Angeles Times,* June 15, 1995, p. A17: "Guillermo Gonzalez Calderoni, former commander of elite federal anti-drug squads—also named in last year's Texas trial as a protector of the Gulf cartel—told investigators that he had personally delivered to Raul recordings of telephone wiretaps of opposition politicians. Said one investigator, 'He said he was aware of the relationship between Gulf cartel chief Juan Garcia Abrego and Raul. He said Raul had meetings with Abrego and that Raul served as a front for Abrego through his companies.'" *Newsweek,* June 12, 1995, p. 37: According to one well-placed U.S. investigator, Garcia dipped into his till to fund a campaign of intimidations and wiretapping that Raul Salinas allegedly conducted in the run-up to Carlos Salinas's fraud-tainted elections. *The New York Times,* February 23, 1997, p. A4: U.S. intelligence officials also reported on meetings where other traffickers gave cash to Raul Salinas, who parceled it out to various senior politicians in the room.

24. *Los Angeles Times,* February 17, 1997, p. A4.

25. Andrew A. Reding, op-ed, "Army Shouldn't Fight War Against Drug Lords," *Los Angeles Times,* June 25, 1995, p. M2.

26. *Los Angeles Times,* December 12, 1996, p. A17.

27. *Los Angeles Times,* February 19, 1997, p. A1.

28. Juan Matta Belestros, Carlos Lehder, Jose Gonzalo Rodriguez Gacha, Pablo Escobar, Fabio Ochoa, Jorge Luis Ochoa, Miguel Angel Rodriguez Orejuela, Gilberto Rodriguez Orejuela, Angel Felix Gallardo, Joaquin Guzman, Hector Luis Palma, Javier Arellano Felix, Benjamin Arellano Felix, Juan Garcia Abrego, Amado Carrillo Fuentes . . .

29. *The Dallas Morning News,* October 12, 1996, p. 1A.

30. Ibid.

31. *The New York Times,* July 30, 1995, p. A1.

32. *The Washington Post,* February 19, 1997, pp. A1, 22.

33. Peter Lupscha, Univ. of New Mexico, KPFK interview with Ian Masters, March 2, 1997; Op-ed, Javier Rodriguez, *Houston Chronicle,* August 18, 1995.

34. "Mexico's Jailed Drug Chief Had Full Briefings in U.S.," *The New York Times,* February 20, 1997.

35. "Clinton Says Mexico's Firmness Is Bright Side of Drug Scandal," *The New York Times,* February 21, 1997, p. A3.

36. U.S. Dept. of State, "Coca and Cocaine," *International Narcotics Control Strategy Report,* March 1996.

37. U.S. Dept. of State, "Estimated Worldwide Potential Illicit Drug Net Production, 1986–1995," *International Narcotics Control Strategy Report,* op. cit.

38. U.S. Dept. of State, "Status of Worldwide Production," *International Narcotics Control Strategy Report,* op. cit.

39. "Annual Trends in Heroin-Related Episodes," NCADI, 1996 DAWN Survey.

40. Professor Peter Lupscha, University of New Mexico, interview with Ian Masters, KPFK, March 2, 1997. According to Lupscha, the DEA estimates the Mexican cocaine trade at $10 billion annually, the Defense Intelligence Agency says it's closer to $17 billion, and Mexican authorities put it as high as $30 billion. If, as some authorities claim, 60 percent goes for bribes, that would put the payoff in the range of $6 billion to $18 billion.

Chapter 8: Mission Impossible

1. Tom Isbell, Supervisory Inspector, U.S. Customs, interview, San Ysidro, California, May 18, 1996.

2. Ibid.

3. "Probe of Customs Targets Corruption Along the Border," *The Washington Post,* February 20, 1996, p. A1.

4. Mike Horner, former Inspector, U.S. Customs, interview, San Diego, California, May 18, 1996.

5. "Corruption Probe Focuses on Ex-Customs Official," *Los Angeles Times*, March 20, 1993, p. A1; *The Washington Post*, February 20, 1996, p. A8; "Trouble on the San Diego Border," *Reader's Digest*, June 1994, p. 73.

6. Terri Price, former U.S. Treasury Department investigator, interview, Los Angeles, California, May 28, 1996.

7. *Hearings, Commerce Subcommittee*, U.S. House of Representatives, 102nd Congress, 2nd Session, March 26 and 27 and April 1, 1992, pp. 2, 32–34.

8. Tom Isbell, interview, May 26, 1996.

9. "Our Drug-Plagued Mexican Border," *Reader's Digest*, January 1996, p. 57.

10. Border Corruption, Associated Press, March 1, 1997, 1:59 P.M.

11. U.S. Immigration and Naturalization Service, "Operation Gatekeeper: Landmark Progress at the Border," October 1995, p. 5.

12. Sheriff Oren Fox, interview, El Centro, California, May 17, 1996.

13. Ibid.

14. Ibid.

15. Inspection tour, January 17, 1994; technical data courtesy of Evergreen America Corp.

16. U.S. Customs Chief Inspector Wayne Kornmann, interview, Long Beach, California, June 7, 1996.

17. U.S. Department of Commerce, imports for 1996: 612,546,148,000 kilos by vessel; 25,000,975,000 kilos by air.

18. General Accounting Office, "Observations on Elements of the Federal Drug Control Strategy, March 1997, GAO/GGD-97-42. An estimated 780 metric tons of cocaine were produced worldwide; 230 tons were seized in 1995. U.S. consumption is estimated at 300 tons of cocaine per year. Of 300 metric tons of heroin produced worldwide, 32 tons were seized. U.S. consumption of heroin was estimated at 10 to 15 tons per year. See also Mathea Falco, *The Making of a Drug-Free America: Programs That Work* (New York: Times Books, 1994), p. 8.

CHAPTER 9: LESSONS FROM THE OLD COUNTRY

1. CBS *60 Minutes*, Sunday, December 27, 1992, segment on Chapel Street Clinic with Ed Bradley.

2. John Marks, Consultant Psychiatrist, Chapel Street Clinic, Widnes, interview, March 15, 1994; Anthony Henman, "Harm-Reduction on Merseyside 1985–1995: The Rise and Fall of a Radical Paradigm of Health Care for Illicit Drug Users," paper presented at conference, "Drug Policy in the '90s: The Changing Climate," John Moores University, Liverpool, June 1995: "Diplomatic sources also describe the storm produced in Washington when the major in-depth US TV news report *60 Minutes* broadcast a favourable report on the Widnes clinic just as President George Bush was whipping up support for a global military offensive against drugs."

3. Arnold S. Trebach, *The Heroin Solution* (New Haven, Conn.: Yale University Press, 1982), pp. 90–95.

4. Bing Spear, Chief Inspector, Home Office Drugs Branch (ret.), interview, Windsor Great Park, March 16, 1994.

5. Trebach, *The Heroin Solution;* Edwin M. Schur, *Narcotic Addiction in Britain and America* (Bloomington: Indiana University Press, 1962); Alfred Ray Lindesmith, *Addiction and Opiates* (Chicago: Aldine Publishing Co., 1968).

6. Edward M. Brecher, *Licit and Illicit Drugs: Consumers Union Report* (Boston: Little, Brown and Co., 1972), pp. 121–25. The British statistics were far more reliable than the American numbers because the British gave heroin to those addicts willing to be counted, whereas the Americans sent them to jail.

7. Trebach, *The Heroin Solution,* p. 109.

8. Ministry of Health and Scottish Home and Health Department, *Drug Addiction: The Second Report of the Interdepartmental Committee* (London: HM Stationery Office, 1971), quoted in Trebach, *The Heroin Solution,* pp. 108–110.

9. Federal regulations regarding the use of methadone, 37 FR 26795, December 15, 1972.

10. Spear, interview, op. cit.

11. Dr. J. A. Marks, interview, February 2, 1995: "Stimson & Openheimer found a fifteen percent mortality among drug users over a ten-year period if you simply leave the addicts to their own devices. We followed cohort of 89 addicts from 1982 to '89 and found a *zero* death rate and *zero* HIV rates. There were no locally acquired cases of HIV infection and no drug-related deaths from 1982 to '89. This information is available from the National Recording Center or the Mersey Regional Health Authority."

12. *New Perspectives:* "Heroin Treatment—New Alternatives." Proceedings of a seminar held in Canberra in 1991 by the Australian Institute of Criminology. Edited by Bammer and Gerrard. Pages 97–108 are by M. Lofts of the Cheshire Drug Squad, "Policing the Merseyside Drug Treatment Program," p. 105: "Between July of 1988 and January of 1990 . . . we evaluated the criminal records of the participants.

July 1988—142 clients—averaged 6.88 convictions for property crimes
Jan. 1990—112 remaining—averaged 0.44 convictions.

"This represents a 15-fold reduction among participating drug users."

13. J. Best et al., *Abstracts of the Proceedings of the Royal College of Psychiatrists,* 1986, p. 43; James Willis, *Drug Dependence* (London: Faber and Faber, 1969).

14. Maureen X. (pseudonym), interview, March 15, 1994, Widnes.

15. Ms. Shain Clarke, Corporate Affairs Directorate, NHS Executive Headquarters, Leeds, letter dated March 15, 1995.

16. Warrington Community Health Council, *Survey to Obtain the Views of Users of the Drug Dependency Clinic,* 1994, quoted in *Drogues Legales, L'experience de Liverpool* (Paris: Editions du Lezard, 1996); Henman, "Harm-reduction on Merseyside 1985–1995," op. cit.

17. Marks, interview, March 24, 1997.

18. Ibid.

19. Marks, interview, February 2, 1995; Henman, "Harm-Reduction on Merseyside 1985–1995," op. cit.

20. "Judge's Plea for Legal Drugs," *Los Angeles Times,* April 19, 1992, p. B9.

21. "Zurich's Open Drug Policy Goes Into Withdrawal," *The New York Times,* March 12, 1995.

22. "Methadone could not be prescribed to the planned number of patients because of the side effects and the problems with acceptability and recruitment. It became evident that the original research plan (250 treatment places for heroin, 250 places for morphine, and 200 for i.v. methadone) had to be adapted." A. Uchtenhagen et al., *Diversified Narcotics-on-Prescription Programme,* Swiss Federal Office of Public Health, Berne, September 1996.

23. A. Uchtenhagen et al., *Programme for a Medical Prescription of Narcotics: Final Report of the Research Representatives,* Swiss Federal Office of Public Health, Berne. July 10, 1997.

24. Uchtenhagen et al., *Diversified Narcotics-on-Prescription Programme*, op. cit.

25. Advisory Committee on Drug Dependence, *The Wootten Report* (U.K. 1968); *The Baan Committee Report* (Netherlands 1972); Canadian Government's Commission of Inquiry, *The Le Dain Report* (Canada 1970); National Commission on Marihuana and Drug Abuse, *The Shafer Commission* (U.S. 1973), abstracted in Theodore R. Vallance, *Prohibition's Second Failure* (Westport, Conn.: Praeger, 1993), Appendix C.

26. Advisory Committee on Drug Dependence, *Cannabis* (The Wootten Report) 1968, quoted in Vallance, *Prohibition's Second Failure*, p. 146.

27. *Drug Policy in the Netherlands*, Ministry of Health, Welfare and Sport, The Netherlands, January 1997.

28. "Europe Finds U.S. Drug War Lacking in Results," *Chicago Tribune*, November 2, 1995, p. A1.

29. *Netherlands Alcohol and Drugs Report, Fact Sheet 7*, Trimbos Institute, Utrecht.

30. Bernard Scholten, Chief Spokesman, Amsterdam Police Department, interview, Police Headquarters, March 21, 1994.

31. L.A. Town Hall Business Forum, February 22, 1995, Matthiew A. Peters, Consul General of the Kingdom of the Netherlands, correcting drug czar Lee Brown.

32. *Reuters*, August 10, 1995, 08:37; *Reuters*, February 18, 1997, 11:49 EST. According to Dutch Statistics, the Netherlands has 1.6 drug addicts per 1,000 head of population, well below about 2.5 per 1,000 in France.

33. Spear, interview, op. cit.

CHAPTER 10: REEFER MADNESS

1. *Los Angeles Times*, October 30, 1996, p. B3.

2. *Los Angeles Times*, November 6, 1996, p. A1.

3. Hendrik Hertzberg, "The Pot Perplex," *The New Yorker*, January 6, 1997, p. 4.

4. Joseph A. Califano, Jr., editorial, "How the Pro-Drug Gang Won the West," *San Jose Mercury News*, December 6, 1996.

5. *Los Angeles Times*, December 10, 1996, p. A1.

6. Ibid.

7. U.S. Dept. of Health, *Preliminary Estimates from the 1995 National Household Survey on Drug Abuse*, August 1996: An estimated

12.8 million Americans were current illicit drug users and 77 percent of the current illicit drug users (9.8 million) were marijuana users.

8. "Pot-Law Critics Call in Big Guns," *The Arizona Republic,* April 9, 1997, p. A1.

9. "Arizona Bill Guts Legalized Drug Initiative," *Los Angeles Times,* April 16, 1997, p. A3.

10. Interview with Carl Rochelle, CNN, December 30, 1996.

11. Vinciguerra et al., "Inhalation Marijuana as an Antiemetic for Cancer Chemotherapy, *New York State Journal of Medicine,* October 1988, pp. 525–27. Fifty-six patients who had no improvement with standard antiemetics were treated with marijuana; 78 percent demonstrated positive response. See also: H. Ekert, K. D. Waters, I. H. Jurk, J. Mobilia, and P. Laughnan, "Amelioration of Cancer Chemotherapy-Induced Nausea and Vomiting by Delta-9-Tetrohydrocannabinol," *The Medical Journal of Australia,* vol. 2 (1979): pp. 657–59; Chang et al., "Delta-9-Tetrahydrocannabinol as an Antiemetic in Cancer Patients Receiving High Dose Methotrexate," *Annals of Internal Medicine,* vol. 91, no. 6, December 1979, pp. 819–24; Leo Hollister, "Hunger and Appetite after Single Doses of Marijuana, Alcohol and Dextroamphetamine," *Clinical Pharmacoloby and Therapeutics,* vol. 12, no. 1, 1970, pp. 44–49 ff.

12. *In the Matter of Marijuana Rescheduling Petition, Docket No.* 86-22, September 6, 1988, Opinion, Recommended Ruling, Findings of Fact, Conclusions of Law, and Decision of Administrative Law Judge, Drug Enforcement Administration.

13. Helen C. Jones and Paul Lovinger, *The Marijuana Question and Science's Search for Answers* (New York: Dodd Mead & Co., 1985), p. 193; Lynn Zimmer, Ph.D., and John P. Morgan, M.D., *Marijuana Myths, Marijuana Facts: A Review of the Scientific Evidence* (New York: The Lindesmith Center, 1997), pp. 59, 60.

14. The National Center on Addiction and Substance Abuse at Columbia University, *Cigarettes, Alcohol, Marijuana: Gateways to Illicit Drug Use,* October 1994, chart 4.

15. *Los Angeles Times,* June 27, 1997, p. A1.

16. "A Bad Case of Deja Vu . . . ," editorial, *New Scientist,* July 5, 1997, p. 3.

17. George F. Koob, Scripps Research Institute, La Jolla, California, quoted in *Los Angeles Times,* June 27, 1997, p. A1.

18. Lester Grinspoon, interview, July 3, 1997.

19. Arnold Trebach, *The Great Drug War* (New York: Macmillan, 1987), pp. 126–27.

20. Ibid.

21. Gabriel Nahas, C. Latour, "The Human Toxicity of Marijuana, *Medical Journal of Australia* 156 (1992), pp. 495–97.

22. McDonald J. Christie and Gregory B. Chesher, "The Human Toxicity of Marijuana: A Critique of a Review by Nahas and Latour," *Drug and Alcohol Review* 13 (1994), pp. 209–16.

23. W. B. O'Shaughnessy, "On the Preparations of the Indian Hemp, or Gunjah: The Effects on the Animal System in Health, and Their Utility in the Treatment of Tetanus and Other Convulsive Disease," *Transactions of the Medical and Physical Society of Bengal*, 1838–1840.

24. Lester Grinspoon, *Marijuana Reconsidered* (Cambridge, Mass.: Harvard University Press, 1971); Lester Grinspoon and James B. Bakalar, *Marihuana, the Forbidden Medicine* (New Haven, Conn.: Yale University Press, 1993).

25. Lester Grinspoon, "A Brief Account of My Participation as a Witness in the Trial of Kerry Wiley," *International Journal of Drug Policy* 2(5), 1991, 11–12; and interviews with Dr. Grinspoon, November 19, 1993, and July 3, 1997.

CHAPTER 11: PRESCRIPTION FOR SANITY

1. *60 Minutes*, December 8, 1996.

2. "No Relief in Sight," Jacob Sullum, *Reason Magazine*, January 1997: "In 1980 researchers at Boston University Medical Center reported that they had reviewed the records of 11,882 hospital patients treated with narcotics and found 'only four cases of reasonably well documented addiction in patients who had no history of addiction.'"

3. *60 Minutes*, op. cit.: "Last year more than 120 doctors who were prescribing . . . narcotics for pain had their licenses revoked or suspended."

4. *Prescription Drug Game*, Virginia State Police, quoted in *The Activist Guide*, Drug Reform Coalition, October 1996, p. 4.

5. *60 Minutes*, op. cit.

6. Richard Lawrence Miller, *Drug Warriors and Their Prey* (Westport, Conn.: Praeger Publishers, 1996). With a remarkable collection of facts, insight, and meticulous research, Miller details the drug war

assault on civil liberties and shows an alarming parallel with the stigmatization of the Jews in Nazi Germany.

7. Lynn Zimmer, Ph.D., and John P. Morgan, M.D., "Exposing Marijuana Myths: A Review of the Scientific Evidence," The Lindesmith Center, New York, 1996.

8. Ethan Nadelmann, director, The Lindesmith Center, New York, interview, *Rolling Stone*, February 20, 1997, p. 51.

9. U.S. Dept. of Health and Human Services, *Preliminary Estimates from the 1995 National Household Survey on Drug Abuse*, August 1996, NCADI. There were an estimated 582,000 frequent cocaine users and 196,000 heroin users in 1995.

10. United Nations International Narcotics Control Board, *Report of the International Narcotics Control Board for 1993*, Vienna, 1993.

11. Drug Enforcement Administration, *National Narcotics Intelligence Consumers Committee Report, 1995*, "The Supply of Illicit Drugs to the United States," August 1996, vii–ix (DEA 96024).

12. United States General Accounting Office, *Drug Control: Observations on the Elements of the Federal Drug Control Strategy*, March 1997, 4 (GAO/GGD-97-42).

13. Leland Atwood, former chairman, North American Rockwell, interview, April 27, 1997. Total cost of the moon program was estimated at $28 billion. In 1990 dollars that would be in the range of $100 billion.

14. Mark Thornton, *The Economics of Prohibition* (Salt Lake City: University of Utah Press, 1991).

15. "Drug Market Takes Hold in Small Towns," *Indianapolis Star*, April 7, 1997, p. B4. Police Captain Dave Van Baalen of Peru, Indiana: "For every one we arrest, two more pop up. . . . Anyone who thinks they are going to run crack out of town is foolish. . . . All drugs are up," and so are drug-related burglaries and thefts.

16. *The Atlantic Monthly*, April 1997, p. 96.

17. Joseph McNamara, op-ed, "A Truce in the War on Drugs," Washington *Times*, April 4, 1997, p. A19.

18. Senator Gomez Hurtado, interview, International Network of Cities on Drug Policy conference, Baltimore, November 17, 1993.

19. Thomas Constantine, Administrator, Drug Enforcement Administration, *How To Hold Your Own in a Drug Legalization Debate*, August 1994.

20. University of Maryland, Center for Substance Abuse Research, *Cesar Fax* 5:42, October 28, 1996.

21. Harry G. Levine, M.D., Queens College, interview, July 3, 1997; see also, Harry Levine and Craig Reinarman, "From Prohibition to Regulation: Lessons from American Alcohol Policy for Drug Policy," in *Confronting Drug Policy,* Ronald Bayer and Gerald Opppenheimer, eds. (New York: Cambridge University Press, 1993), pp. 160–93; National Commission on Marihuana and Drug Abuse (Shafer Commission), *History of Alcohol Prohibition.*

22. *New Perspectives:* "Heroin Treatment—New Alternatives." Proceedings of a seminar held in Canberra in 1991 by the Australian Institute of Criminology. Edited by Bammer and Gerrard. M. Lofts of the Cheshire Drug Squad, "Policing the Merseyside Drug Treatment Program," pp. 97–108; A. Uchtenhagen et al., *Programme for a Medical Prescription of Narcotics: Final Report of the Research Representatives,* Swiss Federal Office of Public Health, Berne, July 10, 1997.

23. L. D. Johnston, P. M. O'Malley, and J. G. Bachman, "Marijuana Decriminalization: The Impact on Youth 1975–1980," Monitoring the Future, Occasional Paper 13, University of Michigan, Institute for Social Research.

24. Michael R. Aldrich, Tod H. Mikuriya, and Gordon S. Brownell, *Fiscal Costs of California Marijuana Law Enforcement 1960–1984* (Berkeley: Medi-Comp Press, 1997). The state saved $360 million in 1984 dollars.

25. Dan Waldorf, Craig Reinarman, and Sheigla Murphy, *Cocaine Changes: The Experience of Using and Quitting* (Philadelphia: Temple University Press, 1991); Craig Reinarman and Harry G. Levine, eds., *Crack In America: Demon Drugs and Social Justice* (Berkeley: University of California Press, 1997).

26. David F. Musto, *The American Disease: Origins of Narcotic Control* (New York: Oxford University Press, 1987), p. 281, n. 13: ". . . most authors who have closely studied the question of the addict-population in the past (Wilbert, Terry, Pellens, Kolb, DuMez, Lindesmith) tend to agree that there was a peak in addiction around 1900 and in the teens of this century this number began to decrease and reached a relatively small number (about 100,000) in the 1920s."

27. Musto, *The American Disease,* p. 22: The Pure Food and Drug Act of 1906 required the listing of narcotics on the labels of patent medicines. "Within a few years of the inclusion of this simple device, it was estimated that patent medicines containing such drugs dropped in sale by about a third."

28. *Los Angeles Times*, November 8, 1996, "Fewer Californians Lighting Up, Study Says." Only 15.5 percent of California adults smoked regularly in 1995, down from 26 percent in 1984.

29. Arnold S. Trebach, *The Heroin Solution* (New Haven, Conn.: Yale University Press, 1982).

30. Lynn Zimmer, Ph.D., and John P. Morgan, M.D., *Marijuana Myths, Marijuana Facts: A Review of the Scientific Evidence* (New York: The Lindesmith Center, 1997), p. xvi.

Index

About the Author

MIKE GRAY, author of the original screenplay for *The China Syndrome,* grew up in Indiana and graduated from Purdue University with a degree in engineering. In 1962 he formed his own film company in Chicago, which produced the award-winning documentaries *American Revolution II* and *The Murder of Fred Hampton.* Since moving to Hollywood in 1972, he has been writing, directing, and producing feature films and series for television. He lives in Los Angeles with his wife, Carol.

About the Type

This book was set in Fairfield, the first typeface from the hand of the distinguished American artist and engraver Rudolph Ruzicka (1883–1978). In its structure Fairfield displays the sober and sane qualities of the master craftsman whose talent has long been dedicated to clarity. It is this trait that accounts for the trim grace and vigor, the spirited design and sensitive balance, of this original typeface.

Rudolph Ruzicka was born in Bohemia and came to America in 1894. He set up his own shop, devoted to wood engraving and printing, in New York in 1913 after a varied career working as a wood engraver, in photoengraving and banknote printing plants, and as an art director and freelance artist. He designed and illustrated many books, and was the creator of a considerable list of individual prints—wood engravings, line engravings on copper, and aquatints.